LORD TIMOTHY DEXTER'S HOUSE.

MANNING, DEL.

MAD and MAGNIFICENT YANKEES

A New England Portrait Gallery

Clarissa M. Silitch
Editor

Carl F. Kirkpatrick
Designer

PUBLISHED BY YANKEE, INC., DUBLIN, NEW HAMPSHIRE

FIRST EDITION

Foreword

"The amount of eccentricity in a society has been proportional to the amount of genius, mental vigor and moral courage it contained. That so few now dare to be eccentric, marks the chief danger of the time." So said 19th-century English philosopher John Stuart Mill in reference to his own "time" (1806-1873) but, of course, without the benefit of the historic perspective we in our century can utilize in judging his. Yet throughout history, and certainly in the present day, there have always been very few who dared to be eccentric. To be sure, those who "deviate from regularity," the old Webster definition of the word, must *necessarily* represent an exceedingly tiny minority.

In terms of population and geographic area, New England, it seems to me, has had far more than its share of those who dared to be eccentric. This book alone attests to the existence of a goodly number. Then consider the additional fact that New England has always been more than amply supplied with "genius, mental vigor and moral courage"—still is!—and you have some logic to support John Stuart Mill's insinuation that the strength of a region is in direct proportion to the number of its eccentrics!

Of course, there is really only one element common to all the New England men and women featured in this book. That element, I submit, is neither eccentricity, madness nor magnificence, though each possesses an abundance of one or plenty of all three. The true common denominator, however, is chance—pure and simple chance. (I personally prefer that word to "fate.") Chance seems to play a discouragingly strong—though far from exclusive—role in either great success or horrendous failure. Happily, both results are magnificent.

Thus, America's first black poet, Phillis Wheatley, whose inspirational story begins 104 pages from here, was "by seeming fate... snatched from Afric's fancy'd happy seat" by a passing Yankee slaver. Charles Corliss (page 183) would most assuredly have founded a city on the Merrimack River but for a freak and violent windstorm which blew down its first building. Poor Frances Hiller (page 169)—her fabulous funeral would not be a source of entertainment today if even a single one of her twenty-three children had lived. If Captain Thunderbolt's friends had obeyed his last wish and buried him with his clothes on, his secret would never have been revealed (page 273). What if Jonathan Lambert (page 161) had been born into a wealthy family? What if Amy Lowell (page 135) had had a good figure? What if Russell Risley (page 110) had lived in Paris or Boston instead of on a remote Vermont farm? What if... what if...?

The possibilities apparent during speculations on "chance" would, I take pleasure in believing, drive amok the most sophisticated of computers. But the majority of the lives about which you'll soon be reading were (or are) successful or disastrous due to both chance and *taking a chance,* which, in essence, is what "deviating from regularity" is all about. Alfred Johnson (page 83) is a simple and uncomplicated example. Everyone laughed when Johnson said he could sail a rowboat across the Atlantic to England. But he tried and he happened to succeed. The feat is important historically because he was successful. The initial laughter created that all-too-common level from which all eccentrics can arise. That he dared to try put him in this book.

It's a pleasure to see some of these old friends between two hard covers. I can recall many of the special situations surrounding their individual appearances in *Yankee* Magazine. For instance, I cannot look at John Taber's "four-dollar-bill" (page 41) without remembering John Kennedy's assassination. I was captioning a photo of it when the news from Dallas was announced by someone who had been listening to a car radio. On a happier note, seeing the Mercer Girls (page 242) reminds me of the birth of my son, Judson, Jr. His mother called to say it was time to drive to the hospital just as I was in the process of press-typing the words "Multiple Romance," the article title when it appeared in *Yankee* back in 1959.

Those two articles and many others from comparatively distant issues were not exposed to many readers. *Yankee's* circulation was small then. So I'm pleased more people will now have the opportunity to enjoy each author's interpretation of these grand eccentrics. Certainly the lessons to be derived from each are relevant now and will remain forever timeless. For, after all, as an ancient quote in the 1974 *Old Farmer's Almanac(k)* states, "We live in deeds, not years; in thoughts, not breaths; in feelings, not in figures on a dial. We should count time by heart-throbs. He most lives who thinks most, feels the noblest, acts the best."

All right, you mad and magnificent Yankees... live on!

Judson D. Hale
Editor, *Yankee* Magazine

Contents

FOREWORD   4-5

SECTION 1. NATIVE GENIUS

Timothy Dexter—**Lord of Newburyport, Earl of Chester, and Merchant
   Extraordinary** *by Ian Nicholas*   10
Ephraim Bull—**He Sowed, Others Reaped** *by John Mason*   20
The Bonesetter Sweets—**A Strange and Wonderful Inheritance**
   by Martha R. McPartland   24
Marian MacDowell—**Maker of Memories** *by Carl Carmer*   30
John Taber—**His Integrity Made Money** *by Sheldon Christian*   38

SECTION 2. CRUSADERS

Prudence Crandall—**Way Ahead of Her Time** *by Martha R. Wright*   44
William Phelps Eno—**Ex Chao, Ordo** *by David K. Witheford*   50
Dorothea Lynde Dix—**A Mountain of Determination** *by William S. Ellis*   55
Henry Daniel Cogswell—**Ice Water and Time Capsules** *by Emil Corwin*   60
Hilda Hamlin—**A Lupine Legacy** *by W. Storrs Lee*   68

SECTION 3. FABULOUS FEATS AND TOWERS OF
            STRENGTH

Elmer Bitgood—**Move Over, Paul Bunyan** *by Richard L. Champlin*   75
Hessie Donahue—**The Lady Who Knocked Out John L. Sullivan**
   by Richard W. O'Donnell   79
Alfred Johnson—**First American to Sail Across the Atlantic Alone**
   by Robert S. Malcolm   83
George Gibson Polley—**Daredevil Original "Human Fly"** *by Richard W.
   O'Donnell*   89
John Krohn—**A Big Wheel Around America** *by William Edward Mason*   95
James Connolly—**A Hop, Step, and a Jump to the First Modern
   Olympic Championship** *by Tom Edwards*   99

SECTION 4. FAVORED BY THE MUSES

Phillis Wheatley—**Boston's Slave Poet** *by Robert E. O'Toole*   104
Russell Risley—**Faces on a Vermont Barn** *by Tennie G. Toussaint*   110
The Saturday Club—**The Purest Intellectual Quintessence**
   by Richard F. Merrifield   115
Lillian Norton—**Splendiferous Prima Donna from Maine**
   by Moreton Abbott   123
Zerah Colburn—**Boy Computer and Mathematical Genius**
   by Don Munson   130
Amy Lowell—**Poet, Boston** *by Laurie Hillyer*   135

SECTION 5. DREAMS THAT CAME TO NAUGHT

Charles Francis Hall—**A Lonely Grave at Thank God Bay**
  by T. W. Paterson   146
William Miller—**The Man Who Drove a Million People Crazy**
  by M. Robert Beasley   154
Jonathan Lambert—**Ill-Fated King of the Isles of Refreshment**
  by Vincent J. Dowdell, Jr.   161
Frances B. Hiller—**Funerals Fit for Pharaohs** *by John Mason*   169
Richard Jordan Gatling—**He Dreamed of Peace and Improved His Gun**
  by Jean Mitchell Boyd   176
Charles Corliss—**The City That Never Was** *by Richard W. O'Donnell* 183

SECTION 6. EMPIRE BUILDERS

Frederic Tudor—**Ice-Cool Ice King** *by W. A. Swanberg*   190
Lydia E. Pinkham—**A Remedy Founded on True Unicorn**
  by Patrice Smart   197
James Fisk, Jr.—**Rapscallion from Vermont** *by W. A. Swanberg*   204
Fannie Merritt Farmer—**Little, Brown Was Doubtful**
  by Gladys N. Hoover   211
George Francis Train—**Space Age Victorian** *by Dawn Anderson*   216

SECTION 7. NEW ENGLAND GRANITE

Rebecca and Abigail Bates—**Victorious Army of Two** *by Alton Hall*
  Blackington   226
The Vermont Version *by Leon W. Dean*   230
George Bloomer—**The World's Greatest Single Rescue Feat**
  by Edward Rowe Snow   234
The Mercer Girls—**Around Cape Horn to Find a Husband**
  by Harold Helfer   242
Warren B. Johnson—**A Yankee Who Went Home... The Hard Way**
  by Laura Page   246
Captain Scullum—**Russia Paid Up** *by Albert P. Hout*   252
Mildred Jewett—**One-Woman Coast Guard Station** *by Harriet Crowley* 255

SECTION 8. LEGENDS IN THEIR OWN TIME

Robert Rogers—**Wabo Madahondo, The White Devil**
  by Simon Cameron   262
John Wilson—**Alias Captain Thunderbolt** *by W. A. Swanberg*   273
Napoleon LaJoie—**New England's Greatest Baseball Player**
  by John U. Ayotte   281
Harry Nelson Pillsbury—**Chess Tyro Who Beat the Masters**
  by Bartlett Gould   288
Daniel Webster—**Lightning from His Eyes, Thunder from His Mouth**
  by Eric Kelly   296
Charles Sherwood Stratton—**P. T. Barnum's Gold Mine**
  by Maudie M. Dabrowski   308

Native Genius

SECTION 1

Lord of Newburyport, Earl of Chester, and Merchant Extraordinary

by Ian Nicholas

"Ime the first Lord in the younited States of Amercary Now of New-buryport it is the voise of the people and I cant Help it and so Let it goue Now as I must be Lord there will foller many more Lords pretty soune for it dont hurt A Cat Nor the mouse Nor the son Nor the water Nor the Eare then goue on all is Easey Now bons broaken all is well all in love Now I begin to Lay the corner ston and the kee ston with grat Remembrence of my father Jorge Washington the grate herow 17 sen-treys past before we found so good a father to his shildren and Now gone to Rest Now to shoue my Lowe to my father and grate Caricters I will shoue the world one of the grate Wonders . . ."

wrote Timothy Dexter of Newburyport, Massachusetts, in his strange little work, *A Pickle for the Knowing Ones* (printed 1801), whose last two pages are filled with punctuation marks with which the reader is in-structed to "solt and peper" the *Pickle*'s pages to suit himself. Timothy was born to be (as he said himself) "one grat man" in Malden, Massa-chusetts in 1747, "when grat powers Rouled," to a poor farm family with no pretensions to nobility. Bound out at the age of eight to a farmer, he served him for seven years before becoming a tanner's apprentice in Charlestown. As was the custom then, Timothy obtained his freedom and a new suit from his tanner master when he came of age. He promptly sold his "freedom suit" for cold cash, walked from Boston to Newburyport, and set up his shop in that thriving seaport.

Timothy Dexter in his famous tricorne hat, out walking with his "strange hairless black dog."

A year later, he found and married Elizabeth Mary Lord Frothingham, a widow of Exeter, New Hampshire, with four children (who little suspected she would one day become a "gost") and a handsome competence, all of which he brought back to Newburyport, where they went into business on High Street. Mrs. Dexter had a small shop on the first floor, while Timothy made leather breeches in the basement. As the Revolutionary War got under way, Timothy saw others like Nathaniel Tracy and Jonathan Jackson (whose fleet included 100 ships) getting rich in the privateering racket. Armed with a letter of marque from the General Court of Massachusetts, their ships could sally forth and capture His Majesty's ships. The sale of those ships and their cargos quickly added up to a small fortune for the investors. Actually privateering was a bit too dangerous for Timothy, but he did take shares in those ships, and everytime a privateer paid off, Timothy got part of the take.

Timothy took his share in Government Bonds and Continental currency. His friends called him a fool. They said, "That idiot Dexter will wake up one of these mornings and all that paper money will be good for is papering the Pantry," but Timothy kept on buying every scrap of scrip he could get his hands on until he had so much paper money he had to stack it up and hide the surplus in boxes and books or behind his bed.

Then the War ended and the bottom dropped out of everything. Men much better off than Timothy failed, including Nathaniel Tracy (and, eventually, his partner, Jackson), and went to the wall.

Returning soldiers, sailors, and marines were told by the storekeepers, "That paper scrip Congress paid you with is no good. In my store I've got to have hard money—dig up some silver!" Things were so bad that a pound of tea cost ten dollars; to buy a new calico dress, a body had to spend $150 in paper currency. Folks were flinging that worthless stuff around like German marks after the First World War. That is, everybody but Timothy Dexter. He had a hunch, and he played it for all it was worth.

Then, overnight something happened which completely changed his life.

Thomas Jefferson and Alexander Hamilton came up with a plan to stop the inflation. They announced a new national banking system. The almost worthless paper scrip was declared valid, and Timothy Dexter, lowly leather worker of Newburyport, had more money than he knew what to do with.

As a gorgeous butterfly emerges from the lowly caterpillar's cocoon to spread its wings in the spring sunshine, so did Timothy Dexter emerge from his tattered shirt and leather apron. The vision that suddenly appeared before the Newburyporters was so startling they still talk about it, and no wonder! Nothing like it had been seen before or has been since.

Like Napoleon (one of his heroes), Timothy Dexter was short and stocky. To make him appear taller, his tailor designed and built a huge tri-cornered hat of red, white, and blue velvet. This remarkable hat was encrusted with gold braid and fringed with tassels that fluttered as he walked. Under the hat he wore a military cloak of bright blue, a shiny white waistcoat, lace cravat, and scarlet trousers.

The very special French shoes designed by Timothy himself to wear for special occasions had long turned-up toes like Persian slippers, with more tassels and silver bells hanging from the tips. Everywhere he went he carried a cane and led "a strange, hairless black dog" that looked like "an elongated pig" and was probably a dachshund.

Having changed the image, he turned to the frame. He'd long had his eye on a big and beautiful mansion—the palatial home of Nathaniel Tracy, shipowner and merchant extraordinary, first citizen of Newburyport. With the rest of the town, Timothy had watched no less a person than George Washington, then recently elected President of the new United States, roll up in his coach to the Tracy mansion where he was to dine and stay the night. When Nathaniel Tracy lost his fortune in the post-war depression, Dexter bought his mansion!

Collecting Continental scrip was not the only wild "spekkelashion" of Timothy Dexter's that succeeded. He carried coal to Newcastle and warming pans and mittens to the tropical West Indies and sold them all at a profit! When Dexter's coal arrived at Newcastle, the great coal-mining center of England, the miners there had been on strike for over a year and every last hunk of Virginia coal sold for ten times its worth.

According to Dexter's own account in the *Pickle*, he bought 42,000 long handled warming pans and shipped the whole lot to the tropical islands. Like his coal venture too, it was the joke of Newburyport. However, when the West Indians came aboard ship to see what was new, the captains trotted out the warming pans and said, "Look, the very latest thing for dipping molasses, a ladle, with a nice long handle." They sold every last one, and Dexter's little book gloated, "They thought I was crazy—but I made 'siventy-nine' percent on that deal."

Timothy's most unusual venture was in, of all things, tom cats. It seems that Newburyport was overrun with cats—little cats, big cats, good cats, and bad cats. At a sizzling Town Meeting, a vote was taken to see if the citizens would vote to get rid of them. When the votes were counted, it was 50–50 for destroying the felines, and Newburyport was right back where it started.

The next day, Newburyport's newspaper, the *Impartial Herald*, carried a full-page ad composed and paid for by Mr. Dexter. In the biggest type they had, it read as follows:

[13]

CATS! CATS! CATS!

During the next 10 days I will purchase any and all felines, for tuppence and thrippence, if they are brought to my wharf—crated for shipment. They will be fed, watered and properly cared for on their long voyage. (T. Dexter)

That night any pussy cat caught roaming the streets was slapped into a gunny sack or basket and hustled to Dexter's wharf. By the end of the week, the tough little rowdies and the regular old rummies had plenty of spare change, and in the dark hold of Dexter's ship the fur was really flying.

Dressed in his usual finery, Timothy met with his captains. "There's an island you haven't touched at," he said, pointing it out on a map. "Take the cats to that island—and remember, you get a good percent of the profits." The island Dexter chose was covered with plantations, and it just so happened that the plantations were covered with field mice and rats. The islanders fought each other to buy the cats in the Yankee cargo. The two thousand cats were sold at an average of $2.50 apiece, some for as much as five and six dollars.

Was it Dick Whittington luck, or had the cagey Mr. Dexter heard about the mice? We shall never know.

As his fortune mounted, so did his eccentricity and capricious bent for self-glorification.

"I will pave the whole of High Street," he said in Town Meeting, "if the citizens will call it Dexter Street." This generous offer was turned down. "The Town Market is a disgrace," he roared. "Dirt and dust blowing all over the vegetables, and a quagmire after a storm. I will build the town a Magnificent Market [like Faneuil Hall] and pay all the costs if it will forever be known as Dexter's market." That offer too was turned down, which infuriated Timothy.

Despite his successful "spekkelashions," fine house and generosity (he built the Essex bridge, first across the Merrimac, and donated beautiful bronze bells to the churches), he was consistently ignored or ridiculed by the élite of Newburyport society, and noticed only by ragamuffins who raced across his lawn, stole his fruit and flowers, and pulled the palings from his fence. Finally, in desperation he put another ad, this time in the *Newburyport Herald:*

ZOUNDS! THIEVES! and LIARS ALL! If any more dead cats and rotten punkins are thrown on my doorstep, I will leave the town and establish my country seat elsewhere!

As the punkins, dead cats and bottles continued, true to his word, Timothy put his mansion up for sale and whizzed off in a cloud of dust for Chester, New Hampshire in 1797.

One of Timothy Dexter's failures (they seem to have been all social, never financial) in Newburyport was the stubborn refusal of the people of that town to address him as "Lord" Dexter. His fancy found more fertile ground in Chester, where folk at first welcomed the advent of this rich merchant family and its retinue, comprising an African servant, a dwarf, cooks, kitchen maids, laundress, waitresses, hostelers and gardeners, each wearing a shield on which was inscribed "$5." By now, the Dexter retinue included one of the strangest of Timothy's whims—his poet laureate, Jonathan Plummer, erstwhile fishmonger, who was paid a princely salary (in kind) to glorify his master in effusive poesies and follow him about wherever he went. One of Plummer's efforts begins:

> Lord Dexter is a man of Fame,
> Most celebrated is his name;
> More precious far than gold that's pure,
> Lord Dexter shines forevermore.

Chester folk didn't mind calling him "Lord" when they found he would repay the effort handsomely in one way or another—a quarter to any child who gave him the much desired title (some say five dollars!). In Chester at last Timothy felt himself recognized as the "grat" man he knew himself to be.

"I will found a Kingdom," he cried—"The Kingdom of Chester." And off he hustled to get Judge Arthur Livermore to draw up the constitution and laws for the "Kingdom" that would make Timothy the official "Earl of Chester." The judge at that moment was short of funds, and Dexter loaned him $1,200. Of this sum, Livermore repaid $200, but claimed the remaining $1,000 as his fee for making out the papers. Dexter said the job was worth only $100. But His Honor refused to pay back any more money and indeed spent most of it on a splendid saddle horse.

Timothy stopped him one day on Chester High Street, saying "I sup-

[15]

Jonathan Jackson's Newburyport mansion after Timothy had it fixed up with a "mouseum"—1810 print identifying the statues by name.

pose you bought that beautiful horse you're riding with my money. Well!
Sir! I want the rest of it." And that isn't all he said. He made the judge
so mad that he struck Lord Dexter six times across the face with his riding
whip. Dexter said afterwards, "My poor face looked like beefsteak fresh
from the grill."

To get even he put an ad in the *Chester Herald* warning his subjects
that they must collect the money from the judge, or—"I will return and
establish myself in ye Newburyport."

It was a sad day for the New Hampshire tax collectors when Lord Dexter sold his house in Chester and turned again toward the seaport town
where he had found fame and fortune. Though he was out $1,000, in
Chester he had gained the title he had coveted for so long, "by the voise
of the people."

Newburyport was glad to have him and his fortune back. Despite Timothy's growing reputation for drinking, wife-beating, and eccentricity, his
generosity to those who did as he wished was unimpaired. He bought the
glorious Georgian mansion built on High Street in 1771 by Jonathan
Jackson—a truly magnificent baronial estate overlooking the sea and the
Isles of Shoals. All it needed was a big gold eagle, and Dexter knew just
the man to make one—young Joseph Wilson, who already had a reputa-

[16]

*Rear view of Timothy Dexter mansion as photographed by Robb Sagendorph,
founder of* Yankee *Magazine, in 1954, when the eagle was still aloft on its roof.*

tion for carving eagles and lifesize figureheads for sailing vessels.

Though perhaps the eagle was all the new Dexter mansion *needed*,
Lord Timothy made its spacious grounds the talk of the town with his ex-
otic and ambitious planting and landscaping, and had even more grandiose schemes in store for it. Briefly, a gallery of statues of people and beasts
considered by Timothy to be the "grat Caricters of the world," starting
off with Adam and Eve, with plenty of carved lions and greyhounds to
guard them. The mad tanner with the title wanted his "mouseum" carved
from granite or marble until he discovered that each figure would cost
him in the neighborhood of $2,000 in stone. Woodcarver Wilson offered
to do the job in wood for $22,000; he also pointed out that wood could
be painted in life-like colors. Wilson was hired forthwith and, though his
patron complained about the time he took to finish the job, eventually
completed some 40 colossal wooden figures whose lofty pedestals encircled
the Dexter-Jackson mansion. On Timothy's list were three American
Presidents (Washington, John Adams, and Jefferson) in the place of
honor atop the tall brick entrance arch; a whole gaggle of kings and emperors; David, Moses, Solomon and other Biblical characters, the Indian
Chief Cornplanter and Black Emperor Toussaint L'Ouverture; as well as
some worthy New Englanders. Although the 1810 print of the celebrity-

[17]

girded mansion lists the statues by name, no definitive list of all the figures exists, for the simple reason that Timothy liked to repaint and relabel them as the whim took him. When the great work was at last completed in late October, 1801, Newburyport was stunned to find the wooden assemblage included none other than Lord Timothy Dexter himself. Not one, but *two* images of milord, each bearing a scroll modestly inscribed "I am the first in the East, the first in the West, and the Greatest Philosopher in the Western World."!

(Timothy explained that if people wouldn't speak to him, at least the statues could say "Good Morning" to each other.)

Some years before the museum was completed, the long-suffering Mrs. Dexter, who had countenanced without demur Timothy's less amusing habits of daily drunkenness (only in the afternoon—mornings strictly reserved for sober business) and wife-beating, complained of the extravagance of this new idea of her husband's. Timothy was furious. And he still remembered her last fall from grace in Chester, New Hampshire. At the mock funeral the new lord had staged there for himself—to find out how people really felt about him—his wife had shed not a tear. The thousands that turned out for the funeral ceremony wondered at the loud noises heard from the kitchen as the mournful procession passed. Lord Dexter was caning his wife for her heartlessness! He considered this new offense the last straw.

At Timothy's request, "Poet Lauriet" Jonathan Plummer wrote her epitaph, and, from that time on, she was known as the "Ghost" and treated as though she were in fact dead. Tiring of this game, Timothy gave her $2,000 to go away and advertised in the papers for another wife. When none applied, he eventually (13 years later) sent the "gost" some more money to come back—and she did!

Although the poor Ghost outlived her unpredictable spouse by only three years, at least she was provided for generously in his will.

The self-created Earl of Chester died at the age of 60 in 1806, ostensibly of alcoholism, and was interred in the old Burying Ground across the pond from Newburyport's Mall (pronounced with a short "a," to rhyme with "Sal"). Although Newburyport did go so far as to mention him specially in the inscription on the cemetery's old stone gateposts, it put quotation marks around his cherished title:

Within Lie Buried More than 50 Sailors and Soldiers of the Revolution, Ministers, Judges, and "Lord" Timothy Dexter . . . 5 French Refugees from Guadeloupe and 7 of the Crew of the Pocahontas.

Surprisingly, his estate totalled only $35 thousand odd, a little less than the amount with which he had first embarked on his amazing career. However, the records show that he gave away approximately $400 thousand, and his Museum and lavish life style undoubtedly absorbed the rest of what everyone had believed to be a huge fortune.

Timothy's essay into the world of Art guarded his "palace" for only 14 years; most of the images were toppled from their pedestals by the great gale of 1815, which left only the three Presidents standing atop the great arch. The fallen figures were sold for pittances, rarely amounting to $5, by Timothy's executors. Of all the statues only one, believed to be that of William Pitt, is still in existence—on display at the Smithsonian Institution in Washington, D.C.

Perhaps the figures would have better withstood the weather had they been less highly placed, and been made of stone as Dexter had planned initially. But the form they did in fact take, and their fate, too, seems more typical of this strange, shrewd, and stubbornly perverse Yankee. His "Kingdom" never came to be, and his "Mouseum" is gone, but his little book, fantastic character, and astonishing history have nevertheless bequeathed to Timothy Dexter quite a durable measure of the fame he craved.   END

The gravestones of Mr. Timothy Dexter and his faith-
ful "gost" in Newburyport's Old Burying Ground.

He Sowed, Others Reaped

by John Mason

The grape, you know, is the oldest fruit cultivated by man. It's mentioned many times in the Bible. Old Man Noah was one of the first grape growers, but he didn't have anything as nice as the Concord. Nobody did in those days. Why, it wasn't until 1800 that any grapes were grown in this country—and *they* were raised down South.

About 1810, two varieties, the Catawba and the Isabella, were introduced into New England—and everybody who had a plot of ground and slats enough to make a trellis started a grape arbor.

But the season was short and the grapes never did ripen. What good is a basket of sour grapes unless you want to make a jugful of that stuff that goes with a loaf of bread and thou? Well, one man was to change all that.

Ephraim W. Bull was born in Boston on the 4th of March in 1806 in a farmhouse that stood just a stone's throw from the little house on Milk Street where Benjamin Franklin was born 100 years before, and near where the old Transcript Building now stands.

Washington Street then was still a country road winding through the village. When Ephraim was a lad, he worked in his father's fields (between Milk and Franklin Streets) and drove the cows back and forth from the grazing grounds on Boston Common. Many a time he picked huckleberries where the State House stands. Unlike the boys who hung around the spicy wharves and noisy taverns, Ephraim preferred his garden. He lugged water for his flowers and vegetables from the town pump at the corner of Congress and Milk Streets.

Ephraim's first job (away from his father's farm) was out in Dorchester where he became apprenticed to a chemist. Later he learned the tricky trade of gold-beating, a profession he worked at, off and on all his life.

When he married, he moved back into the city, taking a small house with a garden on Fayette Street in the South End. He was a first-class gold-beater now, working long hours in a hot, dusty shop on Cornhill. He couldn't wait for the day to end to get home to his little garden and a grapevine that he watched over with loving care and tenderness.

Ephraim never was a rugged chap and, when he had to choose between his profession and his health, he quit the city and bought 17 acres of land on Lexington Road out in Concord. There—in a little white house— Ephraim lived with his wife. He had the vines and flowers he loved, and he did a bit of gold-beating in a tiny shop behind his home.

When the gold business slumped, Ephraim had more time to putter in his garden. Already he had noticed how sandy the soil was on that gently sloping hill that faced the south, and he remembered the Sweetwater grapevine he had left behind on Fayette Street in Boston. One day he dug it up and transplanted it to Concord.

Ephraim tended and pruned the new transplant for two years, but eventually it died. He was disappointed, but he kept on trying—this time with vines he found growing nearby. Yet with all his care and skill, they never did produce as well as the southern vines.

His neighbors wagged their heads and said, "I told you, Bull. You can't raise grapes up here in New England—season's too short. You'd better raise something else."

One day he read about a fellow who achieved success in getting new varieties of pears by planting seeds instead of grafting. He thought he'd try the same stunt with grapes.

He found one vine in Concord that had at least two of the qualities he wanted—good flavor and early ripening. Around the first of October, he dug a hole on the side of his sandy hill and dumped in a handful of ripe grapes—skin and all. He planted them about two inches deep and covered them up with some old boards.

For six long years he cared for those seedlings, but only one vine out of all those plantings showed any promise. Then he planted grapes from that vine. Ten years later, he had what he was looking for.

Imagine the feelings of that persistent farmer, watching the little hard bunches of green grapes get bigger and bigger! How excited he must have been when he compared them with all the other spindly, insignificant grapes and realized that his were *three weeks ahead* of all the other grapes in New England.

One morning in September 1840, when the sun lay in a golden haze across the meadows and the smell of autumn was in the air, Ephraim Bull went out to the trellis behind his house. There it was—a great big bunch of luscious purple loveliness! The Concord grape!

Did he rush to the telephone to call the Associated Press? Oh no. Did he yell to his next door neighbor to come and look? No Siree. He covered 'em up and said nothing. He wanted to be sure that he had what he thought he had.

Five years later, Ephraim Bull (now well past middle age) was ready to tell the world about his discovery. And he decided the best way of publicly announcing his find was to exhibit his new grape at the fall meeting of the Massachusetts Horticultural Society.

When the show opened and the new grape hadn't arrived, two members of the Society went out to Concord and said, "Where are those grapes you promised to send in?"

Quite taken back, Mr. Bull stammered, "I did send them in, by a neighbor. I was too sick to make the trip myself, but I sent them just as I said I would."

Very much puzzled, the committee went back to the horticultural show. They rummaged around and found the grapes hidden in a pile of squashes and turnips and other vegetables. One glance and they knew Ephraim had something!

They looked at the big, round, juicy fruit that had ripened fully two weeks before any other grape and then snitched a couple to eat. They smacked their lips and said, "I'll bet he girdled the vines—we better make sure there's no trickery here."

Back to Concord they hastened—notebooks in hand—and gave poor Mr. Bull quite a going over. But he showed them the vines and some other clusters—far bigger and better than those he had sent to the show.

Once convinced, the committee announced to the world that, at last, a grape had been developed that would grow in New England—bigger and better than any grown before.

The next year, when cuttings from the original vine were offered to the public, $3,200 was realized from the first season's sale.

Unfortunately, poor Mr. Bull was more of an altruist than a business-man. Before he knew what had happened, the grape business had slipped through his fingers.

The Concord grape was the first real table grape and created a sensa-tion. Ephraim Bull lived to see the result of his toil spread all over Amer-ica, bringing fame and fortune to others while he himself was broken in spirit and body.

Next time you visit old Sleepy Hollow Cemetery to see the graves of Thoreau and Alcott, Emerson and Hawthorne, I suggest you look up the simple headstone that stands above the grave of Ephraim Bull—on which is inscribed: "He sowed—others reaped."   END

A Strange and Wonderful Inheritance

by Martha R. McPartland

> Waterman Sweet, bonesetter, hopes to meet the applause of all who may be under the necessity of employing him. He may be found at the Market Cellar, where he has a lot of good butter for sale, fit for table use.

From the Providence Journal
February 16, 1830

In colonial America, graduates of medical schools were few and far between. In Rhode Island there were only five medical school graduates practicing in 1800, and the first medical degree awarded in the state was at Brown University in 1814. Prior to that period, from its founding in 1636, Rhode Island had many men called "Doctor" with little or no qualifications to back up their title. Some were the seventh son of a seventh son, and so believed to be endowed with special healing power; some were charlatans with a smattering of education and glib tongues, who took advantage of misfortune and ignorance; still others had a natural flair for caring for the sick and were able to relieve much suffering. In the last category was a remarkable family from the southern part of Rhode Island called, and still recalled as, the "Bonesetter Sweets."

The Sweets were an old Rhode Island family whose progenitor, John

Top left: *Dr. William Sweet (1802-1888)*; top right: *Martha (Tourgee) Sweet (1803-1880)*. Bottom, from left to right: *their sons, Drs. Benoni, George, and Job Sweet. (Photos courtesy of George Sweet)*

...in his mind's eye he could see every skeletal bone

Sweet (1),* came to the state from Salem, Massachusetts in 1637. Of Welsh extraction, family tradition has it that their forebears in Wales had this innate facility for helping the sick. James Sweet (2),* son of the immigrant, John (1), was the first of the American "Bonesetter Sweets." He was born in 1622, came to Rhode Island with his parents, married Mary Greene and settled in what is commonly called South County, more correctly Washington County. Of the nine children of James and Mary Sweet, only Benoni (3), born in 1663, became a bonesetter. Traditionally, Benoni is said to have had a flowery and polished manner—perhaps a forerunner of the bedside manner possessed by some of today's medical men! He was called "Doctor" Sweet, and his practice consisted of setting bones. He was a respected member of the community and a communicant of the historic Narragansett Church. When he died in 1751, Dr. James McSparren, rector of the church, delivered a glowing eulogy.

The inherited ability to set bones was not regarded by the Sweets as a vocation, but rather as an avocation. They were artisans by calling—stonemasons, blacksmiths, wheelwrights, and carpenters. Bonesetting was a sideline, as is demonstrated by the advertisement from the *Providence Journal* of February 16, 1830, printed at the beginning of this story.

The remarkable part of this family was the fact that they never exploited their natural ability. Not one of them sought fame or fortune through this medium. The father usually selected one or two of his sons, probably those who showed a tendency in that direction, and instructed them in bonesetting. The Sweets did not deem this a magical thing but more an inherited knowledge acquired from their elders. They handled fractures, sprains, and dislocations with a skill to be envied by an orthopedic physician. Their skill was in the manipulation of bones, but they were known to use herbs, ointments, and skunk grease in massaging too. Their knack was thought uncanny, as they so often succeeded where others, more learned and "better trained," had failed. Instances naming local doctors who failed to relieve suffering that was later relieved by one of the "Sweet witches" have become a part of South County folklore.

Dr. Benoni Sweet (3) selected his son, James (4), to carry on the fam-

* The numbers designate the generation, as the given names so often are repeated in the family.

[26]

and knew just where it should be placed...

ily art. James was born in 1688 and not too much is known of his successes, but it was Job Sweet (5), son of James, who gained national recognition and established their bonesetting reputation. Job (5) was born in 1724 and married Jemima Sherman in 1750. He lived all his life in the South County section of Rhode Island. During the Revolutionary War, Dr. Job, as he was called, was sent to Newport to set the bones of French officers, an operation their own doctors would not attempt. After the war, Aaron Burr, later Vice-President of the United States, sent for him to minister to his daughter, Theodosia, who had a dislocated hipbone. Dr. Job, rather reluctantly, journeyed to New York and was there greeted by Colonel Burr, their family doctor, and several other learned medical men. Job was not happy about having an audience. They suggested that a specific hour—ten o'clock the next morning—be set for the operation. After they had left the house, Job talked soothingly to Theodosia, who was in great pain, and explained to her his methods. When he had eased her fears, he asked her father if he could place his hands on her hip to locate the trouble. Colonel Burr consented and, after a few minutes, Job said to her, "Now walk around the room," and much to the surprise of Theodosia and her father she did just that—and without pain. When the medical team arrived the next morning, Job was well on his way back to Rhode Island, and Theodosia's hip was properly set and on the mend.

Two of Job's (5) sons were natural bonesetters, Benoni (6), born in 1762 and Jonathan (6), born 1765. Benoni married and lived in Lebanon, Connecticut, where he continued the Sweet tradition of amazing people with his propensity for healing. Jonathan settled at Sugar Loaf Hill in South Kingstown. He married Sally Sweet and pursued his trade of blacksmithing. He trained his son, Job, in both smithing and bonesetting. The only "hinderance" they asked for their bonesetting services was enough to pay for the time lost in shoeing a horse!

"Shepherd Tom" Hazard (*Recollections of Olden Times* by Thomas Robinson Hazard, J. N. Sanborn, pub. Newport, R.I. c. 1879), a South Kingstown diarist who knew Jonathan Sweet (6), once inquired of him, as he was setting a boy's thigh bone, just how it was done. Jonathan replied that he could not explain it, but that in his mind's eye he could see every skeletal bone and knew just where it should be placed. This same knowledge was displayed by Dr. Job (5) of Aaron Burr fame, when he

[27]

was being shown through a medical science hall in Boston by a learned doctor. Glancing at a skeleton exhibited there, Dr. Job remarked that he had never seen a "tominy" before, but that there was a little bone upside down in the foot of that one. His learned friend protested but on closer examination admitted that such was the case.

Many South County people recall incidents relating to this remarkable family. "Shepherd Tom" Hazard, considered a reputable historian of the area, recalled another incident to illustrate the complete lack of avarice in the Sweet family. Hazard met William (7) Sweet, son of Jonathan, on the street in Peacedale, South Kingstown and, while chatting with him, discovered that he was returning from a visit to Newport where he had been called to set the arm of a man who had fallen from a haymow.

"How much do you charge for a visit across the bay?" inquired Hazard.

"Why," answered Sweet, "I have been very unlucky. In going I was detained all night and most of the next day on Conanicut Island by bad weather, and I got over so late I was obliged to stop all night at a tavern in Newport. Then I had to walk six miles out of town to fix the man's arm, and had to stay another night in Newport. Now it is nearly sundown, and I have not got home yet, so I had to charge him bad, eight dollars."

Hazard figured that from this eight dollars William Sweet had to deduct four ferry fares of 40 to 60 cents each and two tavern bills for food and lodging, to say nothing of travelling some 20 miles on foot and losing four days' work!

In some instances the bonesetting was performed by Sweet descendants not bearing the family name, as was the case of Edward (Bunk) Harvey of South Kingstown, whose mother was Frances Sweet (8), daughter of William. (Though several of the Sweet daughters are said to have possessed the bonesetting gift, none is known to have practiced it.) Edward Harvey was a crossing tender who plied his bonesetting trade in South County. An admirer told of his cousin who, while playing baseball in 1917 as a youngster of 13, was struck in the leg by a ball, which resulted in a large, painful swelling on his lower leg. He was under the care of the most skilled of local doctors and, after three months, was still in the same condition. One of his doctors recommended that he consult "Bunk" Harvey, with the admonition not to tell of the referral.

The boy, some 40 years later, gave the following account of the treatment: "Bunk ran his hand up the front of my leg from the ankle to the knee, then with one quick snap of his thumb he twisted the bunch on my leg. It hurt like hell for a minute, then the pain disappeared, and the

[28]

lump was gone. Bunk told me that two cords had become twisted one on top of the other. That leg hasn't bothered me since."

Generation followed generation of this bonesetting family, and branches appeared in many parts of the country. Some of them went to Upper New York State and others to Massachusetts and Connecticut, where their prowess as bonesetters comes to light in local histories and genealogies. The last practitioner bearing the Sweet name in South County was Dr. Benoni Sweet (8), son of William (7) and Martha (Tourgee) Sweet. Benoni was born in South Kingstown on September 23, 1840. He married Eliza Eaton and settled down in Wakefield, Rhode Island. He was a stonemason and worked at this trade for a number of years, but on the death of his brother, George, in the 1890s, he assumed the family profession of bonesetting. The Rhode Island Medical Society thought enough of Dr. Benoni and his ability to present him with a certificate to practice medicine in Rhode Island. He was unusually successful in his practice and on the very day he died, April 21, 1922, reduced the fracture of a boy's wrist.

In late years the Sweets have gone on to obtain medical degrees. One of these, Dr. John Sweet (1884–1950), was a practicing physician in Newport, Rhode Island. He is quoted in an article by P. P. Swett in the Connecticut Medical Journal for 1946:

> "It is my belief that the reputation of the Sweet family for skill in setting bones was often deserved; but quite frequently the blind faith created by popular superstitions covered up many mistakes in the past which would be revealed by x-ray today.
>
> "The mechanical principles which brought success to the Sweets are the same which are found scientifically sound today.
>
> "Folk stories concerning the achievements of the Sweet family have led to the belief that there was a 'natural gift for bonesetting' and that no training for the art was necessary. This belief is in complete variance with the facts. From early childhood the boys of the family have seen their parents perform 'bonesetting operations' and the principles of the procedures have been explained in careful detail."

Dr. John Sweet's statement bears out the modernization and conversion of the natural bonesetting Sweets into licensed and reputable physicians, as he became a member of the American Board of Orthopedic Surgeons, thus combining his inherent ability with professional knowledge. So, be it North, South, East, or West, any orthopedic surgeon named Sweet may well be a descendant of that unusual and fascinating clan of "Bonesetter Sweets" of South County, Rhode Island.   END

MARIAN MACDOWELL

Maker of Memories

by Carl Carmer

The first I saw of Marian Nevins MacDowell, widow of the American composer Edward MacDowell, was her feet. I heard a step on the floor above and looked up just in time to see black round-toed shoes with a strap across the instep—like the party shoes of a little girl—buckled over white cotton stockings. They came down the stairs like a brook down a sluice. I had no time to rise. Suddenly she was before me, tiny and fragile in a cotton dress of small lavender and white checks. Her round face, crowned by grey hair combed into an old-fashioned "pompadour," was a complex pattern of sharp lines and it crinkled in a smile at my amazement.

"I swung on crutches for years," she said. "Now I'm proud I can come downstairs so fast."

Marian MacDowell with a young friend.

A timorous visitor at Hillcrest, her Peterborough, New Hampshire, home, I sat in her famous "music room." I had come to thank her for my admission to the MacDowell Colony as a Resident Fellow. I told her that I had been a teacher, was now an editor, and hoped to be a writer.

"We have something in common," she said. "I'm working at my third career, too. I was a concert pianist when I met MacDowell. I was his wife for nearly 25 years. The year before he died he told me he wished other artists could have the convenience and solitude he enjoyed here. And so when I was 50 I started a colony with only my own home and an out-building. I wanted it to be a place where professional writers, painters and composers could work without the difficulties that modern living imposes. Now I've been manager for nearly as long as we were married, and we

[31]

have 25 studios, comfortable houses to sleep in, and a community hall.

I said I had heard her play her husband's music at a recent benefit and enjoyed it.

"I don't play well any more," she said, "but I make a lot of noise, and audiences like to hear an old lady play fortissimo."

The next afternoon she came to my studio, isolated in a grove of pines, where I was trying to reconcile myself to the fact that I had been deprived of all the excuses I had previously made to myself for not producing words.

"I feel stunned," I told her. "I keep saying to myself 'They can't do this to me—no telephone, no street noises, no visitors.' "

"It will take you a week or so to get used to it," she said. "After that the work will pour out. Wait and see. Now I want to know if you like this studio. Is your desk in the right light? Is your chair the right height? Have you wood for your fireplace? Is your cot comfortable? Can you afford the $15 a week you're paying for your room, meals, and studio?"

I did not see her again until the end of my three-month stay. Then I went back to Hillcrest to say thanks again and goodbye. I told her she seemed to understand the personal needs of all the writers, painters and composers in the studios scattered over 600 acres of colony woodland.

"I lived with a creative artist for a quarter of a century," she said. "I found out early about the good reasonable things—food, sleep, uninterrupted concentration. The hardest lesson to learn was to tolerate the unreasonable things." She sat up straight with an excited glint in her eyes. "Once MacDowell and I were on our way to a dinner at Mrs. Jack Gardner's in Boston. My husband despised formal affairs, and he scolded me so hard for accepting our invitation that I said 'All right, you go back home and I'll tell Mrs. Gardner an important man from out-of-town wired you to meet him at the Back Bay railroad station and you could not refuse.' MacDowell agreed, and left me. I lied about my husband's absence to Mrs. Gardner, who was gracious and forgiving.

"When we came out of the dining room, however, there stood MacDowell in earnest conversation with one of the guests. Mrs. Gardner went straight to his side and said, 'Did you meet the man from out-of-town all right?'

[32]

" 'What man?' said MacDowell.

"Since then I've known that a worker in the arts cannot be depen
upon for what others call rational behavior. It's not absent-minded
really. It's just that ideas storm into their minds and take complete
session."

During the next decade when I was a frequent resident of the P
borough colony, I came to know what Marian MacDowell had mean
"the unreasonable things." A writer whose chief enemy was alcohol
summoned to Hillcrest and told plainly, "If you *must* get drunk, go d
town and buy a bottle of whiskey. Then come back, lock yourself in
room, and drink it. Your drinking is none of my business unless you i
fere with the work of other colonists or give the colony a bad reput;
by being found in a town gutter. If either of these things happen,
stay will be terminated."

Two weeks later she was forced to send the man away for commi
both of these sins. Later I discovered that the man who had comm
them had been exiled to a hotel high on a New Hampshire mou
where his expenses were being paid from the personal funds of M
MacDowell.

One night, in an excess of good feeling, a new and prominent artis
danced on an elaborately carved Italian marble table that graced th
ony garden, and one of his joyful leaps had cracked its surface. Frigh
and penitent he climbed the rise to Hillcrest to confess and was me
with gales of laughter.

In all of the nearly two-score years she managed the colony, she be
impatient with its residents less than a dozen times—these being
roisterers interfered with the work of their fellow-colonists, or love ;
did the same, or when hoity-toity new arrivals demanded special priv
such as breakfast in bed.

In September of 1938, after I had become one of the directors (
Edward MacDowell Association, a telegram informed me that the
Dowell Colony had been destroyed by a hurricane. It said the (
buildings, including the studios, were still standing but thousands
tall pines that had made the place a peaceful haven lay in pathet
ordered piles on the ground. An immediate meeting of the boar
called for discussion of the crisis. Down from Peterborough came N
MacDowell—calm and unruffled.

"Nature makes quick restorations," she said. "In a few years r
will know that we ever had a hurricane."

[33]

Edward MacDowell, composer
of "To a Wild Rose."

"Think of the cost," wailed a director, "just to clear the fallen trees."

"The day after the blow," said Mrs. MacDowell, "I bought a second-hand sawmill, and our employees and I have been cutting and selling cordwood."

"But the Board did not empower you to buy a sawmill."

"No," she said. "By the time I had permission someone else would have had the sawmill."

The restoration was, nevertheless, very expensive and Marian MacDowell fought for the money to save her project with greater strength than anyone could believe was in her frail, 81-year-old body. She played more concerts. She gave more lectures. She wrote to the Federation of Women's Clubs—and these organizations responded.

It was at this time, too, that she discovered a method of dealing with her Board of Directors when they disagreed with her.

"This may be my last request," she would say. "I'm in my eighties and probably won't be at your next meeting." This sentence won her projects unanimous approval until the directors discovered that she had outlived many of their fellows and suspected she might outlive them as well.

Gradually, during the ninth decade of her life, Americans began to realize the magnitude of her contribution to the national culture. She had created at Peterborough ideal conditions for those whose lives were dedicated to the creative arts, and her plan had begun to show results. Her judgments on applicants had been little short of miraculous. (The current Committee on Admissions wonders how she did it!)

To her delighted surprise, Pulitzer Prizes, Guggenheim Fellowships, awards of the Prix de Rome, began dropping on colonists in a glittering rain. The poet, Edwin Arlington Robinson, had been among her first applicants and he returned each summer for 23 years. His work had not been generally known when he had first gone to Peterborough, nor had the works of the many other colonists whose names are now permanent in the cultured annals of America. Among those to whom she granted residence were Stephen Vincent Benét, William Rose Benét, and DuBose Heyward, who, in collaboration with his wife, Dorothy, turned his novel *Porgy* into a successful play and, later (with the Gershwin brothers), into the opera "Porgy and Bess." Writers Willa Cather, Thornton Wilder, Elinor Wylie, John Gould Fletcher, and composers Aaron Copland, Roy Harris, Charles Wakefield Cadman and Douglas Moore made electric the atmosphere of the MacDowell Colony.

The services which Marian MacDowell offered the colony residents were unobtrusive. While they were eating their breakfasts at Colony Hall, the beds in the houses where they slept were being made. They knew that their basket-lunches would be deposited about noon on the steps of their widely separated studios. Only after six would dinners bring the colonists together after each had had the opportunity of a whole day's concentration.

No one quite realized that the aged woman at Hillcrest was supervising not only the daily schedule but the care of the grounds, the purchase of supplies, the problem presented by visitors who thought they should be allowed to see "artists at work" as if their studios were cages of a zoo. Patient, unpretentious, and wise, she got things done without being seen by those who benefited by her labors. She loved to repeat the story that while plodding along a colony road she had been picked up by a dowager in a big chauffeur-driven limousine. The lady had asked her questions about the colony and she had answered them, then requested to be set down by the kitchen door.

"Thank you for the information," said the dowager. "Doubtless you are one of the help here."

"Yes," said Marian MacDowell, "that 's *just* what I am."

Among my own experiences with her during the three decades I knew her, one of the most vivid in my memory is of meeting her in New York City in 1949 when it had been arranged that in honor of her achievement she was to receive the "Key to the City." I accompanied her to the office of Mayor O'Dwyer where she at once entered a blarney contest with its occupant and more than held her own. We then returned to her hotel and found that the bellboy had rushed to the entrance with a wheelchair for her use. Stimulated by the witty battle she had just won, she strode airily by the waiting conveyance, saying to me, "You ride in that. I'll walk."

When she was well on in her 90s, she discovered to her consternation that her doctors would not allow her to cross the continent from the winter home of her long-time companion, Miss Nina Maude Richardson, in Los Angeles to her loved colony. Offered the position of Corresponding Secretary for the MacDowell Association, she accepted with enthusiasm, and in her 99th year she composed and mailed more than 1,000 letters in the colony's interest.

On the morning of August 24, 1956, Marian MacDowell worked at her job as usual. She died before midnight. Four days later one of the dozen or so letters written that last day was in my mail. She wrote lightly that so many people had told her she must live to be a hundred that she had almost decided to do so. She was happy, she said, over the successes of the recent colony-residents who had come to Peterborough from England. Alec Waugh's *Island in the Sun,* dedicated to her, had made a record in pre-publication awards and the reviews of Rumer Godden's *Episode of Sparrows* had been enthusiastic.

"Everyone in this busy world tends to have something in the way of discomfort," she continued, "but I think most of us try to forget our physical ailments and go ahead with our work . . . I'm not going to write about my ailments. They are just the natural ones that any old woman who is nearly 100 is apt to have . . . It's amusing, isn't it, that next year I'll be a hundred and the Colony will be fifty!"

Even those who knew Marian MacDowell best found her difficult to sum up. They felt at first as I did, that her passing was just another example of her unpredictability, and resented it. Then began sorrowing appraisal. They knew that to every one of the contributions that had been poured from Peterborough into the stream of American culture, she had given accents of her own. Many creative artists soon realized that she had satisfied needs which she understood even better than they. She had

*Edward MacDowell, composer
of "To a Wild Rose."*

"Think of the cost," wailed a director, "just to clear the fallen trees."

"The day after the blow," said Mrs. MacDowell, "I bought a second-hand sawmill, and our employees and I have been cutting and selling cordwood."

"But the Board did not empower you to buy a sawmill."

"No," she said. "By the time I had permission someone else would have had the sawmill."

The restoration was, nevertheless, very expensive and Marian Mac-Dowell fought for the money to save her project with greater strength than anyone could believe was in her frail, 81-year-old body. She played more concerts. She gave more lectures. She wrote to the Federation of Women's Clubs—and these organizations responded.

It was at this time, too, that she discovered a method of dealing with her Board of Directors when they disagreed with her.

"This may be my last request," she would say. "I'm in my eighties and probably won't be at your next meeting." This sentence won her projects unanimous approval until the directors discovered that she had outlived many of their fellows and suspected she might outlive them as well.

" 'What man?' said MacDowell.

"Since then I've known that a worker in the arts cannot be depended upon for what others call rational behavior. It's not absent-mindedness really. It's just that ideas storm into their minds and take complete possession."

During the next decade when I was a frequent resident of the Peterborough colony, I came to know what Marian MacDowell had meant by "the unreasonable things." A writer whose chief enemy was alcohol was summoned to Hillcrest and told plainly, "If you *must* get drunk, go downtown and buy a bottle of whiskey. Then come back, lock yourself in your room, and drink it. Your drinking is none of my business unless you interfere with the work of other colonists or give the colony a bad reputation by being found in a town gutter. If either of these things happen, your stay will be terminated."

Two weeks later she was forced to send the man away for committing both of these sins. Later I discovered that the man who had committed them had been exiled to a hotel high on a New Hampshire mountain where his expenses were being paid from the personal funds of Marian MacDowell.

One night, in an excess of good feeling, a new and prominent artist had danced on an elaborately carved Italian marble table that graced the colony garden, and one of his joyful leaps had cracked its surface. Frightened and penitent he climbed the rise to Hillcrest to confess and was met only with gales of laughter.

In all of the nearly two-score years she managed the colony, she became impatient with its residents less than a dozen times—these being when roisterers interfered with the work of their fellow-colonists, or love affairs did the same, or when hoity-toity new arrivals demanded special privileges such as breakfast in bed.

In September of 1938, after I had become one of the directors of the Edward MacDowell Association, a telegram informed me that the MacDowell Colony had been destroyed by a hurricane. It said the colony buildings, including the studios, were still standing but thousands of the tall pines that had made the place a peaceful haven lay in pathetic disordered piles on the ground. An immediate meeting of the board was called for discussion of the crisis. Down from Peterborough came Marian MacDowell—calm and unruffled.

"Nature makes quick restorations," she said. "In a few years no one will know that we ever had a hurricane."

[33]

offered them rest—because she knew that there were some days when it was better to fish than to work.

Another gift, hard to describe, was stillness! She had firmly believed that in the fields and woods surrounding the cabin-studios at Peterborough, there was a quiet of an especial quality which enabled an artist to face himself, understand himself, identify himself. Perhaps the best of all her gifts to the hundreds of artist-residents, however, had been her personal encouragements. No resident of the Peterborough colony ever left it without bearing away a recollection of her that he regarded as uniquely and personally his own. She was a maker of memories.   END

A basket lunch is deposited at noon on the steps of each studio.

JOHN TABER

His Integrity
Made Money

by Sheldon Christian

Enterprising Yankee business men have thought of many ways of "making a dollar," but it was left to John Taber, of Portland, Maine, in the early 1800s, to think of printing up money as it was needed. He got away with it, too, because what he did was then legal enough; and his money was "sound." But the time came when he had more money than he was worth—and that was what ruined him.

Maine, then a District, was under the jurisdiction of Massachusetts. It would be almost a quarter of a century until, in 1820, she would gain separate Statehood. The Massachusetts General Court had passed a law in 1799 forbidding banks within her jurisdiction to issue bills in denominations of less than five dollars. Silver coins were allowed to be used, but there was very little silver in circulation. Only the small bills issued by the banks of other states, therefore, were available as currency. There was this disadvantage to the currency of other states, however—there was a good deal of counterfeit paper in circulation, and there was therefore an element of risk in handling it.

Until 1802, there was only one bank in all of the District of Maine.

This was The Portland Bank, incorporated as recently as 1799. Within three years, a second Maine bank was founded—The Maine Bank, also located in Portland. It was not until 1805, however, that the Massachusetts law forbidding her banks to issue bank notes in denominations of less than five dollars was repealed. Responding to the "law of supply and demand," John Taber & Son, the year before this, had begun to issue what was in effect "money," in small denominations of one, two, three, and four dollars; and it was so "good," that it actually soon became common currency in Maine. In fact, these notes were the only paper money in these amounts issued in Portland at this time.

Paper money is merely a form of promissory note. United States currency used to promise to pay the bearer in gold, in the amount stated; later the amount became payable only in silver. Now, of course, U.S. paper currency carries no such promise, only the statement that "this note is legal tender . . ." But in the days of metal-based currency, this metal, when actually on "deposit" to the amount of the bills issued to represent it, was deemed to be of intrinsic worth, and therefore served as a medium of exchange having relatively constant value.

The Tabers were Quakers. They had come to Portland from Vassalborough, Maine, where John had been engaged in tanning, and entered into a commercial partnership with Samuel T. Hussey and Isaiah Hacker, who were also Quakers. When this partnership was dissolved, John took his son Daniel into partnership in an export-import business. The business consisted of exporting native products, and importing needed articles from abroad. It was therefore based on shipping. The little promissory notes the Taber firm issued, being in small denominations, facilitated business both for themselves and for their patrons. And, because John Taber's integrity was so highly respected, his "notes" were acceptable to others, and soon passed from hand to hand as "money."

On the side margins of the notes were Latin mottoes: "What are laws without morals," on one side; and on the other, "Rather restrain than punish." On the ends was printed, "Massachusetts, One Dollar," varying with the denomination. The number of the particular "bill" or note would be written in, followed by the printed promissory statement:

We promise to pay (and here was space so a name could be written in) or bearer, on demand, one dollar (or whatever the denomination was) at No. 13 Union Wharf, Portland. (Date of issue.)

John Taber & Son

Attest: N. Pratt

Mr. Pratt was the Taber firm's bookkeeper and cashier. As the cashier, he would redeem these bills for silver if requested. Actually, there were few requests for redemption. On the one hand, it was because people had faith in the Tabers' reliability that they were glad to have their notes to use for money. On the other, a little piece of printed paper, representing in value from one to four dollars, was much easier to carry around in one's pockets or purse than the equivalent in heavy silver.

Not only did Mr. Pratt take care of Taber's books, he also married his daughter, and proceeded to reap considerable dividends on this investment in the form of offspring. Like his employer, however, he had a son who did not fully measure up to his high expectations of him. One night, as he was returning home, a ruffian under heavy disguise, lying in wait for him, suddenly sprang out and roughly demanded that he yield up his money.

Pratt recognized with pain and sorrow that the voice was that of his son, and replied, "Reuben, is this thee!"

The youth, losing his nerve, turned and fled.

Another of his sons was lost to him on the privateer *Dash*, which sailed out of Portland Harbor in 1814, manned by many of the region's finest

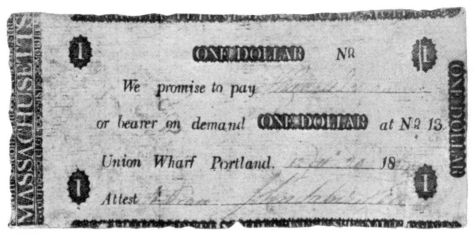

A note promising the bearer one dollar from John Taber's "private mint."

young men and youths, and was never heard from again.

John Taber's son Daniel liked sport, which was nothing against him, but he frequently allowed his love of sport to interfere with the obligations he owed his father's business. He liked to go bird hunting, and William Goold, the Portland historian, relates that he was told by a Portland man who, as a boy, used to go along to retrieve young Taber's birds for him, that Daniel would always reward him generously with one of those Taber bills. The difficulty was that when Daniel needed ready cash—which was most of the time—he would fill out one of those notes without attending to the basic proposition of seeing to it that there was actually an equivalent value in silver set aside on deposit, which the note merely represented. This loose practice on the part of the son did not long pass unobserved; yet, so highly regarded was the elder Taber's integrity that the money came to be called "John Taberson's"—meaning that they trusted the father, if not "& Son." And in spite of Daniel's "watering the stock," John's solid worth would probably have carried the firm through if the events leading up to the War of 1812 had not brought down not only the House of Taber, but many other Portland merchants as well.

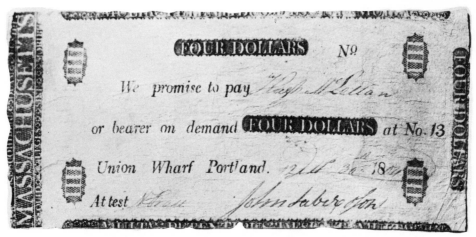

Four-dollar Taber note. (Courtesy of the Maine Historical Society.)

With the beginning of the Napoleonic struggle between England and France, Yankee shipping found itself victimized by the marauding tactics of the two. Napoleon declared a blockade of Great Britain. Great Britain, to gain needed manpower for service on her great ships, arrogantly began stopping American ships on the high seas, boarding and searching them; seizing whomever her officers decided looked like British subjects; and pressing them into her service. Congress replied to this in 1806 with the "Non-Intercourse Acts," following up, in December of 1807, with the declaration of an embargo against foreign trade. The effect of this was ruinous to American shipping, because it simply resulted in the tying up of American bottoms to rot at their wharves. Mercantile communities like Portland, whose life-blood was circulated by navigation, were practically dead on their feet for want of business. Some 30 firms in Portland alone went bankrupt during the first year of the embargo. And among these was John Taber & Son.

After the failure of the firm, John Taber was settling up accounts with his former partner, Samuel F. Hussey. It was ascertained that Taber still had a credit balance of $60.00. Hussey now solemnly and deliberately began to count out the amount due Taber, and handed him the money. But to Taber's consternation, it was in Taber's own, now worthless, notes. Since, financially, Taber's back was against the wall, it was a cruel trick for an old colleague to play on him. He had not expected such sharp practice from one who not only had formerly been his partner but who was a fellow-Quaker to boot.

"Now thee knows, friend Hussey," he remonstrated bitingly, "this money is not good now."

"That is not my fault," Hussey replied. "Thee ought to have made it better!"   END

Crusaders

SECTION 2

Way Ahead of Her Time

by Martha R. Wright

When William Lloyd Garrison in Boston published on January 1, 1831, the first number of the weekly *Liberator*, of which he was both editor and publisher, and when Prudence Crandall later in 1831 opened her Female Boarding School in Canterbury, Connecticut, of which she was both proprietress and principal, neither knew that two years later their interests would be joined in a conflict which in that era would become national in its scope. The conflict concerned the establishment of a private school for Negro girls in the serenely dignified and orderly village of Canterbury, located among the beautiful rolling hills of

Windham County, at the crossroads of the Norwich-Worcester and Hartford-Providence Turnpikes. Whittier's poem to the 26-year-old William Lloyd Garrison beginning

Champion of those who groan beneath
Oppression's iron hand:

might also have been a tribute to the 28-year-old Prudence Crandall, who, with the unswerving determination of the New England Abolitionist, stood unshaken against her opponents, many of them her neighbors and friends.

Prudence Crandall, born in Hopkinton, Rhode Island, in 1803, was brought up in a family of Quakers. As she wrote to Mr. Garrison "I received considerable part of my education at the Friends' Boarding School, Providence, Rhode Island." Her family moved to Plainfield, Connecticut, and in 1813, to Canterbury. In Canterbury in 1831, she purchased a large house in the center of the village at the crossing of the turnpikes facing the Canterbury Green. Here she opened the Canterbury Female Boarding School, a project that met with great success and became well known and prosperous.

"Having been taught from early childhood the sin of slavery," Prudence Crandall was tremendously moved by the articles in the *Liberator* concerning the condition of the Negro in both the slave and free territories. Even at this early date, the *Liberator* advocated immediate emancipation of all slaves. Charles Harris, a Negro whose future wife was employed by Miss Crandall, was the local agent for the *Liberator* and provided her with copies of the publication.

Charles's sister Sarah, a bright young girl who had attended the local school and was a member of the Canterbury church, frequently stopped at Miss Crandall's. Sarah showed great interest in what was being taught at the school and expressed her desire to enroll. She could, it was decided, attend school as a day student, while continuing to live at her father's house some little distance from the village. So, encouraged by the relentless anti-slavery propaganda of the *Liberator*, Miss Crandall permitted Sarah Harris to enter her previously all-white school. "By this act I gave great offense," she stated.

The protests of the residents of Canterbury and surrounding areas rose to the righteous heights of Puritan indignation. Parents of the girls attending the school demanded the immediate withdrawal of Sarah Harris. Miss Crandall refused. The Episcopal clergyman's wife told her that if she permitted that colored girl in her school, it could not remain open. To

[45]

Prudence Crandall's home and school in Canterbury, Connecticut

this Miss Crandall replied that "it might sink, then, for I should not turn her out."

The furor rose, and the greater the furor, the more adamant the principal became. When she realized the prejudice and irrationality of the forces against her, Prudence made up her mind that, if it were possible, she would teach colored girls exclusively. Upon reaching this decision, she wrote to the editor of the *Liberator*.

In her first letter to Garrison, January 18, 1833, Prudence Crandall asked for his opinion "respecting changing white scholars for colored ones." She had decided that, if it were possible, she would devote the remainder of her life to "the people of color." After the exchange of several letters with Garrison and trips to Boston, New York, Providence, and Philadelphia, Miss Crandall was satisfied that she could enroll "twenty or twenty-five young ladies of color to enter the school for the term of one year at the rate of $25. per quarter, including board, washing and tuition." The *Liberator* for March 2, 1833, carried "the advertisement of Miss P. Crandall, (a white lady), of Canterbury, Connecticut, for a High School for young colored ladies and misses." Garrison had been more than enthusiastic and had wholeheartedly endorsed the project. The commencement of the term would be on the first Monday in April.

[46]

For the next year and a half, from January, 1833, to August, 1834, Prudence Crandall and William Lloyd Garrison were to be the central figures in a local dispute which aroused world opinion, led to the founding in Connecticut of a Female Anti-Slavery Society, and set up in Brooklyn, Connecticut, a newspaper, the *Unionist*, to publicize the case.

The uproar in the town of Canterbury extended far beyond the confines of the village. In one week alone, Canterbury held three town meetings. The wealthy and prosperous residents claimed that the school had brought disgrace and ruin on them all. But to all the demands and amid all the clamor, Prudence Crandall, with her small group of 17 Negro students, remained firm. Her attempt to have representation at a town meeting failed. Her principal spokesman, Reverend Samuel J. May from nearby Brooklyn, Connecticut, attended one Canterbury town meeting where, as he states in his recollections, he and his companion were refused recognition at the "Meeting House—one of the old New England pattern —galleries on three sides, with room above and below for a thousand persons, sitting and standing. We found it nearly filled to its utmost capacity." Reverend May records that the tirades and invectives poured out against Miss Crandall and him were accompanied with threats of physical violence.

Undismayed, Miss Prudence Crandall opened her classrooms as planned on April 1, 1833, for the first school for Negro girls.

Reprisals began immediately. Her home was pelted with filth and refuse, and manure was thrown down her well, contaminating her water supply. Townspeople taunted her and her pupils when they appeared in public. Storekeepers would not sell her food; physicians refused to attend the ill at the school. She was beset on all sides. Throughout the ordeal, she was assisted by her father and a close Quaker friend, together with a few other supporters, who carried water and food to the beleaguered school.

Garrison, when he heard the reports of the Canterbury town meetings, gave the caption "Heathenism Outdone" to a *Liberator* article describing the scandalous affair. He put "the names of the principal disturbers in black letter—black as the infamy which will attach to them as long as there exists any recollection of the wrongs of the colored race." So severe was Garrison's attack on the five men whose names he published that even Miss Crandall was to intercede and to write to Garrison "to handle the prejudices of the people of Canterbury with all the *mildness* possible, as everything severe tends merely to heighten the malignity amongst them. 'Soft words turneth away wrath, but grievous words stir up anger.'"

[47]

The "shame of Canterbury" was complete . . .

The persecutors failed in their cruel efforts to intimidate the inmates of the school and failed, too, in the attempt to revive an old Pauper and Vagrancy Statute in Connecticut. Under this statute, town officials could order any person not a legal resident of the state to depart, to fine that person "one dollar and sixty-seven cents for every week he or she remained in said town after receiving such warning, and if the person so warned should not have departed before the expiration of ten days after being sentenced, then he or she should *be whipped on the naked body not exceeding ten stripes.*" However, Miss Crandall and her Negro girls were not to be threatened into submission.

The next move made by the school's detractors came on May 24, 1833, when the Legislature of Connecticut passed the infamous Black Law, designed and phrased to affect the problem of the Canterbury Female Boarding School. This act stated that "no person shall set up or establish in this State any school, academy, or literary institution for the instruction or education of colored persons who are not inhabitants of this State." The act further provided that the education of any colored person not a legal resident of the State must first have the approval of the civil authorities and Selectmen. When news of the passage of the Black Law reached Canterbury, Reverend May records that "joy and exultation ran high in Canterbury. Bells were rung and a cannon was fired until all the inhabitants for miles around were informed of the triumph." The "shame of Canterbury," as one writer has called it, was, indeed, complete.

On June 27, just about a month after the passage of the Black Law, Prudence Crandall was arrested by the sheriff of Windham County and arraigned for trial at the next session of the Superior Court. Having learned even before the passage of the law that the result would be arrest and jailing, Miss Crandall and her advisers had agreed that in order to bring more attention to the egregious infamy of the law and to the relentless malevolence of her persecutors, she should go to jail rather than have bonds posted for her. She wrote, "I am only afraid they will *not* put me in jail." Even the sheriff stated that he was ashamed to make the arrest as he knew the assailants of Miss Crandall would bring disgrace to the State of Connecticut. Prudence Crandall did spend the night in jail, sleeping in the cell vacated by the execution of a wife-murderer. The next day the required bonds were posted by friends. But the news that a young lady of culture had been "imprisoned as a criminal in a murderer's cell in the State of Connecticut for opening a school for colored girls" soon made the papers not only in this country but also in foreign countries.

Prudence Crandall was tried twice for her *crime* of operating a Female Boarding School for Colored Girls. At both trials she was convicted. Her counsel filed a bill of exceptions, and an appeal to the highest legal tribunal in the State, the Court of Errors, was granted. Her lawyers argued on the constitutionality of the Black Law. The court after hearing much eloquence and pleading on both sides evaded a decision, ruling instead that it was "unnecessary for the court to come to any decision upon the question as to the constitutionality of the law." The case was finally dropped on a technicality in July, 1834.

The decision to abandon her philanthropic and noble purpose came to Miss Crandall when, after their failure to get a decision from the Court of Errors, her enemies turned again to physical harassment. They set fire to the school. Though this attempt at total destruction of the school was foiled, soon afterwards her house was again attacked at night by an angry mob armed with heavy clubs, iron bars, stones, and bricks. This time the house was rendered literally uninhabitable. The cost of repairing it, only to invite a repetition of the riot, seemed impracticable. Miss Crandall and her advisers decided to abandon the Canterbury school.

But the cause was never abandoned. In 1834, Prudence Crandall married the Reverend Calvin Philleo, a Baptist minister from Ithaca, New York, and moved with him to Illinois. There, and later in Kansas, she continued to conduct classes for Negroes.

The story of Prudence Crandall and her connection with Connecticut did not end entirely with her marriage and her new home in Illinois. Oddly enough, her life was to be related indirectly many years later to another great man, a great supporter of humanitarianism, whom she never knew . . . Mark Twain. It was through Twain's interest in the lost cause in Canterbury that, on April 6, 1886, a special law was enacted by the Connecticut legislature. By this law Prudence Crandall Philleo was to receive, beginning as of April 1 and continuing throughout the remainder of her life, "$400 a year in equal quarterly payments by way of compensating her for injuries done to her person and property by the citizens of the Town of Canterbury during the years 1833–1834."

Connecticut finally gave Prudence Crandall a place of honor and distinction in the history both of the state and of the nation. For her time, she was, as William Lloyd Garrison wrote, "an unequaled woman." END

Ex Chao, Ordo

by David K. Witheford

"*Ex chao, ordo!*" Out of chaos, order! Carved in a circular seal over the portico of a Georgian building in Saugatuck, Connecticut, these words sum up the goals of one man's life. The chaos was city traffic. The order he brought to it benefits us all.

Below the seal, carved even more prominently, are the words "Highway Traffic Control." They lead many passersby into thinking the building is a police barracks or highway office. But if you go there to report an accident or renew your driver's license, you will be surprised. The heavy mahogany door admits you first to an elegant hall. Its floor of large black and white marble squares, walls panelled in blue and creamlike Wedgwood, and furnishings of venerable origin suggest this is no ordinary office. It is, as the receptionist in the room beyond will tell you, the Eno Foundation. And behind her desk—to lend emphasis—is a life-size portrait of the founder, William Phelps Eno.

He is standing in an erect but relaxed stance, his right arm on the mantel of a dark marble fireplace. He is dressed elegantly in a grey suit and vest, but his slim build, complexion, and confident gaze give the impression of an outdoorsman. His grey hair is cut short and the Vandyke above his stiff high collar is neatly trimmed. If you placed the time at about World War I and judged him then to have been in his late 50s, you would be right.

Down a side hall you could see a replica of the fireplace in the portrait's background. Like the rest of the room, it is a copy from the "big" room of the Eno house in Washington. How big is "big"? Large enough to contain comfortably a 17 x 30-foot Persian rug, a sofa and chairs once belong-

William Phelps Eno (Courtesy of the Eno Foundation)

ing to Napoleon's Josephine, a desk that once was Marshal Ney's, bronze statuary, and ornately framed oil paintings. Another life-size portrait dominates the scene. This one is Mr. Eno's wife, the former Alice Rathbone of New Orleans.

Clearly, the Enos were wealthy. Why did he—a millionaire whose forebears went back to Colonial days—become so concerned about traffic that he founded, and generously funded, an organization dedicated to traffic improvement?

His own words best start the story. As he recalled his New York City boyhood, describing a visit to his father's office on Broadway, he wrote:

"One day I drove down there with my mother in an open carriage, known as a barouche, and on returning home, we were caught in a

[51]

traffic jam on Broadway. It took at least half an hour to get out of it. In those days, many years before the motor car came into use, it seemed as though a dozen vehicles could cause a blockade, since neither drivers nor police, if there were any around, knew anything about the control of traffic or the proper thing to do ... This was my first experience with what disorder could do ..."

Those days "before the motor car" meant 1867, when Billy Eno was nine years old and living way uptown on 23rd Street. His father, a successful businessman turned real estate developer, had built the famous Fifth Avenue Hotel shortly before the Civil War. It was a time of bustling activity and dynamic growth, an exciting place for a nine-year-old boy to be.

Later on, he would call Saugatuck his home. Connecticut was his heritage, after all; his parents had come to New York only in the 1830s, after his father, Amos Richards Eno, had learned the dry goods business in Hartford. And he could trace his Yankee lineage far back. James Enno [sic], on his father's side, sailed from England in 1648 to settle in Windsor, Connecticut. His mother's antecedents in America went back even a few years earlier. William Phelps of Tewkesbury, England, landed in Dorchester, Massachusetts, in 1630, and then went westward as one of the first settlers of Windsor. From those early days both families had established records of distinguished civic and military service.

These influences of family heritage, boyhood interests, "independent means," and then opportunity, conjoined to spur him into his real career at the start of the 20th century. He had just completed the settlement of his father's estate. Now he felt free to leave architecture and real estate and turn to his first interest.

The initial public impact came quickly. In January, 1900, his article "Reform in our Street Traffic Urgently Needed" appeared in the magazine *Rider and Driver*. It was shortly followed by another—"Suggestions for the Management of Carriages at Entertainments." His impatience with delays from carriages making U-turns at the Metropolitan Opera brought that into print.

Public response was immediate. Newspapers picked up and reprinted his suggestions and city officials began to pay attention. He urged New York City Police Commissioners to set up a mounted traffic police squad —and soon a prestige outfit was born. He next prepared a brochure called "Rules for Driving." The Police Department liked the rules but couldn't find money in their budget to make copies. But as soon as the Department endorsed them as the world's first police traffic regulations, Eno paid for and printed 100,000 copies. He then made sure they were widely distributed. From that time on, Eno and "traffic regulations" became virtually synonymous in the public mind. Cities all over the United States wrote in for copies of the New York traffic code and sought Mr. Eno's advice on their problems.

By 1909—the same year that General Motors was incorporated—he had published *Street Traffic Regulation,* the first book ever to deal with traffic. He had also made the first of many trips to London and Paris as a traffic consultant. Motor vehicles were by now crowding out the horses. In the ten years since he had begun his work, their number had grown from only 8,000 to nearly half a million. His pace quickened. He presented papers at meetings, wrote articles for magazines, sent letters to editors, and badgered police commissioners. He also enlisted the support of his influential friends.

To help solve the traffic problems of Paris in 1912, he attacked on several fronts. He got the aid of the American Ambassador, the American Chamber of Commerce in Paris, and the Paris Edition of the *New York Herald-Tribune.* He wrote and then published *Le Problème de la Circulation.* Eventually, he again printed 100,000 folders and 1,000 placards of his regulations. He was getting known for his "Système Eno." Soon he was being called the "Father of Traffic Regulation " in America.

He was designing safety islands and rotaries. He was recommending one-way streets and taxi stands. He was promoting the use of stop and go signals and the use of traffic crow's nests—from which police officers could control the surging traffic. "*Ex chao, ordo!*"

By 1921, there were ten million motor vehicles in the United States, and Mr. Eno was 63 years old. He had not remarried after his wife's death several years before. He had no children, and he foresaw that his chosen work would need to be continued. To assure himself that it would, he set up the Foundation.

Honors began to come his way. In 1923, his efforts were recognized by his alma mater, Yale University. In company with novelist Edith Wharton, Harry Emerson Fosdick, and 12 others, William Phelps Eno was granted an honorary Master of Arts degree. In 1925 he was made a Chevalier of the French Legion of Honor. France, too, recognized the benefits of the traffic organization he had achieved.

Perhaps because he was an ardent and skilled horseman, when Eno began his work he was not convinced that automobiles were here to stay. In fact, he had so little faith in them that the first cars he bought were secondhand. Furthermore, he never drove a car himself—even though by the time he died there were 30 million in America. And though his regulations laid the groundwork for all the traffic laws that followed, he wasn't always right about traffic. At one time he believed that automatically controlled traffic lights were dangerous. Rotaries at every intersection would be better. "Beware of skillful salesmen of mechanical traffic lights," he once warned.

Nevertheless, he had foresight. In 1938, he directed that the Foundation he had set up to help traffic could turn its attention, if it so chose, to problems of noise and water pollution. "The most difficult thing," he wrote, "will be the reduction of noise in the air."

He left the bulk of his sizable estate to his Foundation, which continues to work toward William Phelps Eno's lifelong goal—order out of chaos.

END

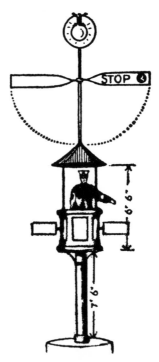

Early traffic light with two sets of "semaphore" arms.

A Mountain
of Determination

by William S. Ellis

D riven by the inexorable dedication of a lonely female with but one purpose in life, Dorothea Lynde Dix almost single-handedly was responsible for instigating "moral management" of the insane in the United States. She stormed through state after state, country after country, and in the ensuing clamor there could always be heard the rattle of chains and the squeal of rusty hinges as the insane were unshackled and led out of their dark, filthy dungeons.

Miss Dix's crusade lasted 40 years. When it was over, America and much of the world had come to realize that cruel and indifferent treatment of the insane could no longer be tolerated by civilized people. In the year of her death, when she was 85, she could point to more than a hundred modern hospitals and asylums and say that she was responsible for their existence. She could know, too, that she had won the profound respect of Americans who, because of the tenor of the times, were weary of crusaders—especially those who wore their hair pulled back and fashioned in a bun.

Before the respect, however, came resentment. Many state legislators greeted hints of scandal with more shrugs than shock. To them, Miss Dix was simply another pinch-lipped feminist who had strayed from the kitchen. But they were soon to learn that the sickly woman with the soft

[55]

voice was a mountain of determination, and that, as William Blake observed, "great things are done when men and mountains meet."

As a friend and disciple of William Ellery Channing, the first great Unitarian divine, Miss Dix was fired with the rich enthusiasm shared by those who subscribed to the ideas for radical social reform being put forth at the time by Channing, Wendell Phillips, Edward Bellamy and, a short time later, Lincoln Steffens. Her desire to help others was without direction until one March day in 1841 when she went to the local jail in East Cambridge, Massachusetts, for the purpose of teaching a Sunday School class.

There, she found two inmates sharing an unheated cell. They were shivering from the cold. When Miss Dix asked the jailer for an explanation, she was told that the two inmates were insane. And as for the unheated cell—well, said the jailer, a person whose mind is gone "can't feel the cold, ma'am."

That experience was Miss Dix's first encounter with a situation scorched to blackness on twin burners of cruelty and ignorance. It started her off on a lifetime of incredible accomplishments.

During the next two years she visited every jail and almshouse in Massachusetts, taking careful notes of highly deplorable conditions. In many of the institutions—indeed, most of them—Miss Dix found insane men and women helplessly trapped in the muck of supreme degradation. The stench was overpowering, and the teeth marks of insolent rats were glaringly visible on many of the chained arms and legs. The human quality of man was not even faintly discernible.

Dorothea Dix filled notebook after notebook with records of her observations.

"—Concord: A woman in a cage; violent, noisy, unmanageable most of the time.

—Dedham: In the almshouse, two females in stalls; lie in wooden bunks filled with straw; always shut up. One of the subjects is supposed curable, but denied hospital treatment because of the expense.

—Barnsdale: Four females in pens and stalls. Two chained.

—Danvers: Young woman . . . there she stood, clinging to or beating upon the bars of her caged apartment, the contracted size of which afforded space only for increasing accumulation of filth. A foul spectacle. There she stood with naked arms and dishevelled hair, the unwashed body invested with fragments of unclean garments, the air so extremely offensive . . . that it was not possible to remain beyond a few moments . . .

Irritation of body, produced by utter filth and exposure, incited her to the horrid process of tearing off her skin . . . disfigured to hideousness."

To the horror expressed by Miss Dix at the situation in the Danvers almshouse, the mistress replied: "Oh, we can't help it. Half the skin is off sometimes. We can't do anything for her." She encountered similar callousness in Lincoln where "an aged woman is chained in a stall, screaming with pain from the cold;" and in Springfield where "a cage, chains and whip were the agents for controlling her (an insane woman), united with harsh tones and profane language."

Dorothea Lynde Dix—oil portrait (taken from a daguerreotype made about 1840) hanging in the New Jersey State Hospital at Trenton.

Such was the state of the mentally ill confined to institutions not only in Massachusetts, but throughout the country, in the mid 19th century. The insane were considered to be dangerous maniacs, immune to all hurts save that of leather cutting into the flesh. But they were funny to watch— oh, wasn't it good sport to visit the local almshouse on Saturday night and, having paid the administrator his asking price (usually between ten and 25 cents), watch the maniacs rant and rave and beat their heads against the unpadded walls of their cells?

Miss Dix completed her two-year study of the institutions and then sat down to write a document with which our history books should be on much more familiar terms. This was her "Memorial to the Legislature of Massachusetts," a report on her findings. When the paper was read to the legislators, there was a shocked silence, for never before had so much damning evidence been so effectively presented.

Although the author of the crushing indictment was a woman—and doing such things was considered beyond the realm of properly womanly conduct—the legislators acted quickly to institute reforms. Miss Dix turned next to Rhode Island, then to New Jersey and Pennsylvania. She went west and south, north to Canada and, finally, across the ocean to Europe. Soon, she was famous throughout the world.

Miss Dix had an extraordinary ability to raise huge sums of money to further her cause. At the time of her death she had raised more money for philanthropic purposes than any other woman in the world. In Rhode Island, she extracted $50,000 from Cyrus Butler, the wealthiest man in the state, to whom she applied for help after her heart-rending encounter with one Abraham Simmons.

Miss Dix found Simmons in the Rhode Island town of Little Compton. He was in a small stone cell, the complete furnishings of which consisted of a thin layer of wet straw. He had been in that cell for three years. Here is Miss Dix's account of finding the man:

"The candle's flickering rays illuminated a spectacle never to be forgotten. The place when closed had no light or ventilation. It was about seven feet by seven, and six and a half feet high . . . There he stood, near the door, motionless and silent; his tangled hair fell about his shoulders; his bare feet pressed the filthy, wet stone floor; he was emaciated to a shadow, etiolated, and more resembling a disinterred corpse than any living creature."

The jailer had warned Miss Dix that Simmons would "kill" her if she entered the cell. Nevertheless, she went to the man and took his hands in hers. The "killer" looked at the woman with pleading eyes and then started to cry.

Miss Dix went directly from Simmons' cell to Butler's mansion. She described what she had seen and asked the wealthy Rhode Islander to donate $50,000. He agreed to give the money, and as a result, construction was started on the now famous Butler Hospital for the mentally ill.

Also constructed as a result of Miss Dix's efforts was Washington's vast St. Elizabeths Hospital (when adopting this name in 1916, Congress for some reason omitted the apostrophe).

When the Civil War erupted, Miss Dix went to Washington, where she was appointed superintendent of woman nurses in the Union Army.

During her wartime service, Dorothea Dix was to supervise the care being provided for Louisa May Alcott, who had come down with typhoid fever while nursing wounded soldiers in Washington. Later, Miss Alcott was to write of Miss Dix: "She is a kind old soul, but very queer and very arbitrary." As the congestion in her lungs became more severe, and as she found it more and more difficult to resist giving in to extreme exhaustion,

After the war, Miss Dix, sicker and more domineering, worked harder than ever to bring about reforms in insane asylums throughout the world. She continued her same tireless investigations, and wherever she was, whatever the findings, there always resulted changes for the better. Finally, in 1881, she could go on no longer.

Dorothea Lynde Dix went to a hospital in Trenton, New Jersey, for a rest. There she died on July 17, 1887. Ironically, she had finished where she had started, for that hospital in Trenton was the first one of many she herself had founded.

In this era of space travel, when the bravery of man is measured by the number of sunsets observed in one day, it seems that America more than ever tends to forget her heroes of the past. Of all our forgotten heroes, Dorothea Lynde Dix's assignment to obscurity seems to be the most unjust. This New England spinster was one of the most useful (and quite possibly the most distinguished) women this country has ever produced. However, it was Miss Dix herself who was chiefly responsible for the fact that today, in her native state of Maine as well as in other sections of the country, her name is recognized by few. She permitted no interviews in her lifetime and allowed no memorials to bear her name. When she was buried near Boston in 1887, the small marble marker contained neither epitaph nor date.

But personal renown was never her aim. Surely the continuing forward progress of the cause to which she devoted her life—the care, understanding, and intelligent therapy of the insane—is in itself sufficient reward for her efforts.   END

Ice Water and Time Capsules

by Emil Corwin

Drawings by Mark Kelley

The gifts of drinking fountains to Boston, Fall River, Pawtucket, Rockville and some two dozen other cities, by Henry Daniel Cogswell, a Connecticut Yankee, in the 1880s, touched off one of the liveliest and angriest artistic controversies of that period. Wherever there are Fine Arts Commissions today to pass on the good taste and suitability of monuments to be erected in public places, acknowledgement must be made to the man who unwittingly started it all.

The fountains were built in a Bridgeport, Connecticut, foundry at a cost of about $4,000 each. Although they varied somewhat in design, features common to most were sculptured likenesses of marine and animal life—sea serpents, dolphins, frogs, horses' heads, pigeons, long-legged birds of the heron or crane family. There were also gargoyles. A curious mixture, and hardly things of beauty. But what proved most annoying was the likeness of the donor himself—a larger-than-life bronze statue of Dr. Cogswell standing atop several of his monuments in full beard and frock coat. In one hand he held a temperance pledge; in the other, an empty glass (for water, of course). Around the base, chiseled in stone were such inspirational Cogswellisms as, "Never Leave Your Work For Others to Do." Or "Indefatigable Perseverance, With Patient Industry, Leads to Fortune." (As it did indeed for Dr. Cogswell.) Hidden somewhere in the masonry of most fountains was a box of mementos "for remote ages to discover." The mementos turned out to be such unspectacular items as one might find in the corner of an attic—local newspapers, photographs of buildings, and various townspeople, including a shot or two of Dr. Cogswell.

Cogswell was proud of his New England heritage and it is not surprising that cities in the region were among the first to be offered free fountains to grace their parks, squares, and streets.

The Rockville, Connecticut, Cogswell fountain as it appeared in 1883, with the donor's statue still aboard. (Photo courtesy of Maurice P. Murray and the Vernon Historical Society)

Born in Tolland, Connecticut, on March 3, 1820, Cogswell was eight years old when his mother died. His father, an architect and builder, brought the boy to live with grandparents in Orwell, New York. Following the death of his father a few years later, young Cogswell, now on his own, returned to New England to make his mark. The going was rough for a boy not yet in his teens. He found work first as a mill hand in Willimantic, Connecticut, and then, presumably for more money, got a job as a dollar-a-week helper in a brick factory in Central Falls, outside of Pawtucket, Rhode Island. He advanced to white collar status in Providence, as apprentice to a jeweler. When the shop went out of business, Cogswell decided to study dentistry, a profession he felt promised some security and a future.

Now dentistry wasn't much of a science in those days. Dentists learned their trade from other dentists. The first dental college opened in Baltimore in 1840, probably just after Cogswell decided to become an appren-

"Man's Free Gift to Man and Beast."

tice in a Providence dental firm. If he had entered the Baltimore institution, one of his classmates would have been William T. G. Morton, who was to become famous for introducing anesthesia at the Massachusetts General Hospital in Boston in October, 1846. But Cogswell, too, was to win fame as a dental innovator and inventor, and an immense fortune.

He opened his own dental office in Providence in 1847 and soon did well enough to marry Caroline E. Richards of Central Falls, daughter of a Providence manufacturer. When gold was discovered in California the young dentist, like a great many other New Englanders, embarked for the West Coast, in 1849, and settled in San Francisco. It was from here, in the late '70s, that Cogswell, now a millionaire from his earnings in dentistry, real estate investments, and mining stocks, launched his great fountain crusade in the name of Temperance.

One of the first fountains went to his beloved Pawtucket. It was erected in Main Street Square and dedicated on November 22, 1880. It was described by one newspaper as "a work of art unsurpassed by anything of its character in the United States." This estimate may have been half right; few could deny it was unsurpassed in character! Made of New Hampshire granite, the 26-foot-high fountain was inscribed as "Man's Free Gift to Man and Beast." Water came out of the mouths of gargoyles, dolphins, bull frogs, and horses. Both people and animals could drink from it. Crowning all was a bronze stork holding an iridescent glass star in its beak. Dedicated to "the citizens of Pawtucket and Central Falls and Their Descendants Forever," the fountain still stands, now shorn of its original ornamentation, at Newport Avenue at the entrance of Slater Park, whence it was removed in 1903. The bronze stork has disappeared, the water no longer flows; but if the box that was placed in the fountain for remote ages to discover is still intact, it will be found to contain a Centennial History of Pawtucket, copies of then current issues of Providence and San Francisco newspapers, several photographs of Dr. Cogswell, and a blueprint of the fountain itself, presumably for the benefit of future planners who might want to build a fountain exactly like it.

A less publicized Cogswell benefaction which is more likely to endure for future generations is the Caroline Cogswell Memorial Clock Tower which overlooks Central Falls from its eminence in Jenks Park. Each Christmas season since it was erected in 1904, the circular stone tower is decorated with colored lights which light up the night sky for miles around.

Perhaps the only Cogswell fountain still functioning stands in Central

It took Boston ten years to get rid of the fountain conferred upon it in 1884.
Dexter Smith termed it "a caricature of art . . . with no claim to mention."
(Photo courtesy of the Society for the Preservation of New England Antiquities.)

Park, Rockville, Connecticut, where he had maintained a dental office. Although the city fathers gladly accepted it when it was offered, in 1882, to the "Town of Vernon and the 'Village of Rockville,'" they were not quite prepared for what they saw on inspecting the finished work at the Bridgeport foundry a year later. The gift was more than a fountain; it was part of an ornate monument surmounted by a statue of Dr. Cogswell himself, his outstretched hands holding the temperance pledge and water glass. "On two sides of it were bubblers for ice water and below each was a basin to catch the overflow and serve the canine population. Beside it was an underground room where the ice which provided the ice water was housed. According to the original agreement the town supplied the ice for it."*

Although Rockville was in no mood to appreciate the temperance motif—the question of liquor licensing was still a hot issue at Town Meetings

* "Vernon Vignettes," a booklet of the Vernon, Ct., Historical Society.

[64]

—the fountain went up anyway in 1883. And so did some tempers. Three years later, on the fourth of July, the statue was "kidnapped" and later found at the bottom of Snipsic Lake. The mud was scrubbed off and the statue restored to its perch on top of the fountain. After another "kidnapping," it remained "lost" until the Centennial Celebration in 1908, when it reappeared, standing beside the fountain with a placard saying, "I've come back for Old Home Week!" Then the statue was carted off to the Town Farm (or poor house), where it remained until sold at the outbreak of World War II to provide metal for the war effort.

Willimantic might have been the second Connecticut city to receive a Cogswell fountain if more interest had been shown. The edifice went instead to Fall River, where it was erected in 1884 outside City Hall. It was to remain there for 78 years—something of a record for survival for most Cogswell fountains. If this gift lacked a statue of the donor, there was no doubt where it came from. One inscription read:

Presented to All Citizens and Mill Operators by H. D. Cogswell, D.D.S., of San Francisco, Who In 1833 as a Factory Boy Marched to the Music Of the Bell.

On another side, etched in granite, one could read:

Citizens and Strangers, Drink Freely of This Cooling Stream. It will Promote Temperance, Faith, Hope and Charity. The Records of 1882 Deposited Within Will Rejoice Antiquarians.

In June, 1962, when the old City Hall was torn down and the fountain with it, the sealed box was found to contain old newspapers and municipal records.

New England was twice blessed in 1884 with Cogswell fountains, the one in Fall River, the other in Boston. The Boston fountain went up in the Common near the West Street Gate. Bacon's *History of Boston* described it (in 1886) as consisting of "a granite edifice, a heavy canopy being supported by four polished columns. On a granite pedestal in the center is a group of two inverted dolphins, in imitation bronze, the faucets being set in the mouths of these pseudo-marine monsters, whose bodies are intertwined. On the canopy is a bronze vase . . . near each of the four corners of the structure is a lamp with colored glass shades. Iced water flows from the fountain during the warm seasons, and is free to all who desire to drink it."

[65]

" . . . *men in working clothes leaped out and battered the statue with crow-bars, severed it from its pedestal, laid it tenderly in the wagon, and it was never seen again publicly . . .* "

The Boston City Council, which accepted the gift, found it "elegant." Few others shared this opinion. The fact that Congress had accepted a similar fountain for the nation's capital in 1882 made little impression on Boston critics. The St. Botolph Club passed a resolution ridiculing the fountain. Moses King's *Handbook of Boston* called it "ugly." Dexter Smith did not include it in the Statues and Monuments section of his *Cyclopedia of Boston and Vicinity* because he found it "a caricature of art, and aside from its useful function of supplying iced water to thirsty throngs, it has no claim to mention."

It was the action of the Paint and Clay Club, however, that set in motion the movement to place in the hands of experts, not politicians, the responsibility of choosing monuments to be erected in public places. In a petition to have the Cogswell fountain removed from the Common, the Club urged the City Council to establish a commission of experts, to serve without pay, to pass on all sculptural and architectural ornamentation offered for the streets and public grounds before their acceptance "in order to guard effectually against such work becoming a reproach to the good taste of the citizens."

And this was done. An Arts Commission was established by an Act of Legislature, in 1890. Under its provisions the commission was to serve without pay; further, it provided that, "No statue, fountain, ornamental arch or gateway monument or memorial of any kind shall be erected in any public street, avenue, square, place, common, park, or municipal building in the City of Boston, unless the design and site for same shall be approved in writing by a majority of said Commission, and their report shall have been made to the City Council."

... *Boston was a model of restraint* ...

Cogswell's Boston fountain was removed in 1894. Two suggestions were made for its disposal: send it to Mount Hope Cemetery or return it to Dr. Cogswell. Where it finally went is not known.

Boston, which put up with the fountain for ten years, was a model of restraint compared with what happened to Cogswell fountains in New York State. The fountain for Rochester (dedicated "to the material wants of our boys and girls who will soon guide our destinies for a brief period, leaving the stamp of their own individuality, and pass on") lasted two years. In his *Rochester Handbook*, Arch Merrill reported that a wagon clattered up to Court House Square Plaza on a March dawn in 1885, and men in working clothes leaped out and battered the statue with crowbars, severed it from its pedestal, laid it tenderly in the wagon, and it was never seen again publicly in Rochester.

The fountains were probably the only major enterprise in Dr. Cogswell's adventurous life that was marked by disappointment and failure. After establishing himself as a dentist in Rhode Island, he became one of the first, if not *the* first, to practice dentistry in San Francisco. A man of inventive mind, he patented a number of useful and practical devices used in dentistry, including a method of securing dental plates in the mouth. Dr. Loren B. Taber, writing in the *Journal of The California State Dental Association*, said that Dr. Cogswell was "possibly the first man in California to use chloroform as an inhalation anesthetic in a dental operation."

If Dr. Cogswell seemed overzealous as a temperance crusader, it was not an unfashionable attitude in his day. The Temperance Movement was one of the leading issues of the time. In offering his fountains, Cogswell reasoned with sound logic that there were plenty of saloons available in most towns and cities but no place where thirsty citizens could get a cool drink of water. He donated fountains to correct the situation, and they made his name famous.

Few remember that Cogswell offered funds to establish a dental college if it would offer free instruction to the needy and permit young ladies of "frugal, sober temperament" to study dentistry. No one would accept the conditions. But he did establish a Polytechnical College where poor boys could learn a trade, and this San Francisco institution, which still serves young people of the region, is Cogswell's most enduring monument. END

A Lupine Legacy

by W. Storrs Lee

Lupines are not indigenous to Maine—not the tall, brilliant garden strains coaxed into bloom from the contents of Burpee packets. The seasons along the northern New England coast are too harsh to perpetuate even hardy dwarfs like those that turn valleys of the West into sapphire lakes, or transform road shoulders into bluebonnet ribbons across the state of Texas.

But early tourists trending Down East in June aren't entirely convinced of this horticultural default, for as they roll down Route 1 through the Brunswick-Bath-Wiscasset country, they are invariably impressed by the roadside splashes of *Lupinus polyphyllus*—not only the ordinary blues, but rank Russells, too, spokes of rose, white, yellow, and the variegated hybrids, growing as naturally along the highway as fields of dandelions and daisies. In fact, many a motorist with a botanical eye pulls in to a gas station for an explanation of the display; and though the Esso oracle may toss off a learned laconism in response, obviously he doesn't know his lupines and couldn't distinguish their life habits from those of a lima bean.

However, if the question were put to a knowledgeable gas-station guide at Newcastle or Damariscotta, chances are that the lupine stalker would be waved off his course and sent down Route 129 toward South Bristol, Christmas Cove, and the sea, and the further he explored that 15-mile detour, the more he would be delighted and mystified by the extravagant patches of color—overgrown front yards abloom with assorted lupines, sunny slopes, abandoned gullies, roadside embankments similarly blanketed, all leading to a sort of lupinesque climax at the headland on which Christmas Cove couches.

That thoroughfare eventually disintegrates into a cul-de-sac; Christmas

Cove was never engineered for through tourist traffic. As Route 129 comes within a half mile or so of the Atlantic, it forks into two very narrow, winding lanes—liberally landscaped with lupine, of course—and both come to a dead end a few yards from the rocky shore, in a confusion of entrances to private drives. Take the left fork. It leads to "Juniper Knoll," and to a solution of the mystery surrounding the origin of so many of those bright patches. The Knoll, sometimes a spectacular floral escarpment, marks the end of the lupine trail.

Intruding upon the margin of an inconsiderable turn-around, sprawls an untidy woodpile, year in and year out, with a neat, hand-drafted notice propped against one of the chunks: "If friends of Hilda Hamlin would tote a few sticks of wood to her cottage, they would be doubly welcome." The weather-beaten cottage that crowns Juniper Knoll is hers. Hilda it was who, years ago, long before anyone ever heard of Ladybird Johnson's national highway beautification program, began this rejuvenation of the Maine roadside.

Burdened with an armful of split seasoned oak, you stumble up the only access avenue to Mrs. Hamlin's aerie, a rough little trail through a jungle of juniper, spruce, rampant blackberry vines and lupine. You emerge from the woods directly onto an open deck to be greeted by an ebullient hostess, whose accumulation of years you would never suspect, and a breathtaking sweep of sea and rugged coast, extending from Damariscove Island to Pemaquid Point, and to Monhegan, a dozen miles out.

For almost three-quarters of a century, Juniper Knoll has been Hilda Hamlin's summer hideout. Here she first began "flinging" lupine seed, imported from her native England, over the thin soil of the headland. They took hold. The biennials grew and blossomed in glorious wild pro-

A rare snapshot of camera-shy Hilda Hamlin, waist deep in the lupines of her back yard at Juniper Knoll.

[69]

fusion, until her hillsides became the garden show of Lincoln County. Every August, she harvested bundles of dried stalks, shook out the seeds and strewed them over a wider area. Handfuls were doled out to neighbors, who started lupine patches in their own back yards, and they in turn made community contributions of more "boughten" seed. From the first there was a contagion about the dissemination.

Then Hilda adopted the habit of filling a pocket with seeds, and on her tramps to the post office, would fling a few into roadside thickets, work them into the soil at a curve in the road where there was a pleasant backdrop of boulders or balsam, or cast them generously down an ugly embankment. A sixth sense and a green thumb dictated where they would do best. She discovered, for instance, that they germinated readily and grew most profusely on the site of old woods' fires.

From Christmas Cove she went farther afield. Though she never drove a car herself, her friends did, and when they took her for a spin, she was prone to toss handfuls of seed from the car windows into spots she felt needed floral decoration. The mature plants, of course, self-seeded and spread, but under the best conditions of soil and climate in Maine, lupine tends to "run out" after a few seasons. New stock is necessary if the show is to carry on. Any number of unknown disciples have appreciated that fact, supplied the seed, and emulated the original strewer.

Like her disciples, Hilda has always kept her plantings strictly anonymous. Only her closest friends were wise to her avocation. Even exclamations expressed in her presence about the beauty of the approach to Christmas Cove were commonly received in poker-faced agreement, with nary an admission of her complicity. It was her practical jest on the public and nature—her private secret. Only on one occasion did she break down and confess all to a complete stranger.

"I was en route to the P.O. on a mid-June morning when the roadside lupines were unusually fine and numerous," she recounts. "Suddenly I heard a queer squeaking sound, and around a bend in the road came a Model T Ford, complete with running board and all the other accoutrements of a Tin Lizzie. Behind the wheel sat a sort of Platonic *idea* of a desiccated virgin, a regular old-time New England schoolmarm, her gray hair done up in a bun and her prim figure rigged out in a high-necked, long-sleeved cotton dress. She stopped the car, begged pardon for the intrusion and inquired: 'Madam, can you explain the origin of these beautiful cultivated lupines growing along the roadside like wild flowers?'

" 'Yes,' said I, 'at the end of the road lives a queer old bird who has so many hundreds of lupines on her land that she has acquired the habit of scattering the seed when it ripens. Her friends call her Hilda Lupina.'

" 'What a delightful hobby,' she said. 'She must be related to Johnnie Appleseed!'

" 'Yes, there's no question of that," said I, 'but it's a very distant relationship.'

" 'Wonderful!' said the old gal. 'How I'd like to meet her and shake her by the hand and thank her.'

" 'Would you?' said I, extending a paw. 'Shake. I am Hilda Lupina.' "

The schoolmarm was dispatched down the road to inspect Juniper Knoll by herself, and the jokester jogged on to the post office. They never crossed paths again.

Miss Lupina's tenure at Christmas Cove antedates even the Tin Lizzie. She arrived there from Bristol, England, in 1904, at the age of 15, with a rich British accent which she has never entirely shaken. She came on invitation of a bachelor uncle, a distinguished professor of philosophy at Smith College; Professor H. Norman Gardiner had built the cottage the year before, only to find it all too isolated and lonely for his tastes. There was no road to the Cove in those days; the only way to reach the tip of the peninsula was by train to Newcastle and then by mail launch down the Damariscotta River. Hilda fell in love with the setting on first sight, and her radiant presence quickly solved the professor's problem of sequestration.

Her invitation had distinctly specified 15 months, but season after season it was charitably extended, until her stay has stretched to a total of 67 years. At the end of the first summer, she went back to Northampton with her uncle, graduated from Smith in 1912, and three years later was married to architect Talbot Faulkner Hamlin, professor and librarian at Columbia, and later Pulitzer Prize recipient for his definitive biography of America's first architect, Benjamin Henry Latrobe. But during all the following years, in which she was raising a family and traveling with her husband, she always managed to get back to Christmas Cove for the summer.

[71]

Separated from her husband in Paris in 1926, she returned to Northampton, where until recently she was a Reader for courses in English, Art
and Religion at her alma mater. That started a close association with students and a perennial addiction to auditing courses. (" 'Culture vulture,'
the gals call me," says she.) Students matriculate and graduate at Smith,
but Hilda Hamlin stays on forever, bridging the generation gaps. Never
does a week pass during the academic year without a full calendar of invitations to undergraduate dinners and doings. The last we knew, she
was attending refreshers in Greek Art, Restoration Literature and Modern
Music.

Come June, she is off again to Christmas Cove and her lupines. She has
outlived the mail-boat run down the Damariscotta River; outlived the
lively and romantic era of the Boston boats to Bath and the coastal steam-
ers from there to the resorts; witnessed the construction of a dusty, horse-
and-buggy highway down the peninsula, and seen that turn into broad
macadam. She has lived through the period when Christmas Cove was a
booming shore resort, with the *big* hotel and any number of flourishing
boarding houses; watched that revert to a quiet cottage community; and
she can count off four and five generations of families that have fre-
quented the Cove continuously during the years.

For them, and for the latter-day tourists, she has established a tradition,
a lupine legacy, that will long outlive her.   END

EDITOR'S NOTE: Mrs. Hamlin was overwhelmed with hundreds of letters and almost as many visitors following publication of the original article in the June, 1971,
YANKEE; most of the correspondents and callers begged for sample seeds. Out of
deference for Mrs. Hamlin's advanced years, the editor feels called upon to remind
would-be roadside gardeners that "Hilda Lupina" is not in competition with Burpee
and other seed suppliers, and, happy as Hilda is with her fan mail, she is no longer up
to distributing souvenir seeds or receiving and entertaining hordes of callers at Juniper
Knoll.

Fabulous Feats
and Towers
of Strength

SECTION
3

Move Over, Paul Bunyan

by Richard L. Champlin

Pebbles tossed into Beach Pond send rings to both Connecticut and Rhode Island shores. A legend begun near there concerning an actual weight-lifter, Elmer Bitgood, who died in 1938, promises to send ripples far beyond. When Paul Bunyan left New England's logging camps for the Great Lakes country, his departure created a strongman vacuum. Will the legend of Elmer Bitgood fill that vacuum?

In the early days of autos, when the fame of Elmer's strength had already reached beyond his Voluntown, Connecticut, home, a caller chugged up to the Bitgood farm where a farmhand of unusual strength was busy *pushing* a plow through the field. The visitor, obviously impressed, exclaimed, "You must be Elmer Bitgood, the strong man." "Oh, no," came the reply. "I'm Doane, his brother." Then, lifting the plow single handedly out of the furrow, he pointed, "That's Elmer over there."

Again, one of the old model cars went rumbling down Crooked Hill Road past Elmer's home in mud time. It bogged down in its own ruts, wouldn't go forward or back. Elmer to the rescue. This 250-pounder came out with, of all things, a harness. He harnessed himself to the car, hauled it uphill with the passengers still inside, and refused to take so much as a penny for his trouble.

Still to be seen near this Connecticut Yankee's homestead are the dumbbells he assembled using rocks the size of double cakes of ice linked by an iron bar, also loose rocks with metal rings attached. These, so the story goes, he lifted with a single finger. Putting on exhibitions at rural get-togethers where they had ox-pulls and greased pig chases, he made a business of muscular feats. He would mount a platform and press the

Left: *Elmer Bitgood, Connecticut's Voluntown Samson.*

[75]

weights up and overhead before gasping spectators, not, however, without first taking up a collection. Only after passing the hat would he perform.

An article on this Voluntown Samson appeared in the *Providence Sunday Journal* for February 24, 1946. According to the author, G. Y. Loveridge, Elmer could squat under a table loaded with stone weighing 2400 pounds, place his hands on a small stool, and with his shoulders and back raise the table three or four inches off the platform. (Must have been a strong table, too!) He could press a 230-pound dumbbell over his head and hold out at arm's length a rock weighing over 150 pounds. Not both at once, of course; but then, let the legend ripen a little, and who knows!

At age 25 Elmer weighed 290 pounds, and just about this time he lifted the front end of a freight car off the track at Danielson. Furthermore, he offered to put it back for a price. He had a right arm like a leg of mutton, but Miss Annie Bitgood of Oneco, who remembers her distinguished relative, assures me that this story has gotten out of hand. Not everything they tell about Elmer happened just that way. "Why, you know how stories grow," she commented. "You start with a feather in the mawnin', and by night it's a feather bed."

What sort of chap was Elmer, anyhow? He had a speech defect, according to one informer, and out with a work party one day a fellow worker nagged and taunted him because of it. Finally annoyed beyond endurance, Elmer strode up to the tease and lifted him up by the scruff of the neck, causing his feet to dangle in mid-air. "Don't you make me mad," snarled Elmer. "Don't you make me mad." And after that, no more trouble.

Reportedly, for all his strength Bitgood was never overly ambitious. Sent by his mother to the woodpile for logs to stoke the fire, he would return with one or two, no more. He conserved his strength for special occasions. Neighbors found it hard to hire Elmer for more than a day at a time. But for a spell he did work with a logging crew at Rice City, Rhode Island, and lodged at the home of a Mrs. Love. On moving in, he warned her that he had a good appetite, and he would pay her board for two, but he didn't want to be restricted at the table.

Perhaps it was while on this job that he performed the feat which has become the stock story about him. In those days sawmills, driven by steam, were set up wherever the loggers worked. Part of the machinery consisted of a sizable steam boiler. One day they needed to raise the boiler to hook it onto a wagon. Elmer saw the need and obliged. Equipping himself with a flat board, he squatted beneath one end of the boiler, placing

The Bitgood brothers—Doane left, Elmer right.

the board across his shoulders to save them. Then he lifted the behemoth into place.

Another person, who didn't know the Bitgoods personally, but said he wouldn't tell me a lie, 'cause that's the way he was brought up, had it straight from one Emory Sweet that Elmer and Doane shouldered a log "20 foot long and 16 inches through on the butt."

If loggers remember him as a logger, orchardmen recall his feats with them. One apple-grower related how the pickers would pile crate after crate of apples onto a wagon, but they weren't sure how much of a load the horse could haul off, weren't sure, that is, until Elmer Bitgood came along. If he managed to raise one wheel of the laden wagon off the ground, then the horses could be expected to undertake the load.

And speaking of horses, the Brothers Bitgood, it is said, once hitched up the horse and headed for the village to buy a barrel of flour. On the way home, as they climbed a steep hill, the horse balked at the load, so Elmer hopped off the wagon, if a 300-pounder can be said to hop, and rolled the barrel onto his shoulder, whereupon he toted it to the hilltop while Doane came along with the horse. Then Elmer unloaded, and the party went jogging along under horse power.

Not only his weight-lifting deeds have caught the imagination, but his capacity to stash away volumes of food. On another occasion the errand was to buy crackers, not just *some* crackers, but a barrelful. Before they reached home, the brothers had finished off the last cracker and tossed the empty barrel by the wayside. (Elmer's mother cooked his meals in a washtub.)

One individual who had competed against Elmer at lifting two stuffed nail kegs joined by a bar, and had lost, told how Elmer went to a farmer once, asking for some milk. The farmer pointed to a 10-quart milk can and told him to help himself. Minutes later Elmer reappeared asking for —some milk! Exasperated, the farmer repeated, "I told you to help yourself. There's the can." But Elmer had already quaffed that off and was back for more.

Churches in financial straits during the early 1900s used to put on baked bean suppers to raise money. "Fifteen cents for all you can eat," they advertised. But it didn't take long for the committee to realize that they lost money if those Bitgoods were on hand to clean up everything. So when the word got around that there'd be a bean supper Saturday night, the clause was added, "and don't tell the Bitgoods." Nevertheless, Doane and Elmer did show up, and one time they paid for five meals. They emptied every platter in sight, including the six-quart bean pot.

Then there was the fellow who wanted to cut down some big trees in his maple swamp. He did so, and next winter went in with a pair of oxen to get them out. However, the beasts pulled and tugged and thrashed about, but they couldn't move the logs. "Better get the Bitgoods," someone suggested. Elmer and Doane came to move the logs. They marched out of the swamp easily. Trouble was, the weight of those logs up on their shoulders pushed their legs into the frozen ground up to their knees.

Finally one more from the legend, the tale of our hero hoisting bales of wool up to the third story loft of a woolen mill. (Elmer Bitgood got around.) He stood there near the edge, too near at one point, for he unbalanced himself and tumbled. On the way down, realizing that this would be a once-in-a-lifetime experience, he glimpsed an open door on the first floor and some wool lying around, so he changed course in mid-air, sailed through the door and came to rest on a pile of springy wool. Lucky for him—and for the legend.

Before his death in 1938, Elmer had reduced considerably under doctor's orders. He might be seen of a holiday or Sunday over at Beach Pond watching the swimming and diving. His lifting days were over, but the legend had gotten a firm footing.

And so, Paul Bunyan, move over. END

The Lady Who Knocked Out John L. Sullivan

by Richard W. O'Donnell

Maybe ex-champion Bobby Riggs proved something on the tennis courts when at the age of 55 he beat World's Champion woman tennis player Margaret Court in 1973, but it seems doubtful in view of what Hessie Wanner Donahue, that doughty dame of South Boston, did. In March, 1892, Hessie *knocked out* John L. Sullivan, the vaunted "Boston Strong Boy," in an Arkansas boxing exhibition—flattened the gladiator who claimed he could lick any *man* in the house!

When she was interviewed in 1961 at the grand age of 87, Hessie's blue eyes sparkled as she brought to life the events that projected a handsome young woman into the same ring with the great John L. For the record, it should be pointed out Mrs. Donahue's victory over Sullivan was strictly accidental.

"I married my first husband in 1891, when I was just eighteen," recalled Mrs. Donahue as she rocked comfortably in a favorite kitchen chair in her West Ninth Street home. "His name was Charles Converse, and he ran a school for boxers in Worcester, Massachusetts, where I was born. John L. Sullivan used to come there quite a bit. He was a great friend of my husband and they used to do quite a bit of sparring together.

"Even before I married Charles, I spent a great deal of time at the training school watching the fighters. In fact, after we were married my husband used to ask me to watch certain men and point out mistakes.

[79]

"Sometimes, strictly for fun, I'd get into the ring with Charles and we'd box a couple of rounds together. I was a powerful woman, and my husband never tried to hit me hard, so I was in no danger. Sullivan got quite a kick out of watching us together."

Boston's pride and joy was, in fact, so delighted by the ring antics of Mr. and Mrs. Converse, he invited them to join his theatrical tour. It was only natural that Sullivan would take to the stage. He was champion of the world and attracted crowds wherever he appeared. Barnstorming meant more money for the lavish Sullivan.

"My husband's school was losing money," continued Hessie, "and he had to close it. The tour gave him a chance to earn money by giving a punching bag exhibition. My husband was also able to pick up extra cash as a sparring partner with Sullivan, when needed.

"I don't know who thought of the idea of my sparring with John L. I can't recall. I do remember Sullivan thought it would be quite an attraction. As far as I was concerned, it was a chance to make $15 for a few minutes' work, so I didn't mind. That was good money in those days. We worked out quite an act together. The audience really loved it."

According to Hessie: "Sullivan would stand up and shout, 'I can lick any man in the house.' He offered cash and volunteers would come up. They didn't stand a chance. He knocked most of them out with a punch.

"If the volunteers were reluctant, I'd go on as a substitute. The announcer would shout, 'And now we have a woman who has volunteered to fight John L. Sullivan.' I'd come out wearing a blouse, skirt, bloomers, long stockings, and my boxing gloves."

Alas, the buster who could "lick any man in the house"—no idle boast

Hessie Donahue

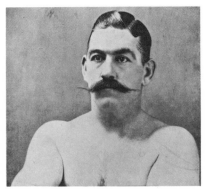
John L. Sullivan

—soon got his come-uppance at the hands of the more dangerous of the species.

That March day in Arkansas, Hessie weighed "about 145 pounds and was a mighty powerful woman." Her opponent tipped the scales "about a pudgy 195 pounds and was out of condition. He was a tired man."

"It was in the third round," recalled Hessie. "I can't remember the name of the town, but it must have been a big one. The hall was crowded that night. John hit me in the face. It was a hard blow and hurt. I became very angry at him.

"After he hit me, John was off-balance for a second. He was always awkward. I swung back at him in anger with a right and and hit him flush on the jaw. He went down. Yes, John L. was out—for about a minute—no doubt about that. He was out cold as a corpse.

"The referee saw he was dazed, but went through with the regular finish to our act. John got up slowly, with a funny look in his eyes. A lot of the people in the audience knew he had really gone down for the count and began giving him a horselaugh when he got up. You should have heard the words he muttered to me when he was on his feet. I wouldn't dare repeat them.

"John didn't remain angry long though. He was too good-natured. He knew it was an accident. We resumed our act together a few days later."

Mrs. Donahue said her boxing exhibitions with John L. always ended with a "knockout."

"The audience would roar," the lady pugilist recounted. "Sullivan would let me punch him all over the ring. That may seem silly now, but everyone enjoyed it in those days. At the end of round three, I'd hit Sullivan and he'd go down. It was all an act. I'd put my foot on his chest. The referee would hold my hand up and say I was the new champion. Then John would bounce up laughing. He got as big a laugh out of the act as our audiences did."

That same year, 1892, an out-of-shape Strong Boy stunned the fighting world when he lost his championship to an excellently conditioned Californian named James J. Corbett. But the moustachioed muscleman remained a great attraction, and he was off on another tour at the start of 1893. He starred in a play about a true-blue blacksmith, entitled "Honest Heart and Willing Hands." His performance at the Old Howard in this drama wowed Boston audiences.

"My husband and I went all over the country with him," stated Hessie. "I'd give my boxing exhibitions whenever possible. Sometimes between

[81]

acts, or whenever Sullivan would give an exhibition on the side, and needed me. The crowds always loved our act."

During her theatrical tours with John L. Sullivan, Hessie Donahue met "practically all the great ones," and formed her own opinions of them.

Of Buffalo Bill Cody, she said: "He was a peacock. He spent so much time in front of a mirror preening himself, I wonder he ever had time enough left to shoot a buffalo."

According to Hessie, "Lillian Russell owed most of her fame to the fact she had a good corset and was able to stuff herself inside it."

"Gentleman Jim" Corbett "was no gentleman. He was conceited too. I wanted to go on the stage with him, but he wanted our bout to end in a draw. He didn't want to have it said he lost to a woman—even as a joke. Besides, he hit too hard."

Famed dancer Pat Rooney, Sr., "was nimble enough to be an excellent boxer. But he probably had a glass chin and would never have got by the first round."

Annie Oakley "dressed like a man in those Wild West britches, and could shoot a hole in a playing card from several yards away. She should have worn more dresses and tried to act dainty. Buffalo Bill was prettier than she was!"

Hessie Donahue was married four times and was a widow four times. Her first husband, Charles Converse, died in 1899, and in 1903 she married Fred Proctor, retired from theatrical life, and settled down in South Boston where she lived out her days.

Proctor died in 1913, and four years later she married Arnold Wanner, who died in 1952. In 1955, she married a South Boston neighbor, Joseph Donahue, when she was in her eighties. Donahue was an invalid, and died a year later.

Of all the "great ones" Hessie encountered over the years, John L. Sullivan was her favorite.

"He was a big show-off, but the people loved him," she said. "There were no movies, radios, television, or things of that sort in those days. A man like John L. was important to the people. He was a hero. Everybody adored him and flocked to wherever he happened to be. Why, men used to pay money to sit in the barber chair he used.

"When he was in shape, John L. Sullivan could really lick any man in the house," concluded the silver-haired Hessie. "He was that strong. He was a powerhouse. Looking back, it's a miracle that I *was* ever able to knock him out."   END

First American to Sail Across the Atlantic Alone

by Robert S. Malcolm

In the middle of the second day of sea fury, the spendthrift power of the great wind began to wane. The enormous rolls of water lengthened and leveled out to long swells, and the solitary man in the 20-foot boat fell forward on the deck to sleep, his eyes running with the shameless tears of sheer exhaustion.

There was nothing in sight but the sweep of sea and the weeping skies. A thousand miles astern lay the sailor's home port of Gloucester, Massachusetts; two thousand miles ahead and to the northeast lay his destination, Liverpool, England.

He should have slept now, but a piercing earache would not let him rest, and vague pains had just begun in his molar teeth. His clothes were soaked and stiff with salt, and his skin was rasped raw. A maximum misery ate into the man's soul.

As the breeze freshened, a topsail schooner winged out of the west, reefed her sails, and stood close to the dory. The captain, flanked at the rail by most of his crew, hailed the lone sailor. "Are you in need of help?"

The voice, vast from the megaphone, boomed into his semi-consciousness. This schooner offered warmth, hot food, companionship, emollient for his aching nerves. Most of all, it offered a reasonable, an excusable, retreat from his vow to reach England alone.

He cupped his hands and his ear twinged brutally as he shouted, "I do not need assistance. I am able to proceed alone. Thank you."

They tried hard to persuade him, for he looked to be in poor shape, but he ignored their coaxing. Finally, the skipper spread sail and the schooner stood away in dignity to the east. As the last mast vanished below the horizon and the great grey emptiness folded about him once again, the sailor cursed the day his stubborn stupidity had committed him to this insane voyage.

It was back in Gloucester, six months earlier, on a bitter, windswept winter night in 1876.

Alfred ("Johnny") Johnson, his face dour and humorless, had looked around the small circle of men who sat under the kerosene lamp in the plain cottage parlor. They were all members of Gloucester's halibut fleet, gathered for an evening of talk, tobacco, and simple fun. The flaring logs crackled in the fireplace and radiated the disinfectant smell of pine wood. Outside, the driving wind raked the unpeopled streets and a soulless cold immobilized the town.

At 29, Johnson was the youngest of the group and a man with a thin sense of humor—the natural butt of the friendly fun of the older men. An argument had just been started about the seaworthiness of the boats of the fleet. Willie Walker, a thin, wiry man with sharp, grey eyes and the poker-faced mien of the practical joker, spoke up in support of the *Susan Lawdor*, a broad-beamed, clumsy boat that none of the halibut men liked being on. "A fine boat," he said. "Slick and easy to handle."

Johnson's clear blue eyes and heavy yellow eyebrows gleamed in the fireglow. You're talking nonsense," he said. "I'd rather sail a rowboat clear across the Atlantic to England than be aboard the *Lawdor* in soft weather."

The general laughter provoked by this remark irritated him. He had an overwhelming desire to be the match of these fine, experienced men. Their very professionalism dwarfed him in his own eyes. "I mean it," he said, looking with challenge at every man around the table.

And when testy Amos MacPherson told him bluntly not to be a fool, Johnson stood up, gazed at his companions with an extraordinary dignity, and went out into the welter of wind.

By the end of May 1876, using the few hundred dollars he had saved at the halibut hunt, Johnson was about ready for the trip. He had bought a dory, the type of strong rowboat used by the whalers, and incorporated in her a few ideas of his own.

She was 20' long, 5½' in the beam, and about 2½' deep amidships. He decked her over, leaving a snug well for himself a little aft, and hinged the foot of the mast that he stepped forward of the *Centennial*, as he named her. The hinge was to enable him to unship mast and sail, in a hurry if need be.

Below deck, he fitted compartments and made them as watertight as possible to preserve food supplies and fresh water from flooding seas. To the stump of the lower part of the mast, where it protruded from the deck, he fastened about 25 feet of stout line. In heavy weather, Johnson intended to tie this line around his waist so that if he were washed overboard he would stay in contact with his boat.

Despite the pleas and protestations of concerned friends, this stubborn man loaded his provisions in the little holds and, on the 16th of June, he cleared Cape Ann lighthouse and set his craggy jaw toward 3,000 miles of wild water and a strange land.

The weather held clear and sparkling for a week. Johnson's only real discomfort was that there was no position on that deck or in the well that would give him adequate rest. He was young and supple, however, and, by changing the lay of his limbs frequently, he did well enough.

At the end of that first week, the sailor got his first taste of the traps of the Atlantic.

Fog, sulphurous and clotted, closed in and stood about *Centennial*, imbuing Johnson with the superstitious horror of the unseen deep and the real dread of being ridden down into the sea by invisible ships.

Despite his prayers, the swirling vapors remained with him for six days. When they finally began to lift and the first rays of the sun streamed through to him, the lone voyager was astounded at how quickly his fear vanished.

His regrets at having persisted in keeping his vow faded, only to redouble on the 6th of July when a great storm fell on him suddenly, battering him and *Centennial* for over 36 hours. At the waning of the wind, the schooner had appeared and offered him rescue; Johnson's fear of failing to keep his word won out against his fear of death in the great sea. By this act, he committed himself irrevocably to finishing his task, alone, as he had sworn, without the aid of any man.

A few days of nearly warm weather set in now, and he managed to get himself dry at last—after about three weeks in continuously wet clothes.

Then, early one morning, as he was finishing his breakfast of canned peaches and soaked bread, a cannon of a wind boomed out of the southwest and hurled a tremendous sea against him.

This was the worst yet. There was no regularity of timing or direction in the rushing of the hilly waters. Solid blows came at *Centennial* from all points of the compass. The little vessel was spun about and smashed against walls of water as against the walls of a great arena. Her master's sinews, unable to brace against the unpredictable angles of attack, were wrenched brutally and, finally, Johnson was knocked senseless against the rim of the well, just after he had managed to unstep the mast and secure it to the deck.

He lolled, unconscious, for a few hours. The blow was not serious, and he awoke at the sudden ending of the storm with nothing more than a bloodied head and a reawakened earache. He washed with sea water, set up the mast and once more faced his fate northeast.

The solitary mariner was now far into the regular Atlantic shipping lanes and he rejected many offers of rescue from the big ships he met, despite his increasing pain, intense personal discomfort, and the certainty of more rough weather awaiting him in the cold northern seas.

In early August, as *Centennial* stood within 300 miles of the south of Ireland, the skies and the seas turned the color of charcoal and once more the might of the waters marched against the adventurer. He unstepped the mast, checked the knot of his lifeline, and waited.

In less than a half hour, amid the drumming waves, a ten-foot wall of water smashed the boat broadside and turned her deck under the surface. Johnson was hurled overboard far from the craft.

The lifeline held. Against the massive thrust of the waves, he pulled himself to the boat and hung onto the keel with frozen fingers. He could not, unassisted, pull the dory upright against the powerful suction of the high seas, and he hung on, grimly awaiting another unusually tall wave to give him the extra leverage he needed.

It was several icy hours and a dozen tries later before a wave struck at the right angle and the last kick of which Johnson was capable turned the boat deck up once more. He was utterly weary, but the last embers of his strength had to be used to pump the well free of water.

As the wind died and the waters stilled, the skies appeared to descend to the face of the sea and a copious rain began to fall. It fell without limit for four days and four nights, giving the man no rest, and in all that time *Centennial* moved not a single mile nearer England.

This realization, piled upon his exhaustion and pain, robbed Johnson of any gratification he felt at having come so near to completing his voyage. His supplies were very low, and there were almost two weeks of sailing still to be done.

His mind grew doughish, conscious of little but piercing pain and the acid of final defeat. Of the early confidence, of the occasional exultation at beating the storms, of the hard will to win, there was left now only the cold ash of remembered ambition.

With the return of the light winds, he sailed on because there was nothing else to do. He was too weary even to realize how near he was to the last point of exhaustion. His movements were sluggish and infrequent.

On August 10, the lone sailor was startled by the appearance of the blank Welsh cliffs off the starboard bow. At first, this meant nothing to him, but as he began to realize that success was actually possible, his mind came slowly out of the anesthesia of defeat, and he regained a measure of his former confidence. He rationed his meager food and water to the borders of rank miserliness, and gripped the tiller with a new power.

Days later, *Centennial* approached the mouth of the River Mersey. A dozen crowded ships came out to meet her and give her master a tumultuous welcome. He acknowledged their cheers with a lump in his throat, for he had not expected anything like this, but declined their offers to take him aboard.

He sailed on just past Liverpool and docked at a landing to the east of the city. A crowd met him at the stage and told him that all England had followed his progress across the great sea from reports given by the ships he had met.

As he checked in at a riverside hotel, stiff and aching, for the best feed and the best rest of his life, Johnson looked back at his boat. *Centennial* rode, tiny and sweet, on the breast of the water. He could not believe that the ordeal was finished.

It was August 21, 1876.

After some weeks of earning his passage home by exhibiting his boat, Alfred Johnson returned to Gloucester and the halibut fleet. There were two changes in him. He had lost his contempt for the *Susan Lawdor*, and, when his friends turned a joke against him, he smiled and joined in it.

It was good to be home. END

Daredevil
Original
"Human Fly"

by Richard W. O'Donnell
(Pictures courtesy of G. Gibson Polley, Jr.)

The climber had reached the 30th floor. He had only 27 more floors to go to reach the top!

That memorable spring day in 1920, the man from Marblehead, Massachusetts, had inched his way, slowly but surely, up the outside of New York's famous Woolworth Building, which, at the time, was the highest building in the United States.

In the street below, tens of thousands of New Yorkers, all of them nervous, stared up at the intrepid climber. Traffic was stalled for blocks around. The city was at a standstill.

Would he make it all the way to the top, or wouldn't he?

When the daredevil reached the 30th floor, something happened, and his heroic climb came to an end. That brave climber did not fall—nothing like that. It was the long arm of the law that got in his way. When the chap reached the 30th floor, a police sergeant stuck his head out a window and asked: "Have you got a permit from the City of New York to do this?"

The man dangling on the outside of the skyscraper informed the law enforcement official that he had neglected to obtain a permit.

"Then, sir," said the sergeant solemnly, "I'll have to ask you to come inside. You've snarled traffic all over downtown New York. Nothing's moving. Everybody's in the street below looking up at you. I'm sorry, sir, but you are under arrest for climbing a building without a permit."

Thus was the great climb ended by what was probably the most unusual arrest ever made by a New York police officer.

Left: *George Gibson Polley, on the way up.*

[89]

A triumphant headstand atop an edifice just scaled.

In his day, George Gibson Polley, who died in 1927, climbed an estimated 2000 buildings in the United States. Never once did he slip or lose his grip. He was known as "The Original Human Fly," and his building-climbing accomplishments stagger the imagination.

In Boston, he climbed up the side of the Custom House and the Little Building. In Lynn, he climbed the old City Hall. He also climbed the City Hall in Portland, Maine. In Manchester, New Hampshire, he went all the way up the side of the tallest hotel in town. Over in Vermont, the "Tarzan of the Cities," as he was being billed, climbed up the side of a Montpelier department store. The building was only four floors high, but it was the tallest thing Polley could find in town.

In Hartford, Connecticut, Polley climbed the sides of three buildings in one day. And over in Providence, Rhode Island, for a change of pace, he once put on a blindfold and shinnied all the way to the top of the tallest flagpole in town.

Polley climbed the old Cregg Building at Common and Amesbury Streets in Lawrence, Massachusetts, so many times that he could go up the outside of that structure wearing a blindfold too.

"My father was a daredevil, but he never took any unnecessary chances," recalled his son, G. Gibson Polley, a realtor in Marblehead and Hamilton, Massachusetts. "Before he went up the side of a building, he always checked out the exterior to make sure there were no loose bricks, or that the wood hadn't rotted away. He used to grab drainpipes as he was going up, and if they were weak, he would not risk a climb. If he considered the outside of a building dangerous, he'd find another one in the same town. Or, if necessary, he'd cancel his climb.

"He used to say he was 'a daredevil but not a fool.' And before he started up the side of a building, he would make a short speech warning youngsters not to try what he was going to do. He made it clear to the youngsters that it took a great deal of training to do what he did. My father didn't drink, or smoke, or even swear. He always kept himself in top physical condition. He was quite a man."

Actually, George Polley's career as a human fly started when he was a mere lad in Richmond, Virginia, where he was born. He loved to play baseball, and one day during a sandlot game, he hit a home run and the only baseball available ended up on the roof of a six-story school building. So George climbed up the side of the structure and recovered the baseball.

In 1910, when he was 12, George's family moved to Chicago, and he got a job delivering newspapers. One afternoon, after delivering a paper to a well known Chicago clothing store, he spotted an expensive suit hanging on the rack.

"Boy!" he told the store owner, "I'd stand on my head on the top of this building if I could have a suit like that."

Naturally, the clothing-store owner thought the lad was joking. "If you do that," he said with a friendly smile, "I'll be glad to give you the suit."

So young Polley went outside, took off his coat, climbed to the top of the three-story building, and stood on his head. The newsboy had a new suit. In later years he sometimes wore a sign on his back naming the product or organization he was publicizing.

Polley's climb up the side of the clothing store attracted a great deal of attention, and he was offered a contract by a local theatre manager. Thus was his career launched. The great Houdini taught the youngster some tricks of magic and, at the age of 13, he was billed as "The World's Youngest Magician." With Houdini's help, he also became an outstanding escape artist. But it was his daring as "The Human Fly" that brought Polley his greatest fame.

Much of his success was due to his flare for showmanship. His arrival in a town was treated as headline news by the local press; he invited reporters to join him when he inspected the buildings he was scheduled to climb, and he always announced that the particular building he was going to climb on that day was "one of the most dangerous" he had come across.

He usually wore a white suit and sneakers as he went up the side of a

George G. Polley, the *Human Fly.*

Polley—here in mid-air—would deliberately "slip," and drop a floor to the next ledge below.

"Fly's-eye" view of a typical Polley audience.

building. And if he thought it could be done safely, he would deliberately "slip" and drop a floor to the next ledge below at least once during a climb.

When World War I broke out, Polley joined the army and served in France as a sergeant in the Observation Balloon Corps.

"After the war, my father would never accept a penny when he performed for the American Legion or the Salvation Army," said his son Gibson. "He was a member of the Legion and was always willing to perform when they wanted to raise funds. He remembered how the Salvation Army kept serving coffee and donuts to the boys up front during the war, and he was happy to help the Salvation Army when that fine organization needed to raise money."

After the war, Polley met and married the former Helen Stillman, who is now Mrs. Horace Snow of Marblehead. His wife was a singer, and they appeared many times together on the stage. After their marriage, the couple settled in Helen's hometown of Marblehead. In addition to Gibson, they had two other sons: Herbert, who was killed in action with the army during the Second World War, and Stillman Polley, a Miami businessman.

During the '20s, many so-called "human flies" crept up buildings in various parts of the nation. But Polley was the originator of the daredevil act and easily the most successful.

He would climb buildings in order to attract crowds to his magic shows in local theaters. Or he would be hired by store owners to attract crowds to their grand openings, or to lure people to carnivals sponsored by civic organizations.

His standard fee for climbing a building was $200. A Springfield, Massachusetts, newspaper used to hire him every December to climb a building in that city and, while he was climbing, newsboys would circulate through the crowd below and collect funds to buy toys for the poor children of the community. It should be noted that Polley added his own salary to this particular collection.

"Human Fly" Polley was also an automobile salesman. In fact, he was probably the most successful salesman the old Essex car company ever had. He would arrive in a town and inform the press that he was about to climb the tallest building available. The press would headline the news and, at the appointed time, Polley would appear and climb the building. Then he would climb back down, and start shaking hands with every person present. He would also hand a small card to each one he greeted, urging one and all to visit the local distributor of Essex motor cars. Finally, he would saunter over to his own magnificent new Essex, start up the engine, and head for the next town where more potential customers were anxiously waiting for him to climb one of their buildings.

Besides standing on his head when he reached the roof of a building, Polley sometimes rode a bicycle around the edge of the roof. Actually, the wheels of the bike were in the drainpipe at the side of the building, which made the feat all the more sensational.

In scaling skyscrapers in practically every major city in the nation, he had his share of close shaves. Once, while going up a building in a southern community, it was necessary for him to grab two copper pipes to boost himself up to the roof. As he was raising his body, one of the pipes broke and struck him on the side of the head. Polley, though bleeding, managed to reach the top safely, but the wound required several stitches.

George Gibson Polley, who had defied death practically every day of his adult life, passed away at the age of 29, during an operation for a brain tumor.

He once told an interviewer: "I regard my vocation strictly as a business, and I assure you I am very glad when a climb is completed. I've climbed more than 2000 buildings during my career, and haven't fallen yet. And I don't expect to."

He never did!   END

A Big Wheel
Around America

by William Edward Mason

In the early years of the twentieth century, when there were no wars, space flights, or fears of a nuclear holocaust or of overburdening our planet, the papers were filled with accounts of daredevils who bounced over Niagara Falls in barrels, "human flies" (see page 89) who scaled the walls of skyscrapers, and a number of long distance walkers. In the latter category was former newspaperman John Albert Krohn, a 35-year-old Newburyport resident who walked all the way around the perimeter of the United States, trundling a wheelbarrow in front of him. In the course of 357 days, "Colonial Jack," as he called himself, walked a distance of 9,024 miles. Newspaper readers of the period (1908) followed his daily progress avidly. The morgues of New England newspapers contain reams of yellowing, crumbling clippings attesting to tall, frail Jack Krohn's fortitude and endurance. Dubbed a "nut" by some, he was praised by legions for his courage and lauded by physical culturists for his stamina. Though the practical value of his accomplishment is questionable, unquestionably no one has ever duplicated the feat.

It all began on a hot sunny day—June 1, 1908—when Jack, dressed in homespun and broad-brimmed hat like a Colonial farmer, appeared before a large crowd in front of the City Hall at Portland, Maine, pushing his wheelbarrow. This consisted of a light spoked and rubber-tired wheel between two shafts on which was mounted a pyramid-shaped box containing his scanty baggage. He carried with him letters from Portland's Mayor, Adam P. Leighton, which he was to present to the Mayor of Portland, Oregon, when he got there, and a letter from D. W. Hoegg, editor of the

Aluminum token commemorating John Krohn's walk.

(Courtesy Leo F. Bennett)

[95]

"Colonial Jack" Krohn and his wheelbarrow, here covered with cards and letters.

(Courtesy Vernon E. Sauvan)

Portland, Maine, *Evening Express*, addressed to the city editor of the Portland, Oregon, *Oregonian*.

To defray his expenses en route, Jack had provided himself with a supply of aluminum tokens which he hoped to sell to persons encountered along his long and torturous route. On one side of the token appeared a representation of himself and his wheelbarrow; the other side explained: "Colonial Jack is walking and pushing his wheelbarrow around the border of the United States, a distance of 9,000 miles in 400 days (except Sundays), starting and ending in Portland, Maine." He did sell quantities of these metal souvenirs and managed to cover the not inconsiderable cost of his great walk by the income gained from their sale, supplemented occasionally by money collected at public appearances and talks.

The wheelbarrow man traversed the northern tier of New England states from Maine through New Hampshire and Vermont and into New York with nothing but pleasant memories, aside from a few doubtful dogs (as he recorded in a journal published upon his return). He was usually accorded a friendly welcome by the curious New England villagers who eagerly purchased his tokens, keeping the walker well supplied with pocket money.

Jack's first real fright came near East Alburgh, Vermont, when he escaped what seemed certain death. He was crossing a railroad bridge with his wheelbarrow; to his horror, when he was in the middle of the bridge, he found a train fast approaching the further end. Cool thinking and fast action saved the day. He quickly lowered his wheelbarrow over the edge of the bridge so that it hung from a strap which he wore over his shoulders attached to the handles. He then dropped flat, lying beside the rails so that the train rushed past without touching him. It took him some time, he said, to get over "my first big scare."

The shoes he wore at the start of his journey had to be replaced by new ones when he reached Charlotte, New York—a distance of 613 miles. The pneumatic tire on his wheelbarrow lasted into the third week; he bought a solid tire in New York state.

Onward he plodded across the states on the southern shores of the Great Lakes, on into Michigan and Minnesota. Walking down a lonely road in Michigan, a day of high winds and driving rain, he fainted—one of the several times he did collapse during his marathon. But his stamina was such that he always recovered strength after a good night's rest and was able to continue. In Bay City, Michigan, Jack was "arrested" by the chief of police for being a "highwayman"—and he was sentenced to the "best meal at the best hotel in town—all free of charge." This happened more than once, as his purposed exploit had caught the imagination of the American people. Throughout his long walk, Jack was offered free meals and lodging in a great many places, usually by police officials, local editors, or other prominent persons. In fact, he slept indoors every night until he reached the Minnesota wilderness—his first camping ground.

Proceeding westward into Idaho in his 21st week, Jack bade goodbye to his wife, who had been meeting him every weekend en route until then. Poor health forced her to return home to Newburyport.

The trip through the northwest to the Pacific coast tested Jack's endurance to the limit. Where possible he followed main roads, but his best progress was made along railroad tracks. To relieve the monotony of the lonely hours, Jack would count the number of telegraph poles along the railroad tracks—they averaged 35 poles to the mile. Often he had to resort to woods roads or wagon trails, and sometimes there were no roads at all.

In Portland, Oregon, he delivered his Portland, Maine, letters and headed down the west coast. He crossed San Francisco Bay to Oakland on a ferry.

Coming into desert country, Jack prepared for it by purchasing new supplies that added 101 pounds to his wheelbarrow, including large water canteens, a small stove, frying pan, heavy blanket, and other camping equipment which up to now he had not needed. Lest the desert prove too much for him, Jack Krohn pinned a note inside his breast pocket: "To whom it may concern. If you should find my lifeless body, communicate immediately with Mrs. J. A. Krohn, Newburyport, Mass. (signed) Colonial Jack, long-distance hiker." But again the railroad proved a helpful guide. By following the tracks across the sandy wastelands and carefully husbanding his supplies, he emerged safely from the desert. In one 24-hour period in Texas, Krohn covered 46 miles—his record mileage for any one day.

The railroad tracks led him through Louisiana, Mississippi, Alabama, and Florida and then up the east coast through Georgia, South and North Carolina. Now at last he was headed into the home stretch.

In New York City, his unusual garb attracted much attention, and the hiker suffered pointed comments and often insults from what he called "the natives." Crossing the New York-Connecticut boundary line into New England made him very happy, and then, at a more leisurely pace, he sauntered up through Massachusetts and along the New Hampshire seacoast into Maine, finally reaching his goal of Portland, Maine, 357 days after he left it originally.

Krohn's numerical profile of his unique undertaking is thought-provoking: days lost through illness—19; towns or cities visited—1,209; pairs of shoes used—11; pairs of socks worn out—112; five wheels and three tires on wheelbarrow, expenses—total $1,356.60; average per day, $3.25; average mileage per day—25.

History records no more walks for Jack Krohn—he settled down to the less strenuous life of a gardener; his strawberries were much in demand by Newburyporters.

Why would anyone *want* to walk all the way around the United States, much less *do* it? Perhaps because, like the mountain, it was there. But perhaps also because John Krohn wanted to see America and his own two feet provided the simplest and most financially feasible means of locomotion. In these days of the energy crisis, when the days of the gasoline-powered automobile seem numbered, other New Englanders might do well to consider Colonial Jack's solution to the problem of vacation travel!

END

The first modern Olympic Games, held in Athens, Greece, in April, 1896. From Krout: "Annals of American Sport" (v.15, YALE PAGEANT OF AMERICA), United States Publishers Assn. Inc.

JAMES CONNOLLY

A Hop, Step, and a Jump to the First Modern Olympic Championship

by Tom Edwards

Of the many United States athletes who have earned gold medals in the Olympic Games, few have paid so dearly for victory as did James Brendan Connolly of South Boston in Athens at the first Olympic Games in modern times (1896).

Not only did he pay his own way to Greece to become the first winner of a modern Olympic event, but, because he chose to participate, James Connolly was expelled from college.

Connolly had entered Harvard in 1895 at 27, having spent three years as a clerk, inspector, and surveyor with a U.S. Corps of Engineers in Sa-

[99]

vannah, Georgia. By late 1895, a Frenchman, Baron Pierre de Coubertin, who had been working for several years to establish some type of international athletic competition, had persuaded some eight different countries to take part in what was to become the Olympic Games the following spring—Greece, England, France, Germany, Denmark, Hungary, Switzerland, and the United States. If it hadn't been for the Boston Athletic Association, which, under the gentle prodding of member Arthur Burnham, had decided to get together a team, it is unlikely that the United States would have taken part at all, and even then our participation was doubtful. Three days before the team was due to sail, funds to cover their travel and living expenses were still insufficient.

Another Yankee stepped into the breach. Oliver Ames, a former governor of Massachusetts, went to work and performed as admirably as any Olympic champion. He begged and pleaded and cajoled friends, contributed substantially himself, and raised enough funds within the short time allotted so that the nine Boston A.A. athletes did embark from Boston, assured not only of the voyage to Athens but of a return ticket as well.

Two other athletes had independently decided to join the team in Athens. One was Robert S. Garrett, a Princeton student whose specialty was discus throwing, who sailed for Greece with the blessing of his University. The other was Connolly—who was less fortunate. Months earlier he had applied to Harvard for a leave of absence so that he might make the trip. As days, then weeks, crept by, he anxiously awaited word from the college. When it did come he was disheartened. His request had been denied. Connolly was told that if he went to Athens he would be expelled from Harvard. With anger and misgivings, he resolved to represent his country nonetheless.

Thus, on April 6, 1896, when King George I of Greece stood in the Royal Box at Athens to open the modern Olympic Games, among the athletes who stood below him on the playing field behind their national flags was the now ex-Harvard student, James B. Connolly.

Twelve pounds overweight when he arrived in Athens, Connolly wasn't worried—he had planned his arrival 12 days before the date that the games were due to open—plenty of time for practice and acclimatization. But he and the other members of what the *New York Times'* Arthur Daley referred to as the "catch-as-catch-can" American Olympic team had made their plans according to the *Roman* calendar, not the Hellenic calendar then still in force in Greece. They found that they had to compete the very next day after they disembarked. More bad news for Jim was

James Brendan Connolly
(Courtesy of the Boston Globe)

that the style required in the hop, step, and jump (or triple jump) event was one long outmoded in America, plus the fact that the competing ground was deep, soft turf instead of the hard surface he was used to.

The first final event scheduled was Connolly's, who was the last to jump. This he did. On landing, he was surprised by the roar welling up from the crowd. "What's that racket all about?" he asked. "By Jove, man," answered an English competitor, "you're a mile in front." Three feet, three inches, to be exact.

By 3 P.M. the competition was over. The crowd hushed as a smallish, wiry, black-haired youth was escorted to the center of the field. The olive wreath of victory was placed on his head, the band struck up the "Star-Spangled Banner," and the American flag was raised aloft on a 200-foot pole at the end of the stadium. As the music ended, King George carefully and distinctly read the name of the first modern Olympic champion— James Brendan Connolly of South Boston, United States of America, who had won the event with a jump of 45 feet.* After receiving the olive wreath, he commented simply: "All my life I shall be weighted with responsibility."

Did he ever go back to Harvard? Not as a student. As Connolly said

---

* The World Almanac, 1897—*the record reads: "Running two hops & jump, without w'ts. J. B. Connolly (A.) 49' 1½"." According to the author, Connolly must have set this record at some place other than the Olympic Games as a number of completely reliable sources set his Olympic distance as 45 feet.*

himself, "I walked out and didn't set foot on Harvard ground until about twenty years later, when I went there by invitation to deliver a talk on literature."

Literature?

His friend, President Theodore Roosevelt, said of Connolly that he was "mentally and physically vigorous and straight as a whip." Not one to rest on his laurels, this Olympic champion kept right on going, reaching excellence in an astonishing number of fields. Soldier Connolly fought with the 9th Massachusetts regiment at San Juan Hill and the siege of Santiago, while Journalist Connolly wrote up what he saw for the *Boston Globe* as its Spanish-American War correspondent.

Sailor Connolly shipped with the Gloucester fleet to fish the Grand Banks, with the German fleet in the Baltic, and with the English fleet in the North Sea. No wonder the stories that rolled out regularly from Author Connolly's salty pen from 1902 to 1944 gained him the title "dean of American sea-story writers."

When Connolly's famous "Out of Gloucester," was first published in 1902, *The Reader*, a literary journal, commented: "This is the sort of thing Kipling tried to do in "Captains Courageous." He failed because, clever as he was, he could not get inside the life, could not become a veritable part of it, and so could not describe . . . (it) . . . accurately."

Connolly could. His stories caught and preserved in print the essence of that great era of New England's fishing fleets because he knew it all so well—the people, the ships, the life, and above all, the sea. The short stories are history with the names changed; their writer swore that every incident in them really happened, even to a ship he described as rolling completely over to right itself again. All his fictional characters, too, are based on real people. Sometimes he wrote straight history, with real names and dates, sometimes biography, such as the lives of Robert Bennet Forbes of Boston and Amasa Delano of Duxbury, Massachusetts—two great New England sea captains. But many feel the most amazing life he ever wrote about was his own, in his autobiography, *Thirty Years Avoyaging*, published in 1944.

So that's why Harvard asked him to come and talk about literature.* Brains, brawn, talent, and courage—Harvard expelled a real broth of a boy in James Brendan Connolly, our first Olympic champion.   END

* They even got around to awarding him a major letter "H" in 1949, 53 years after Connolly left Cambridge for Athens.

Favored by the Muses

SECTION
4

Boston's Slave Poet by Robert E. O'Toole

A seven-year-old negro girl stood on the Boston auction platform shivering and afraid; she was naked, except for a piece of dirty carpet which she clutched to her breast. She was a pitiful sight; with coarse, wiry hair enclosed by a piece of dirty blue cloth. She had lost all her teeth on the trip from Africa. Her legs were thin and crooked, and her whole form depicted physical suffering. This black, illiterate child was to make her mark on American Literature.

The slave (Phillis Wheatley) was born in Senegal, French West Africa about 1753. She was kidnapped shortly after her birth and sold by her countrymen into slavery; she found herself eventually in the slave market of Boston.

The black orphan's life changed that day on the block, for she was purchased by John Wheatley, a Boston tailor. Wheatley was a kind, considerate man. He bought the slave to serve as a domestic servant to his wife. Susannah Wheatley took a liking to the girl on their first meeting; she had her bathed and clothed properly, and gave her the name Phillis. Phillis Wheatley prospered in her new environment; she was accepted as an equal in the Wheatley home, and she performed her menial duties with great care and ability. However, Phillis Wheatley was destined to become more than a servant.

From her earliest entrance into the Wheatley home, Phillis was seen making letters and figures on the walls with pieces of chalk or charcoal. This phenomenon delighted Phillis's mistress; she was amazed that her new servant was able to write and was inquisitive. This was the beginning of the end of Phillis Wheatley, servant; and the start of Phillis Wheatley, poet.

Susannah Wheatley appointed her daughter Mary as instructor to Phillis; she believed that her new protegée could be taught to read and write English. Consequently, she relieved her of domestic duties and had Phillis' belongings moved from the servants' quarters to the main part of

[105]

the house. Phillis became a close companion to her mistress, and she was treated by her master as a member of the family.

Mary Wheatley (later Mrs. Lothrop) was dumbfounded at the rapid progress of her student. At the end of 16 months, Phillis could read and write English fluently; she was extremely fond of English and Latin literature. She loved the poetry of Alexander Pope, whom she imitated in her later literary career. Latin was no obstacle to Phillis; she learned the dead language and translated a short piece by Ovid. Phillis read Greek and Norse mythology; she was a religious person and received her most enjoyable hours from her readings in the Old and New Testaments. In her poem *On Being Brought from Africa* Phillis displays her ardent devotion to Christianity:

> 'Twas mercy brought me from my Pagan land,
> Taught my benighted soul to understand
> That there's a God—that there's a Saviour too.
> Once I redemption neither sought nor knew.
> Some view our sable race with scornful eye—
> "Their color is a diabolic dye."
> Remember, Christians, Negroes black as Cain
> May be refined, and join the Angelic train.

The Boston intelligentsia quickly saw in Phillis the makings of a good poet, and they supplied her with books and pamphlets. Phillis Wheatley soon became one of the centers of literary attraction in Boston. She, after all, was a black who could read and write.

In spite of this new-won notoriety and honor, Phillis remained unchanged. A grandniece of Susannah Wheatley wrote in her *Memoirs*: "She never for a moment lost sight of that modest, unassuming, demeanor, which first won the heart of her mistress in the slave market."

Phillis Wheatley was often invited to dinner by the most prominent Bostonians; however, when Phillis accepted an invitation she was a humble guest. Aware of the feeling toward her race, Phillis would request that she be seated at a separate table; she always dined alone at banquets given in her honor.

Phillis' mistress was delighted at her servant's new fame, but worried constantly about her protegée while she was absent from home. An anecdote in the aforementioned *Memoirs* describes Susannah Wheatley's state of mind during one of Phillis' outings:

[106]

"On one of these visits, the weather changed and Mrs. Wheatley afraid of Phillis' poor health sent Prince (slave) with the chaise to bring Phillis home. When the chaise returned she drew near the window, and explained—'Do but look at the saucy varlet—if he hasn't the impudence to sit upon the same seat with my Phillis!' "

Mistress Wheatley could not do enough for Phillis; she saw to it that she had a candle and writing materials at her bedside when she retired. She also installed a stove in Phillis's room during the cold winter months. Phillis was not allowed to spend all her time studying. She was encouraged by her mistress to learn knitting and other genteel hobbies.

Throughout this early period, Phillis progressed rapidly from an ignorant slave girl to one of the most intelligent of her sex. She loved life. Her mind hungered for knowledge; and her imagination ran rampant.

In the winter of 1773, Phillis's health (poor since childhood) was at its lowest ebb. She was 20 years old and in such poor condition that she was advised by a physician to take a sea voyage. John Wheatley made preparations for her to journey to England with his son Nathaniel in the summer of '73.

Nathaniel Wheatley's business in England was to arrange a mercantile correspondence for his father; he also had the distinction of introducing his mother's protegée to the literary personages of the mother country. Before Phillis left Boston for England, her mistress gave her legal freedom.

Phillis Wheatley was received as a distinguished personage in England; she met Lady Huntingdon, Lord Dartmouth, and Mr. Thornton, a benefactor of Dartmouth College. During her stay in London, the Lord Mayor of that city presented her with a copy of John Milton's *Paradise Lost*, which she cherished until her tragic death. The book was sold after her death, and is now in the Harvard College library.

While on her English vacation, Phillis Wheatley gave her poetry to the world. The poems published under the title: *Poems on Various Subjects Religious and Moral, By Phillis Wheatley, Negro Servant to Mr. John Wheatley, of Boston*, were dedicated to the Countess of Huntingdon (patroness of George Whitfield) and were accompanied with an engraving of the authoress. Phillis sent a copy of her poems back to her beloved mistress.

Phillis longed to meet the reigning English monarch, George III. However, she was destined never to meet the king; for she received sad news from Boston. Susannah Wheatley's health had slipped rapidly, and she was dying. She died shortly after Phillis' return in 1774, and she was soon followed by her husband John and daughter Mary.

Phillis did not know what her future would bring. Though she lived for a while with a close friend of Mrs. Wheatley, eventually she took a room by herself, and continued writing.

In 1775, Phillis Wheatley commemorated the installation of George Washington as General of the Continental Army by the poem—*His Excellency General Washington.*

Washington was so impressed by Phillis' poem that he wrote her the following letter:

Cambridge, Feb. 28, 1776

Miss Phillis—

"I thank you most sincerely for your polite notice of me in the elegant lines you enclosed; and however undeserving I may be of such encomium and panegyric, the style and manner exhibit a striking proof of your poetical talents; in honor of which, and as a tribute justly due to you, I would have published the poem had I not been apprehensive that, while I only meant to give the world this new instance of your genius, I might have incurred the imputation of vanity. This, and nothing else, determined me not to give it place in the public prints.

"If you should ever come to Cambridge, or near headquarters, I shall be happy to see a person so favored by the muses, and to whom nature has been so liberal in her dispensations."

GEO. WASHINGTON

When the British evacuated Boston, Phillis Wheatley did visit the Commander-in-Chief's camp. She was received with marked attention and respect by Washington and his staff.

Poverty stalked Phillis Wheatley; she found it hard to make a living. America's trouble with England made the times hard, and the future of the colonies was indefinite. It was during these depressing days that Phillis received a marriage proposal from a Boston negro, John Peters.

John Peters was a dandy; he wore a wig and carried a brassheaded cane. He loathed the servile work performed by his fellow negroes. Peters was arrogant and vain. He owned a grocery store on Court Street in Boston. Phillis fell in love with Peters, and the negro couple married.

The marriage from the beginning was a failure. Peters was the complete opposite of Phillis. He was envious of his wife's poetical talent and was jealous of her fame and recognition. Peters was illiterate.

After three years of marriage, the negro poetess found herself with three sickly, frail children. Phillis was a loving mother; the love that she showed for Susannah Wheatley was tripled on her children.

But, Phillis was a realist. She put away her pen for the last time and took up the hard task of servitude.

From 1781 to 1784 Phillis Wheatley disappeared from the public scene. However, a relative of Mrs. Wheatley's heard of Phillis' whereabouts in November of 1784. She found the poetess ill and living in dire poverty in a cheap boarding house.

Phillis, who walked with royalty, now trod the path to oblivion; the pendulum had made a full swing for Phillis Wheatley. She was dying; two of her children were already dead, and the third was dying. She died in obscure poverty on the second floor of a boarding house on December 5, 1784—she was 31.

Phillis Wheatley was once referred to as "a kind of poet laureate in the domestic circles of Boston." Her poetry is occasional, and nearly half of her poems are elegies; six treat public events of importance. She loved her adopted country; she speaks of her slavery and kidnap in the poem to the Earl of Dartmouth:

> Should you my lord, while you peruse my song
> Wonder from whence my love of freedom sprung,
> Whence flow these wishes for the common good,
> By feeling hearts alone but understood,
> I, young in life, by seeming fate
> Was snatched from Afric's fancy'd happy seat:
> What pangs excruciating must molest,
> What sorrows labour in my parents breast?
> Steel'd was that soul and by no misery mov'd
> That from a father seiz'd his babe belov'd:
> Such, such my case, And can I then but pray
> Others may never feel tyrannic sway?

END

Faces on a Vermont Barn

by Tennie G. Toussaint

On a back-beyond farm in the sparsely settled town of Kirby, Vermont, there once lived a man by the name of Russell Risley, who was an enigma to his neighbors and to the many curious people who came to his farm from miles around to see his works of art, and his ingenious inventions.

He painted life-size pictures on the sides of his barn of his neighbors and nationally known people with ordinary house paint. So natural appearing, they were recognized instantly, and one had to get close to realize they weren't alive and standing against the barn! Familiar faces appeared on some of the hardwood chunks from the woodpile, and some wooden animals were scattered here and there. In the house every inch of available wall space was covered with his paintings, even between the pantry shelves, there were landscapes, people, and animals, some framed and some not. Painted on canvas, boards, pasteboard and the back of oil-cloth. Out in the pasture stood busts of familiar people cut out of granite stones.

Russell Risley was born on the farm in 1842, and lived there until some ten years before his death on November 17, 1927, at the age of 85 years. After the death of their parents, Mr. Risley and his two sisters, Achsah and Hannah continued to carry on the home farm, as none of the three ever married.

The Risleys were really timid people, and didn't care too much for visitors, especially curious ones. For some years, there was a sign on the gate-post at the foot of the hill leading up to their house, which warned in large red letters, SMALL POX.

Rus Risley was a medium-sized man with a short beard and very sharp eyes. He always wore small checkered brown and white frocks gathered into a waistband at the waist with large pockets on them, which his sisters made for him, even to the large handmade buttonholes.

He was called "kind of queer," but he was in fact a very talented man. He was a school director in Kirby for several years. When he was quite

Above: *Risley's barn with seven life-size figures visible.*
Below: *Four of the portraits painted on the Risley barn. The man on the left is Cot Dunn, local blacksmith at the time; second from left is unknown; third is Charles M. Chase, then editor of the* Lyndonville (Vt.) Journal. *The lady is Sophronia Grout, sister of Governor Grout whose famous farm was just over the hill from the Risleys'.*

[111]

A corner of the Risley woodpile.

an old man he obtained some French textbooks and learned to read French, then subscribed to a weekly French newspaper, which he read regularly and thoroughly. Rus invented a trapeze on wires to take him back and forth between barn and house. A similar device carried his milk pails.

His sisters were large, strong women, but shy. Hannah was the more sociable one, and if you called at the house Hannah would answer the door, but you might see Achsah peeping out from behind the door. Hannah helped Rus with the farm work, saving the cost of a hired man. She was the better-looking sister, but she didn't dress as well as Achsah.

In winter the Risleys rode in a handmade board-runner sleigh with sides a foot and a half high. Inside the dasher and outside the sleigh Rus

Even the pasture granite was carved . . .

had painted colorful landscapes, and with good fur robes and the little Morgan mare with Rus or a sister driving, there was something to see and remember.

People today who remember the Risleys say they were hard-working, thrifty people, who seldom left the farm. A neighbor said, "Rus Risley was a temperamental old codger. Sometimes he would talk and sometimes he wouldn't, but chances were ten minutes after you left his place he would have your face carved on a piece of wood!"

He owned an adjoining farm, making 300 acres, and kept a small dairy of ten or a dozen cows, the average for his time. He carried on two large sugar places, with two sugar-camps, situated on the side hill above his place. This area was, and still is, called "Sugar Hill." A lot of the sap was piped into the sugar-camps, one of the very first, if not *the* first, pipe-line operations.

Folks always thought Rus was pretty well fixed for money, but they never realized how well, until one day in a talkative mood he told a friend he had $100,000! "What are you going to do with it all?" his friend asked in astonishment. Rus's only reply was, "It's too much responsibility for one person!"

Mrs. Gertrude Rich of East St. Johnsbury, who was a neighbor of the Risleys years ago, said when she was a child she went with other children up to Mr. Risley's place. "We loved to see the funny-looking wooden faces and animals he had carved out of blocks of wood. Sometimes we even saw him carving out a face with his sharp axe. The pictures on the barn always fascinated us, because some of them were pictures of people we knew. For a long time there was a picture of a shapely young woman in the nude painted on the barn that we stole furtive embarrassed glances at whenever we could. We had heard our parents talk about that picture. They thought it was a disgrace for an old bachelor like Mr. Risley to paint anything like that right on the outside of his barn!

"We kids knew the Risleys had plenty of money. The sisters used to let us look at some books to amuse us that were on a corner shelf in the

[113]

kitchen. Our eyes popped the first time we ran across some dollar bills used as bookmarks! 'Here's some money!' we told them excitedly. 'So there is,' Hannah said, 'well, leave it be there,' she told us.

"Mr. Risley once told me that he had never wanted for money. The Risleys accumulated their money through the years by hard work and careful planning and living, with perhaps some inheritance from relatives. It is said Rus Risley never sold a painting or piece of sculpture. Such things were considered foolishness and a waste of valuable time, and people of that time and area didn't set much value on art of any kind."

Mr. Risley looked for natural three-legged branches of trees in the woods, and when he found one that suited him, and was sturdy, he carved a wooden torso and head and fastened it to the tripod so it would stand up. "Once," Mrs. Rich said, "my father, Mr. Bugbee, opened the door of his sugar-camp one morning and met a wooden image of himself looking at him! How Mr. Risley would laugh and chuckle. He was always chuckling at the jokes he played on people," she said.

The Risleys continued to work and live on the home farm until Achsah and Hannah both died of pneumonia in 1914. Hannah died on April 6, aged 79 years, and Achsah died eight days later at the age of 82.

Soon after their deaths, Russell Risley walked out of the house, leaving everything as it was, pictures and all, to go to St. Johnsbury, where he lived in the home of a lady on Eastern Avenue, and where he died on November 17, 1927, aged 85 and nine months.

His money had dwindled away; after a few small personal bequests, he left $100.00 to the Sunset Home in St. Johnsbury, and the same amount to the old family church in East St. Johnsbury. Some $8000 was bequeathed to the North Congregational Church in St. Johnsbury, and a like amount to the American Board of Foreign Missions of New York City.

The last of the old farm buildings fell into decay in the early 1940s, and no one knows what became of all the paintings and sculptures. Diligent search has found only two portraits, and one granite head that can be identified as Rus Risley's work.

But in his heyday, it must have been a queer sensation to drive along that remote mountain road and suddenly come upon a barn with portraits of friends or prominent people painted on the sides—a beautiful mermaid painted high over a manure pile—chunks of wood from the woodpile carved to resemble people and animals lying around the yard, and stones in the pasture cut to resemble people! END

Boston's Parker House

The Purest Intellectual Quintessence

by Richard F. Merrifield

One afternoon in the late 1850s, fourteen distinguished men approached Boston's Parker House.

Some merely strolled up from their business district offices; others walked over from Cambridge professorships; a few sauntered down Beacon Hill. A lone scholar or two had come a longer way for those days— even from so distant a place as Concord, Massachusetts, by rail.

With the deep inner excitement of men of taste, each as he walked relished the familiar scene: Brimstone Corner where Park Street Church presided over the Common; King's Chapel umbrous and squat in shadow; the rear windows of the Athenaeum, alcoved Paradise of open-shelved tomes; and busy Tremont Street agog with people, carriages and carts.

To those of the fourteen who had read Nathaniel Hawthorne's *The Scarlet Letter*, published a few years before this meeting, the scene was especially hallowed, for it was in the very heart of it that the tragedy had been so vividly imagined.

The fourteen's destination, however, was the opposite of tragic in mood and atmosphere—an enchanted interior of Turkey red carpets, black and white marble floors, steeplechase wallpaper, gas-lit magnificence

[115]

and culinary sumptuousness. The Parker House was already celebrated as a rendezvous of the literati—and for rolls.

Let us suppose ourselves present, making fifteen. We are visitors invited by these elect, so that we, too, are in The Room.

Horatio Woodman is there, in that second floor dining room—the feast's high steward, a Maine man and country teacher turned Boston lawyer. He is alert, slight, reddish of hair, and sports English whiskers. There is something Boswellian about him, in his worship of men of genius, himself not one. Busy at cooking mushrooms on the table, and seeing that the sherry, sauterne and claret are well placed, he rambles on with humor and pride about the beginnings of The Saturday Club.

There had been, Woodman tells us, a wistful start—informal gatherings at Concord, Boston and Medford. Some of the meetings were called Symposiums, and there were other philosophic or poetic designations. One group of philosophers had met for sublime speculation, only to sit in hapless silence, chewing at russets, mute as pelicans in conclave.

Then there had been the letters exchanged by Ralph Waldo Emerson of Concord, an ex-minister who was doing a little writing, and young Samuel Gray Ward, the Boston businessman. Mr. Emerson proposed a Town and Country Club, a haven for lonely scholars. He was hankering for meetings of minds on his Boston trips. Ward was glad to help. An amateur of arts and letters, he lived in Louisburg Square, read Livy before breakfast, rode horseback after supper and sang Italian songs in the evening.

Late in 1855 the club took informal shape. By 1856 there were eleven members; by 1857, fourteen: Emerson, Louis Agassiz, Richard Henry Dana, Jr., John Sullivan Dwight; Ebenezer Rockwood Hoar, James Russel Lowell, John Lothrop Motley, Benjamin Peirce, Samuel Gray Ward, Edwin Percy Whipple, Horatio Woodman, Oliver Wendell Holmes, Sr., Cornelius Conway Felton, and Henry Wadsworth Longfellow.

The very names make Horatio Woodman's deepset eyes gleam with reflected pride—and we catch his excitement as The Saturday Club members arrive. Their greetings are not hail-fellow-well-met. There is no backslapping. A quiet decorum is one of the Club rules; besides, these are men of unique distinction, scholarly, all of certain gifts, and a few have genius. But there is an undercurrent of exhilaration, for from the present hour of three until late there will be conversation of the rarest excellence, not heard on either side of the Atlantic since the days of Dr. Johnson.

| Ralph Waldo Emerson | Louis Agassiz |

Top hats, shawls, capes, greatcoats and canes are set aside; the Club members take their places. The room is small, but the acoustics are good, the table is inviting, and two paintings warm the walls—one of the Parker House's Harvey D. Parker, the other an equestrian portrait of Charles Flint, President of the State Agricultural Society.

Scientist Louis Agassiz settles at the head. Professor of Natural History at Harvard College, he will be the leading man in his field on either side of the ocean until Charles Darwin publishes his study of evolution, in 1859. Then Darwinians will call Agassiz "an impediment in the path of science" for refusing to accept their theory. Swiss-French, the life of the party, Agassiz has an immense good fellowship. His dark eyes are mobile and large. With his full black locks a-curl on his shoulders, he lounges in his chair, listening eagerly, his very ears appearing to twitch with the intensity of his universal interest. "Fat and plenteous," Emerson described him, but the Concord poet nevertheless relishes Agassiz and harkens alertly whenever the big laughing giant speaks of some domain of Nature.

Wines are poured, and now the conversation is avid, for these men can converse upon great topics for eight hours without stopping, and begin again the next evening. Their talk struggles to obey the rule that it be general, but it tends to center at the table's two ends.

Opposite Agassiz sits a man of singularly noble aspect—Henry Wadsworth Longfellow. At this time his Dundrearies are expanding into a beard. Heavy hair rolls over his forehead. His brows are straight, his eyes sad, humorous, bright and blue-gray. His lips are generous and wide. He has lost one wife by death, and, though he knows it not, will in a few

[117]

Henry Wadsworth Longfellow   *Oliver Wendell Holmes, Sr.*

years face his darkest blow, the death by fire of his second wife, of whom he will write poetry in private agony while maintaining his grace and dignity before the world. "The absolute ideal of what a poet should be," as the critic William Winter will one day say of him, Longfellow is perhaps the most personally beloved man in the room. He exchanges warm greetings with Agassiz, but is soon absorbed in a topic at his own end of the table, after pausing just long enough to commend Woodman for not having plover again out of season.

A vibrant, smiling, chattering little man enters and briskly takes his place at Longfellow's right, "so as," says the little man, chuckling all about, "to have my back to the windows." You glance over his sloping shoulders at the long windows and the Franklin statue in front of City Hall. This is a busy Boston doctor who knows every cranny of his city as a mouse knows its cheese. Merrily he rubs his hands, makes a quip about their "Mutual Admiration Society" and promptly begins a rapid-fire discussion with Lowell. It is hard for us (though certainly it never was for his thronging students) to equate Oliver Wendell Holmes, the poet, wit and brilliant table talker, with Dr. Holmes, the earnest teacher of anatomy, or Dr. Holmes the physician crusading against puerperal fever. For here we find him, with gusts of laughter all around him, sailing into the mighty Lowell on a question of satiric verse.

James Russell Lowell is breaking one of the Club's few rules—that talk must be general, without tête-à-têtes. We observe what has tempted him—proximity to Judge Ebenezer Rockwood Hoar, who is at this time in private practice but is destined for the state's highest judicial circle. Lowell and Hoar are talking college matters, and someone tells us that

[118]

Ebenezer Rockwell Hoar   *James Russell Lowell*

this is a familiar peccadillo of Lowell's at the Club. For all know that
it is more of a joy to hear them in general conversation, Lowell keeping
"the whole table on a roar," as Holmes will put it later. Harvard Greek
Professor Lowell is editor of the just founded *Atlantic Monthly,* and his
exact memory, stored with all of Europe, can pour forth a massive flood
of cosmopolitan talk, always with vast goodwill.

Lowell is making an appreciative comment on "the cider of the Judge's
wit," while beaming at the Concord jurist, who sits erect, columnar. Judge
Hoar turns his whole torso toward his friend, blue eyes bright and keen
behind gold-bowed spectacles. A smile stirs his light-brown beard. A mild
quotation from *The Book of Common Prayer* (his pet quotation source)
reproves Lowell gently—but with the after-knowledge of ghostly visitors
we know that it is to Hoar, his ancient friend, the dying Lowell will send
almost his last note—twitting him about his gout.

At Longfellow's end of the table sits also a spare, black-suited man
with a countrified shawl about his shoulders. He leans back, relighting
a cigar brought from Concord, a cigar that had been carefully set down
on the picket fence before he entered his house after a stroll in his Muse-
enchanted woods. Knowing his economic prudence, we suspect that he
had retrieved the cigar as he left for the Boston dinner. His eagle-bright
eyes show his intense relish of the gathering, although he says little. For
his valuation of this chorale of noble discourse is truer perhaps and higher
than that of any other man in the room. He is Ralph Waldo Emerson,
here for a day of, to him, the purest intellectual quintessence.

You have scant time in which to recognize the rest, as the conversation
builds with vitality and range. Richard Henry Dana, Jr. is here, you note.

Edwin Percy Whipple   Richard Henry Dana, Jr.

Not a wit, he has just contributed a tale from his seafaring years, experienced before he settled into Boston maritime law. As the author of *Two Years Before the Mast* he is deferred to in matters nautical.

Figures less familiar attract your attention, and by discreet inquiry of Woodman you identify them. One man leans first toward Agassiz's end of the table, then toward Longfellow's, earnest to be in on all aspects of the topic, which is now a tilt of the Transcendentalists and the Naturalists. This is Edwin Percy Whipple, slight, alert, almost ecclesiastical in his black suit, an impression helped by his white neckcloth, square face, large glasses and bulging eyes. Although he comes faithfully down for every Saturday Club Dinner from his dim little Pinckney Street home, he has a quiet and playful wit about the group, and may whisper in one's ear that the Club is "a society based on mutual repulsion." A Gloucesterman, bank clerk, ardent reader, he has done an important article on Macaulay. Here he is delighted with the wines and courses, and with the assemblage, of which he will write: "Probably not even the club of which Johnson, Burke, Reynolds, Garrick and Goldsmith were members brought so many forcible individuals into such good-natured opposition."

Near Whipple is a handsome man, whose fine features and "beautiful" eyes (as they were described) would have drawn female attention had any ladies been present. He has worked all day at his writing, at home, but is eager now for talk and social companionship. No one present has excelled him in achievements, for he is John Lothrop Motley, author of the vast *History of the Rise of the Dutch Republic*. At the moment he is confiding to Whipple his desire to produce great works, and the self-distrust that deeply worries him.

[120]

John Lothrop Motley   *John Sullivan Dwight*

Cornelius Conway Felton is one of the older men present (without long to live, although he is nearing the top of a brilliant career that soon will make him President of Harvard). His large, burly body supports an out-size, dark-complected head, which in its turn has a penumbra of black, massy hair. The talk is fortunately not on Abolitionism, or his opinions would have been less welcome in this anti-slavery group. In the present Transcendentalism versus Naturalism argument, he is in his best vein, his impulsive voice tossing forth treasures of Greek and Latin scholarship. Longfellow bends one of his most archangelic smiles upon Felton—it will be Longfellow who will write, in 1862, that Felton's death made him feel "as if the world were reeling and sinking under my feet."

Countering Felton's literary classicism with mathematical authority, now is heard the voice of Benjamin Peirce, possibly one of the greatest mathematicians of all time. He is basically an idealist, but a point involving his specialty, geometry, has placed him on the side of Agassiz. Full of personal charm, better at a self-effacing tête-à-tête than general talk, he huddles with the Swiss scientist, intense, his long beard agitated.

Only one of the members takes no part in the conversation. He is John Sullivan Dwight, the only musician here—unless Emerson with his Æolian harp in his Concord study window may qualify. Dwight has spent his morning in lodgings at the Harvard Musical Association, just off Charles Street, on the lower slope of Beacon Hill. There, poor, simple, unworldly, a ministerial failure, he has sat playing soft improvisations on his flute and piano, or bits of his beloved Mozart and Beethoven. He is editor of *Dwight's Journal of Music*. A sweet, white-bearded dreamer, he smiles sunnily, whispering to Emerson that Thoreau, Hawthorne and

[121]

Alcott should be present. Emerson may remind him that Thoreau peered in once, when the Club was not dining, but preferred the railroad depot to this conviviality, or the Maine forests (where he is on this occasion); that Alcott, for all that he is "Man thinking," is also Man talking to the probable exclusion of all other conversation, and is in Walpole, New Hampshire, anyway; and that Hawthorne is in Rome working on a novel, *The Marble Faun*.

The old room grows dim and hushed as we try to catch the actual words there spoken, the reputed mighty discourse. For these are men of large mind, who move easily along peaks of speculation—the nature of Deity, or Being, of Mind, of Good and Evil, and the Ideal and the Real. Born as the 19th century opened, they are moving away from the reasoned, perfect universe of their fathers; they feel themselves positioned at a promontory of thought. All is possibility; a gigantic hope is alight in their hearts, a hope particularly for America, which appears to them a new Athens arising out of primordial vegetation. To these ruddy, inspired men, a man is a divine miracle, not a culprit; he is a prism through which the highest rays may shine. So thinks the happy philosopher-poet of Concord, sitting beside Longfellow, elated at the Club of which he had dreamed.

We cannot hear their voices; we can only surmise. Reluctantly, now, we withdraw. Our last glimpse is a final, quick look around at their apostolic faces—Emerson, Agassiz, Dwight, Hoar, Lowell, Motley, Peirce, Ward, Whipple, Woodman, Holmes, Dana, Felton, and Longfellow.

Their Saturday Club went on. There came a time when Dr. Holmes was the only one left of the originals. Yet the Club lived along—and still lives. And all its members would regret, along with its late president M. A. DeWolfe Howe, that there was not, in the old, first days, "a single chiel amang them takin' notes."   END

Splendiferous Prima Donna from Maine

by Moreton Abbott

Throwing its cap in the air, the Farmington, Maine, *Chronicle* of August 23, 1911, exulted, "Last Thursday was a day that needs no red letter to make it remembered. It will never be forgotten." For a conservative paper, this unqualified prediction might seem like going out on a limb. But the *Chronicle* knew what it was saying; the limb was sturdy. Thursday, August 17, had been the day of Lily Norton's concert in Merrill Hall.

The celebrated prima donna had arrived by train Monday for a week's vacation in her old home town. It was her first visit in over 20 years, and her reception at the depot had been tumultuous—at least as tumultuous as the good folk of Franklin County, of whom self-control was characteristic, could make it. Hundreds of admirers had gathered on the station platform to greet the homecoming diva with shouted welcomes and waving handkerchiefs. Among the noisiest had been the children, none of whom had seen the object of their enthusiasm before. But there was not a single child who had not heard his or her parents speak proudly of their own dear Lily and her achievements in the musical world.

Admittedly, Lily's glorious soprano voice was God-given. But don't forget! She had studied hard, practiced her scales faithfully, and, as a result of her determination, been the only one of her original class at the New England Conservatory in Boston to finish her courses and graduate. Within three months she was in New York singing with the great Gil-

[123]

more's Band in a *Grand Jubilee Centennial Programme*. (That was in 1876, 100 years after the signing of the Declaration of Independence.) And then Lily had toured Europe with the Band, and then, barely 22, made her operatic debut in Italy. The Italians had gone wild about her. But they had not been able to twist their tongues around the name "Norton." So her Italian teacher had changed her name to "Nordica" and the Italians had called her "La Giglia Nordica" which, translated, means Lily of the North. Everybody in Farmington knew *that* much Italian! And from then on her career had been one triumph after another, Lily always studying, learning different languages and new roles, working hard, but earning honors. She had gone on and on, up and up, singing before the crowned heads of Europe, even dining with them, accepting their tributes of diamonds, emeralds, pearls, performing in the world's greatest opera houses, giving concerts before hundreds of thousands of people.

Her concert gowns, designed by Worth of Paris, had never cost less than $1,000 each. One of the costumes she had worn in the opera *La Gioconda*—just one—had cost $3,000. In London, where she had been the city's darling, she had been cited as one of the best-dressed women in public life. And *that* included the Queen! But there had never been anything highfalutin' about Lily Norton. There's a story that once, when some London lady asked her if she did embroidery or some kind of needlework to quiet her nerves, Lily answered, "Heavens no!" Then she added, quickly, "But I can patch . . . and make as neat a patch as any New England housewife."

Three years before the event in Farmington, at age 51 she had toured the United States by train like a queen in her own private car named "Brunnhilde" (after one of her most famous operatic roles) and had given 60 concerts in 50 cities. Since then there had been a dozen other tours. You just couldn't stop her. Lily would sing at the drop of a hat. And not always for money, either. She had sung at dedications, patriotic rallies, benefits—hundreds of things—and all without charging. And now she was to sing in Farmington, where she first saw the light of day!

There had been some confusion among the townspeople as to how their most famous daughter should be addressed. In the outside world she had often been referred to as the American Songbird, but that would hardly do in Farmington. Should she be called Lily Norton or Madame Nordica? The confusion was compounded by the fact that her legal name was Mrs. George Washington Young. Lily put everyone at ease; she asked that she be called Lily. Walking happily about the village, she dropped in on relatives, of whom there were many, and old friends. She visited her cousin's dry goods store and watched while self-conscious customers purchased something, any little thing, just to observe the great prima donna at close range. Most of her time, however, she spent at her birthplace, the old Norton homestead, a simple farmhouse pleasantly located two miles from the village on Titcomb Hill.

A young reporter from the *Boston Sunday Post*, calling on her there, asked if she was having a good time in the country. Lily's answer was typically unequivocal. "Don't ask foolish questions," she said. "I'm having the time of my life. The town is one of the prettiest in the world, and I think the house where I was born is the best one I know." She then set her questioner to work helping her rearrange the furniture. The long, illustrated interview in the next *Sunday Post* praised the great diva's "unfailing democracy."

When a group of townspeople approached Lily and timidly asked if she could be persuaded to give a public concert, Lily promptly picked up the hat. And, she added, it would be free. Everyone would be welcome. It was decided that Merrill Hall on the State Normal School campus, seating about 900 people, was the only auditorium large enough to hold the crowd which would want to attend. The platform, little more than a dais raised four steps above the floor, was large enough to accommodate a grand piano, Madame's accompanist, Madame herself, any flowing draperies she might choose to wear, and two large baskets of golden glow, then at its height. The concert would be at four in the afternoon. There would be no printed program. The affair would be simple and informal.

As soon as she had helped make these decisions, Lily wired her favorite accompanist, then in New York, to come—and bring her jewels with him. Farmington, that vale of fertile farmland and rolling hills, was to get the full treatment. She would sing in Merrill Hall before her townspeople exactly as though she were appearing before thousands in New York's Carnegie Hall or London's Covent Garden.

The day of the concert dawned bright and clear. Flowers—petunias, nasturtiums, golden glow, early asters—in every yard, in borders and beds, iron kettles and lard buckets—all seemed abloom with anticipation. In every household, men, women and children eagerly donned their Sunday best, including ruffles. By three o'clock hundreds had descended upon Merrill Hall. They had come on foot, by carriage, by automobile, and by train. In almost less time than it takes to tell, the pleasant room, its arched windows bearing a tinge of Tudor and looking out over broad

[125]

The Nordica Homestead, Lily's birthplace.

lawns and ancient trees, was filled. Extra chairs were placed in the aisles. The back of the room was crowded with standees. Corridors and anterooms held some of the overflow; those who could not get in clustered outside the open windows, hoping to hear even if they could not see.

At exactly four o'clock, Mr. David Knowlton, a prominent citizen, stepped to the dais to make an introductory speech. It was hardly necessary. It did serve, however, to remind his listeners that Madame Lillian Nordica had sung twice before in Farmington, once in 1878 in the Methodist Church where her illustrious grandfather, the popular revivalist "Camp Meeting" John Allen, had been a pastor, and again in 1883 at the then new Music Hall, when the great artist, generous as always (as his presently assembled listeners should know) had turned over the admission fees of 25, 35 and 50 cents to the town for kerosene street lamps, since replaced. Mr. Knowlton, overcome with the honor of introducing the world famous Nordica, ended by remarking that this was the proudest moment of his life. To which the *Chronicle* would add, "not only a proud moment for Mr. Knowlton but for every one present."

No sooner had Mr. Knowlton bowed and taken his place in the audience than a door beside the dais opened and in swept Lily led, most elegantly, by her Cousin Hiram, a 24-year-old farmer who was holding his cousin's gloved hand aloft, smiling and acting like a continental dandy. A radiant Lily floated upward to the dais, her white gown trailing behind her. At the dazzling spectacle, everyone rose, clapped their hands as wildly as "self-control" would allow and enthusiastically waved their handkerchiefs, an act which in Farmington seems to have been as much a sign of joyous welcome as of fond farewell.

Such was the excitement and emotion of the occasion that accounts

[126]

vary as to just what Madame was wearing. It is safe to say, however, that her gown was of white crepe "artistically" draped over white satin. Without doubt it touched the floor in front (See Madame's book, *Hints to Singers*) and was enhanced, according to the *Chronicle*, by a "demi-train." On her stately head she wore either a diamond tiara, or a "rosette" which anchored a spray of black aigrettes, or both. Sparkling diamond and pearl pendants fell from her ears. A "few" emeralds adorned her neck, which was bare. Ropes of pearls reached her waist. Brilliant diamond and pearl bracelets encircled her long white "kids." Farmington was indeed getting the works.

Cousin Hiram vanished into the audience. The applause subsided. Those in the audience who had seats resumed a sitting position and Madame's accompanist took his place at the piano. An expectant silence fell over the room.

Madame began without delay. She sang three simple songs by Charles Wakefield Cadman. (As she wrote in her *Hints*, "To begin too early with the pyrotechnics is a mistake.") These were probably from the composer's American Indian suite, "From the Land of the Sky Blue Water." Next came a German folk song; then Debussy's *Mandoline*—all prefaced, as the *Chronicle* said, by brief explanations given "with sweetness and simplicity . . . and with a voice which is as beautiful in conversation as it is in song."

At this point, a huge basket of roses was brought forward. Madame showed her appreciation by plucking one rose from the basket and tucking it in her "corsage." Then came a Handel aria.

Madame left the platform, her "demi-train" trailing behind her. Her accompanist left, too, but returned almost immediately to render a Chopin polonaise. It was greatly applauded and the *Chronicle* implied that an encore would have been in order, but Madame quickly reappeared.

Now she resumed her program. The pyrotechnics were on the way. Several operatic numbers, each of increasing intensity, led to an explosive climax, Wagner's blood-curdling war whoop, the "Ho-jo-to-ho!" from *Die Walküre*. It was executed with fervor and with gestures, just as if the great opera singer, clothed in Brunnhilde's silver cuirass and winged helmet and brandishing a spear in one hand and a shield in the other, were once again charging up the Metropolitan's rickety rocks to even wobblier heights. The applause was deafening. Few, if any, had heard or seen such overpowering singing and acting.

[127]

This might officially have been the program's end. But the wily Nordica had more tricks up her long white "kids." When the applause had died down, she sang—very quietly and simply—"Annie Laurie." People were beginning to weep. But not, according to Madame's way of thinking, enough. Turning slightly and looking out the open windows toward her birthplace two miles away, she sang—once again, very quietly and simply —"Home, Sweet Home." The effect was overwhelming. The audience rose as one, applauded mightily and waved their handkerchiefs, moist as many of them might be.

After many bows of grateful appreciation, Lily retired—whether to recover or to let the audience recover would be hard to say. But in a moment she was back, standing before the dais to shake hands with and speak to hundreds who came forward wanting to shake the hand of their own dear Lily.

Writing of this concert, Ira Glackens, in his perceptive and rewarding biography, *Yankee Diva*, says, "It was the most dramatic, because the most romantic in its implications, of any appearance of her career." It was also one of the happiest.

The rest of the week in Farmington passed only too quickly. There were several receptions, a family reunion at the homestead, a trip to the Rangeley Lakes. On August 21 there were fond farewells at the depot accompanied, unquestionably, by more waving handkerchiefs.

Within a month Lily was touring again. Once, in upper New York State, because of a train wreck, she tramped two miles through mud in the early dawn to keep an engagement. In Boston and Chicago, she sang Isolde in four performances of Wagner's *Tristan und Isolde*. In London, she appeared before royalty with a new orchestra conducted by a young Mr. Leopold Stokowski and was recalled to the stage 12 times. At a concert in New York she sang Wagner's war whoop as an encore "gloriously and spontaneously," according to the *New York Sun* critic. Spontaneously —after all those years! In San Francisco, standing beside President Taft, she sang "The Star Spangled Banner" at the ground-breaking ceremonies for the Panama-Pacific Exposition. In New York, at the Metropolitan, she sang the National Anthem in a Woman's Suffrage pageant; President Theodore Roosevelt spoke. Later, from the same stage, she sang at a benefit for the victims of families whose relatives had drowned on the *Titanic*.

But now neuritis began to plague Lily; fatigue and shortness of breath became noticeable. Once, in a morose mood, she told a friend that at her funeral she wanted a singer to sing Wotan's Farewell, an orchestra to play

Lillian Norton on her last visit to Farmington, Maine— August, 1911.

the Funeral March from *Götterdammerung* and a speaker to say . . . Then, unhappy, bewildered, at a loss for words, she had hesitated. Oh, well, she had continued helplessly, let him say, "She did her damnedest."

Nothing, however, could stop America's Songbird from singing. In 1913 Lily sailed to the Far East on a tour which was planned to take her to Hawaii, Australia, New Zealand, Java and China; then to Moscow and St. Petersburg; then to Italy; then to Paris and London. In Melbourne Lily became ill. Her doctor ordered a rest. When she resumed her tour, determined as ever, she had to be carried up the ship's gangplank. Ten days at sea, the ship struck a coral reef. The hull was ripped open. Finally tugged free, the ship managed to continue but ran into a storm. The captain advised the passengers to stay on deck; the lifeboats were readied. Eventually the ship arrived at Sunday Island, where Lily remained for three months in a small tin-roofed hospital suffering from exhaustion and pneumonia. When the doctor once again permitted her to travel, Lily was carried aboard a ship sailing for Batavia, where, at the Hotel des Indes, feverish and bedridden, she lingered on for three weeks, rallying occasionally to speak of more concerts, more appearances, and to dream, possibly, of returning once again to her hilltop Farmington home on the other side of the earth. On May 10, 1914, she died. No one could say that *La Giglia Nordica* had not done her damnedest.   END

(Courtesy of the Vermont Historical Society.)

Mathematical Genius and Boy Computer

by Don Munson

At an age when most boys were happily playing marbles, Zerah Colburn was dazzling the scientists of two continents with his mathematical genius. By the time he was eight years old he was famous.

This strange and wonderful boy, born in Cabot, Vermont, in 1804 and growing up in one of the most dramatic periods of world history, possessed a brain that was one of the most remarkable of all time. He glanced briefly at mathematics and knew all about it.

Rumors spread all over Caledonia County to the effect that Abiah Colburn's little boy possessed magic powers. As the story spread, the country folk gathered.

"How much is 13 times 97?" one of the men asked, no doubt passing a wink around the circle of skeptics.

"1,261," the child replied instantly, he being six years old at the time.

Following a hasty conference and much computing, the elders decided the answer was correct. "Wal, I swan!" they chorused, finding this phenomenon difficult to believe, but impossible to deny. Then they went to work to cook up even more difficult problems for the eager child—to whom it was all play.

Zerah's father was a joiner, something like what is now called a cabinet maker, and it was while he was at work at his bench that the strange story had its beginning.

Zerah, playing in the chips on the workshop floor, broke into a kind of chant: "5 times 7 are 35; 6 times 8 are 48..."

Colburn dropped his tools in astonishment. The child, after all, was only six, and had not been to school at all except for a few weeks during the previous summer. Second thought suggested that perhaps only a few multiplications had happened to stick in his mind. Not at all! He had more mathematical answers than his father had questions. A neighbor who had dropped in during the revelation, left the house spraying news bulletins to right and to left. This is what brought on the inquisitors.

Abiah Colburn, who had waged a bitter struggle to make a living between his joiner's bench and his farm, now saw the family's horizons broadening. If little Zerah was one of the wonders of the world, as the sages of Cabot agreed, there should be a fortune in it.

That, of course, meant leaving Cabot. First stop Danville, the county seat, where members of the Court questioned the boy; then to Montpelier to give members of the State Legislature the same opportunity; to Burlington; to Hanover, New Hampshire; and, at last, Boston, Massachusetts, popularly described as "the Athens of America."

Here in the American Athens, a distinguished panel, including James Perkins, Daniel Sargent, Josiah Quincy, William Sullivan, and William S. Shaw confronted the boy from Vermont.

"How many," one of the inquisitors demanded, unfairly it would seem, "how many seconds in 2,000 years?"

For just a fraction of a minute, according to witnesses, the boy's body "assumed certain contortions." Then the triumphant treble: "730,000 days, 17,520,000 hours, 1,051,200,000 minutes, 63,072,000,000 seconds." Again the elders checked out and confirmed Zerah's findings.

As ever, the attempt was made to press the questions to the point of impossibility. So far as contemporary report goes, the boy occasionally suffered a little more, but never failed.

One question stopped him for a moment during the great public appearances that followed. A lady in Boston who presumably wanted, herself, to go around astonishing people, asked: "How do you get these answers?"

Zerah frowned in puzzlement, and then said: "God put it into my head and I cannot put it into yours."

There followed a tour of most metropolitan centers of importance on the Eastern Seaboard: New York, Philadelphia, Washington, Fredericksburg, Richmond, Charleston, and Norfolk. Then to Europe, a stormy passage of 38 days under sail before facing the scrutiny of the intellectual and aristocratic *élite* of Great Britain.

Promises of sponsored education and other fulfillment flickered ever more brightly in England, but deeds were laggard in following the words. A shrewd Yankee assessment of this led the harassed father to take his marvelous red-headed son across the Channel.

In one of the salons of Paris, two most extraordinary Americans crossed paths: the Vermont boy and Washington Irving. The handsome and gifted Irving greeted the Colburns with delight, as did William H. Crawford, United States Minister to the Court of Louis XVIII, and other distinguished Americans sojourning on the Seine.

Probably the most extraordinary conjunction was that with the famous mathematician, La Place, who took a very serious interest in the boy and suggested to the King that he be accepted for study at the Lyceum. Louis ("the fat hog," his people called him) was too busy mincing about to get around to the application.

Shortly, Napoleon returned to France for his "one hundred days." He was fully capable of admiring Zerah's mind, having one of equal com-

[132]

plexity, and managed to find time away from fighting off all Europe to favor the boy with a scholarship at the Lyceum Napoleon.

Other than the distinguished associations and the scholarship, Zerah's visit to Paris showed little profit. Perhaps the French were so dazzled by Napoleon's martial exploits that they had little appetite left for astonishment.

There were still friends in England, and the Colburns gave it another try. Thanks to the generosity of the Earl of Bristol, Zerah received a scholarship at Westminster School, and studied there for almost four years before returning to the States.

When he sailed from Southampton, the few years of education in France and England were all he had to show for 10 years of alternating high hopes and crushing disappointments. Parisians didn't warm up very much to lightning calculation, most of them probably being convinced that the most important mathematical knowledge is that one and one make two. The British showed greater ardor, especially the Earl of Bristol, who continued as Zerah's patron after almost everyone else had fallen away.

Zerah sailed for home not only without the promised fortune (he had his passage and $50 in his pocket, thanks to the Earl of Bristol), but without his father, who had succumbed to tuberculosis.

The voyage marked a complete break in the career of this incredible prodigy. So far as the records show, he never again displayed his mathematical wizardry before a crowded and breathless auditorium. Evidently people were channeling their interests in other directions, and Zerah was seeking a new avenue of accomplishment.

Always since the age of six a wanderer, though a fabulous and feted one, Zerah upon arrival in America headed right for Cabot, Vermont, where he found an aged woman who didn't recognize her long-lost son, and found six brothers and two sisters—all living in impoverished circumstances.

Though the house was small and humble, Zerah was welcome and could feel for the first time in 15 years that he was home. He could also feel deeply about the family problem. How to help?

He tried the academic career first at "an academy of Fairfield, State of New York, connected with Hamilton College." (In the little writing he did, the style is a peculiar mixture of terse flatness with circumlocution and general disorganization. He was exact chiefly in lightning calculation.)

[133]

After only a few months he resigned from the Academy, having found "his prospects there quite different from what he had anticipated," and returned to Cabot. (He usually spoke of himself in the third person.) Nobody but Zerah should have been surprised. The difficulties of patiently drilling the young would certainly seem tedious after years of easily astonishing the elders.

Finally, Zerah decided, after his adventures abroad and his disappointment in his first attempt at teaching, to try preaching.

In the spiritual area he encountered difficulties easily as serious as those that had discouraged him in the educational field. A mathematical mind is addicted to having everything exact, which involves keeping a firm grip on seeing things in the small, where religion finds its exactitude mostly through seeing things in the large.

During this struggle to check out his faith as to its exactness, he joined the Congregational Church in Burlington, Vermont, and after further soulful computation, withdrew and was received into the Methodist Church. For nine years Zerah was a Methodist preacher, serving seven different circuits in Vermont, meanwhile acquiring a wife and three girls.

One wonders if the small-town preaching seemed dull to him after Boston and London and Dublin and Paris, and after the Earl of Bristol, La Place, and Napoleon.

After almost a decade on the preaching circuits, he went back to teaching, giving as the reason his increased family responsibilities. During the last five years of his amazing life, he served as professor of languages at Norwich University at Norwich, Vermont.

Somehow, he didn't "belong," never could belong, because he was so different from other people. Questions that would seem impossible to us, he answered with ease. "Us?" To put it that way makes him an outsider, doesn't it?

One question that Zerah Colburn was never able to answer successfully was what to do with his life. He was born to mystery, lived with it, and returned to it.   END

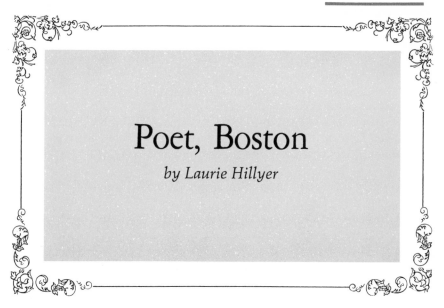

Poet, Boston

by Laurie Hillyer

Though Amy Lowell is presently in eclipse as a poet, and may remain so, she has left several enduring memorials as a person. The Boston Athenaeum, for instance, that treasure house for lovers of good books, stands where it is because she fought to keep it there. Her gift of approximately 2000 rare volumes is a priceless asset to the Houghton Library at Harvard. Her sponsorship of Imagist poetry is not to be forgotten. And she also left to posterity a stream of amusing anecdotes founded on her eccentricities and determined independence.

She was born in 1874 and died in 1925, having lived 51 full, sad, gay, crowded, courageous years as poet, book collector, philanthropist, lover and biographer of Keats, staunch friend, traveler, lecturer, feminist, and defier of conventions.

The Lowell estate in Brookline, Massachusetts, where she was born, was called, after her birth, "Sevenels"—there being seven Lowells, parents and five children. She was named after her great-aunt, Rebecca Amory Lowell, who was always called Amory; but Mrs. Augustus Lowell, Amy's mother, disliked a surname as a Christian name for a girl, so Amory was changed to Amy, a name the poet always loathed as being inappropriate, foolish, and fancy.

The young Amy Lowell

Since she had arrived 12 years after the fourth child, she was known as the "postscript" and became the darling of the family, a spoiled little girl, quick at learning—she read all the Rollo books when she was six—and at finding an original way out of a difficult situation. An early letter to her mother is signed, "Your loving son, Amy"—"because," she explained to her father, "I can't spell daughter."

The family life at Sevenels and at the Lowell town house, first on Beacon Street, later on Commonwealth Avenue, was a happy one. Amy was taken abroad, made friends easily, liked school. She was a lucky child until her adolescence when, because of a glandular disturbance, her figure became heavy and mature. This avoirdupois ruined her years as a debutante and, according to one rumor, was responsible for her being jilted. Handicapped by the weight of her body, she found solace in the wealth of her mind. She read, thought and began to write poetry. She had fallen in love with John Keats when she was 15, and the Keats biography, which she did not complete until the last years of her life, was always something to think about and plan. Her first volume of poetry, A Dome of Many-Colored Glass, published in 1912, contains her most autobiographical poem, "Fairy Tale," an elegy for her enchanted childhood:

> I am no more a child, and what I see
> Is not a fairy tale, but life, my life.
> The gifts are there, the many pleasant things:
> Health, wealth, long-settled friendships, with a name
> Which honors all who bear it, and the power
> Of making words obedient. This is much;
> But overshadowing all is still the curse,
> That never shall I be fulfilled by love!
> Along the parching highroad of the world
> No other soul shall bear mine company.*

Some of her happiest hours were spent browsing, studying, writing, reading at the Boston Athenaeum, 10½ Beacon Street. She would open the great red-leather doors studded with brass nails and enter the outer foyer where a bronze plaque stated briefly that here remained a retreat for those who would enjoy the humanity of books.

The Athenaeum has a distinguished history. It was incorporated in 1807, moved to its present quarters in 1847. One of Amy's ancestors, John Lowell III, was a founder and first treasurer. It dedicated itself to "An attempt to buy every book that should find a place in a gentleman's library with a reasonable proportion of that flotsam and jetsam that lies upon the literary stream of the day." To read the records is to read a roster of well known Boston names—Adams, Bowditch, Coolidge, Hemenway, Longfellow, Lothrop, Lowell, Lyman, Perkins, Putnam, Sears, Thorndike, Wendell, etc.

* Reprinted from *The Complete Works of Amy Lowell* with the permission of Houghton Mifflin Co., Boston.

"two ladies had discourteously defeated

A study of the minutes, bound in copy books and kindly produced by Mr. Walter Muir Whitehill, historian and present director of the Athenaeum, unearthed the story of Amy Lowell vs. the Athenaeum trustees.

On May 31, 1901, at a special meeting of the proprietors, Mr. John G. Gray put through a motion authorizing the trustees to sell the land and building at 10½ Beacon Street and purchase land at Arlington Street (where the Ritz now stands). Mr. J. H. Beaton, Jr. at once (heatedly, one imagines) moved to table the motion, but his motion failed to pass and the trustees were authorized to build a new library. Plans were drawn up for a new building which, in the words of Mr. Whitehill, were "dreary."

The reason for the move was need for extensive repairs in the old building plus the fact that the city was moving uptown. Although the membership was divided on the issue, the dissenters needed a leader both plucky and persevering. Amy Lowell elected herself to this job and conducted a campaign which lasted nearly two years. At the annual meeting on February 9, 1903, a motion was passed requesting the trustees to postpone further action in the matter of the proposed sale. At this meeting Amy Lowell and her friend, Elizabeth Perkins, were defeated in their bid for election to the board of trustees, but Dr. Lawrence Lowell, Amy's brother, was one of the 15 victors.

The next day a letter appeared in the *Boston Transcript*, signed by William Sloan Kennedy, who protested that "two ladies had discourteously defeated two years' unremunerated labor of the self-sacrificing trustees who had worked on plans for removal." This was later followed by a letter from Percival Lowell, another brother. "Our forefathers," he wrote, "spent all their time cutting down all the trees they could lay their hands on, we are now spending time and money planting others." Saving the Athenaeum, he said, is "a thing of vital interest to all of us who are not blind to art" and to want "the newest and the largest is only an aping of the semblance of progress without its excuse."

two years' unremunerated labor..."

Although she had been defeated in her bid for election to the board, Amy Lowell had three voting shares, one inherited from her grandfather, one from her father, and one which she herself had bought and later sold. Three proprietors, Richard Dana, William D. Sohier, and Robert Treat Paine were persuaded to sign a circular headed "Reasons for Preserving Our Present Building." "Too late," it said, "we have regretted the destruction of some of Boston's most interesting landmarks—Hancock Mansion, Province House, etc." "Let us preserve," it encouraged, "this old-time library, its atmosphere, traditions, associations, its quiet and peaceful outlook on the Old Granary Burying Ground." "St. Gaudens," it pointed out, "always admired the simple dignity of the façade as a specimen of the best work of the period and for its intrinsic merit." "Arlington Street," it asserted with distaste, "is a noisy thoroughfare, the horses' hoofs resound upon the asphalt pavement. There is also noise from the continued stream of Boylston Street electric cars."

A postcard vote was now put through and 349 stockholders voted to remain, 284 to move. Amy's three votes, plus 62 others, had won the day. The vote to remain included disposal, by sale or lease, of the Arlington Street site and suggestions for repairing, cleaning, painting, heating, strengthening of floors, fireproofing, and improving toilet facilities in the present building. By 1906 all repairs were made; the bone of contention had vanished from the records.

A poem which Amy Lowell wrote during the period of uncertainty about the fate of the Athenaeum was published several years later in *A Dome of Many-Colored Glass*.

The Boston Athenaeum

Thou dear and well-loved haunt of happy hours,
How often in some distant gallery,
Gained by a little painful spiral stair,

[139]

This photograph, taken at her house "Sevenels" in Brookline, Mass., was one of Miss Lowell's favorites. (Courtesy of the Boston Athenaeum.).

Far from the halls and corridors where throng
The crowd of casual readers, have I passed
Long, peaceful hours seated on the floor
Of some retired nook, all lined with books,
Where reverie and quiet reign supreme! ...
The shifting sun pierces the young green leaves
Of elm trees, newly coming into bud,
And splashes on the floor and on the books
Through old, high, rounded windows, dim with age.
The noisy city-sounds of modern life
Float softened to us across the old graveyard ...
The dear, old, sleepy place is full of spells
For us, by right of long inheritance ...
And must they take away this treasure house,
To us so full of thoughts and memories; ...*

Amy Lowell's battles had by no means ended. She battled with her publishers to have her books published when and how she wanted them published. At first it was a battle to have them published at all. She fought for Ezra Pound and the new poetry; for recognition of D. H. Lawrence, who had become a valued friend and who was at times financially dependent upon her; for the Women's Municipal League; and—bravo, Amy—for the Suppression of Unnecessary Noise. She fought against increasing ill health, and she fought to become known not only as a poet but as a personality, exaggerating her eccentricities beyond belief.

She smoked cigars at a time when few women were smoking cigarettes. A friend told me of meeting Miss Lowell at the College Club in Boston; she was peering around for an ashtray where none was to be had.

She had become a celebrity—a letter addressed to *Amy Lowell, Poet, Boston* was duly delivered—and when a mechanic who had repaired her car refused her personal check, she was outraged. "Call my brother, the president of Harvard College," she ordered; "he'll identify me."

"What's this woman doing?" asked Dr. Lowell.

"Sitting across the road on a stone wall," replied the mechanic dourly, "smoking a cigar."

* Reprinted from *The Complete Works of Amy Lowell* with the permission of Houghton Mifflin Co., Boston.

"That's my sister," said Dr. Lowell. "You can take her check." He perhaps cast a rueful glance toward the highest and least accessible shelf in his study where his sister's books were kept.

Amy's parents had died when she was in her twenties, and she lived alone at Sevenels and at her summer place in Dublin, New Hampshire. Ada Dwyer Russell, a former actress, had become her beloved companion, lived with her, and alleviated, as nearly as anyone ever could, that "parching highroad" of her life. For she was not, one judges, a happy woman, and her egocentricities undoubtedly stemmed from a dissatisfaction with herself. Although her second volume of poems, *Sword Blades and Poppy Seed*, published when she was 40, made a small sensation, she was not a first-rate poet and knew it (she never, surprisingly, fought critics hostile to her work); she was stout and would have liked to be slim; she was increasingly ill, with poor eyesight, and longed to be well. But she was famous.

To be invited to dine at Sevenels was both an accolade and an experience.

Mrs. Russell welcomed the guests at eight, cocktails lasted an hour, dinner was announced at nine, Miss Lowell then made her first appearance, in a rich dark satin gown, her patrician fingers flashing with rings. The food and wine were ambrosial, the talk·lively. Coffee was served in the drawing room, at which time the seven sheep dogs whom Miss Lowell called her "children" appeared and were served carefully carved steak in seven exquisite bowls. The butler distributed a large bath towel to each guest as protection against affectionate onslaughts from the "children." (When meat was rationed during the First World War and the dogs were fed horse meat, they all, alas, died.)

Mrs. Russell gave the signal for departure at eleven, the guests left, Mrs. Russell went to bed, and Amy Lowell's working day began. She sometimes wrote all night, scattering scribbled sheets she did not want on the floor, to be picked up and burned in the morning. Work to be copied was piled up for her secretary to type.

She slept most of the day, usually going to theatre, concert, opera, or dinner party in the evening. She sat in the front row at the theatre, her companion bearing a footstool for the slippered Lowell feet. She was a theatre buff, liked and befriended stage people, and adored Eleonora Duse both as an actress and a friend.

When Miss Lowell traveled, her hotel—the old Belmont, if it was New York—was warned well in advance of her arrival, accompanied by Mrs. Russell, a secretary, and a maid. Sixteen pillows were·placed on her bed, all clocks were stopped, all mirrors were shrouded in black—the reflections bothered her when she worked all night—and she occupied a six-room suite, the rooms on either side of her own being vacant, to insure quiet. Her wardrobe was always carefully sorted and packed for speed and efficiency in dressing—gowns in one suitcase, toilet articles in another, underwear in a third. The trunk containing the underwear once slipped into the harbor at Piraeus when the landing net broke, and Miss Lowell stood on the Greek pier wringing her hands and moaning, "My drawers, oh, my drawers." She had the harbor dredged and recovered them.

If her pillows were not fluffy enough she cut them open and removed some of the feathers, covering herself with down; if the sleeping car was stuffy, she asked for a hammer and broke the glass. "Send me the bill," she would say.

The Lowell fortune and the Lowell name smoothed her path but she was determined that she herself, and not they, should be what the world thought of when they heard the name Amy Lowell; as if, since her weight made her odd, she would be, in defiance, very odd indeed.

"Impossible manners with a golden heart," Ellery Sedgwick said of her, and her manners could, indeed, be impossible.

At a dinner party in Cambridge, prior to our entering the First World War, one of the guests was a British submarine officer, son of a baronet. When talk turned to the unusual sight of uniforms on the Boston streets, the officer said he was often mistaken for a policeman and a woman with a baby had once asked him to direct her to the South Station. "My cue, of course, to misdirect her," he said. Miss Lowell grew scarlet with fury. "Excuse me for saying so," she hurled across the table, "but you are a complete cad." The dinner deteriorated as a social success, and when the

[143]

young officer left, she thumbed her nose at him.

She was a non-conformist and her best-known poem, "Patterns," ends with her best-known line: *Christ! What are patterns for?*

Here own pattern ended when she was 51. She had had a stroke, she was ill, worn, exhausted, and ready to sleep. "Peter, I'm done for," she said to Mrs. Russell.

On May 15 she was buried in the family plot at Mt. Auburn, and her will was filed.

She left a long list of publications, including articles, pamphlets, and reviews; a few poems which will be remembered; gifts to those who loved her; and books, manuscripts, and a traveling scholarship to Harvard. She also left a wider understanding of free verse and—the most worthwhile memorial, after all—friends deeply to mourn her going.

The Lowell town house stood—and stands—on the sunny side of the Commonwealth Avenue mall, opposite the bronze statue of William Lloyd Garrison whose ringing words Amy Lowell might well have taken for her own: *I will not excuse, I will not retreat a single inch and I will be heard.*   END

Dreams That Came to Naught

SECTION 5

A Lonely Grave
at Thank God Bay

by T. W. Paterson

In September, 1965, Canadian scientist Dr. E. F. Roots searched lonely King William Island for the grave of Sir John Franklin, legendary Arctic explorer who vanished in 1847 with 128 men while seeking the Northwest passage. A century before Dr. Roots, American Charles Francis Hall claimed this ice-bound island held the secret of Franklin's mysterious fate.

Born in Rochester, New Hampshire, in 1821, "Crazy" Charley Hall was not a scientist or even an explorer. He had never been to the Far North in his youth and knew only that about it which he had read in books. But from 1861 until his death 12 years later, this scorned blacksmith-printer pursued the elusive facts surrounding Franklin's death and almost reached the North Pole!

While owner of the short-lived Cincinnati (Ohio) *Penny Post*, bear-like Charley Hall heard of Sir John, and what started as mild interest became an obsession; all his humdrum life Hall had been seeking a goal, a cause to which he could devote his tireless, but aimless, energy. At last he had found it—"rescue" of the long-lost explorers!

Although history had all but closed the books on Franklin, Hall argued: "We know only that one-fourth of the expedition died. What of the others? Eskimos survive—why not the others?"

Thus one of the Arctic's strangest adventures had begun. Hall read every book on the subject. He wrote Lady Franklin and questioned every authority. Everyone except Lady Jane thought the rough, uneducated 40-

*New Hampshire's unlikely but determined
Arctic explorer, Charles Francis Hall.*

year-old printer comical, pathetic—even mad. Still he continued his lonely course until, finally, he was ready to go north. All he needed was money.

While most people laughed derisively at the would-be explorer, there were those who did not know what to think. Among the interested but dubious citizens was future President Rutherford B. Hayes.

Apparently Hayes could not resist Hall's childlike innocence and missionary zeal, for he signed a public appeal for contributions. It was all Charley needed. Within weeks he had sufficient funds to equip a small—very small—expedition. The exploration party consisted of Charley and a heartful of dreams. But it was enough.

Booking passage aboard the whaler *George Henry*, Hall began his remarkable odyssey. Lashed to the whaler's deck was his little boat, containing a handful of supplies and the old navigation instruments he had scrounged.

But when the *Henry* anchored in Ookoolear Bay, a gale was threatening. As the ships battened down, Charley insisted his boat be launched. Capt. Sydney O. Buddington was near speechless with amazement.

Charley persisted though, and the boat was lowered; with two Eskimos he had hired, he set off to fulfill his dreams . . . and to make history.

All that night the storm raged, the whalers fighting to remain afloat. With morning came calm—and Charley. His boat had been wrecked, he said, and surely Captain Buddington wouldn't mind lending him another?

". . . a gale was threatening. . . "

Charley lived with the Eskimos, learned their customs, and gained their confidence.

Buddington knew better than to argue. Waving his hands in despair, he cursed the grinning lunatic and ordered his men to give Hall the *Henry's* poorest whaleboat. Charley thanked the skipper profusely and launched his new command (described as being "old, rotten, leaky, and ice-beaten").

Finally reaching Frobisher Bay in Baffin Land, he set his plan into action. By living with the Eskimos, learning their customs, and gaining their confidence, he hoped to discover information about Franklin. Hall spent two seasons with the friendly Innuits.

But the initial loss of his sturdy boat quashed intentions of exploring Fury and Hecla Straits, although he did make the historically important discovery of Martin Frobisher (1556) relics in Frobisher Bay. Moreover, he had learned to live and travel like the Eskimos and now spoke their dialect; these would prove invaluable.

Returning home in 1862, he began his second drive for funds, accompanied by the Eskimos Joe (Ebierbuig) and Hannah (Tookoolito), who had visited England in 1853. But Hall's series of lectures were fruitless.

The Civil War crowded everyone's thoughts. Without the generous contributions of Henry Grinnell (who had financed earlier Arctic exploration), Charley would have been unable even to support himself and companions. And he had little to show for his Franklin search—beyond himself. For many had predicted he would vanish in the North as had Franklin. But here he was, loud as ever, and the skeptics grudgingly conceded he had proved them wrong in that respect, at least. But they gave no money.

[149]

Charley was on his way...

Charley was desperate. Joe and Hannah's baby, Tuk-e, had died; the grieving parents wished to return home. Finally, R. H. Chapell offered the disheartened trio passage northward in one of his New London whalers. Old friend Henry Grinnell mustered his friends and collected enough to grubstake Charley. Again, it was all the irrepressible Hall needed.

He spent the next five years tracking the Arctic wilderness in the "final determination of all the mysterious matters relative to Sir John Franklin's expedition," filling in the "gap on (the) coast between Parry's and Rae's explorations." He also learned "one of Franklin's vessels had actually accomplished the Northwest Passage while five of her crew were still on board," and collected 150 relics of the tragic expedition.

This time he succeeded in searching Repulse Bay, and Fury and Hecla Straits, but did not reach his true goal, King William's Land, his native guides fearing that region's fierce inhabitants.

During this period, Charley quelled a mutiny. He had engaged several men from whalers wintering in Repulse Bay, promising payment when he returned to New York. The men worked diligently for some time. But for all Charley's talents, he lacked the prime requisite—leadership. This shortcoming led to a shooting which ruined his hopes for his cherished Franklin project and eventually may have caused Charley's own demise.

After months of exhausting and unremunerated labor, during which relations between the whalers and Hall deteriorated drastically, one of the men, Patrick Coleman, quit on the spot, exhorting his comrades to follow his lead. Hall ordered the glowering seaman to honor his contract. When Coleman advanced menacingly, Hall raised his ancient shotgun and ordered him to halt. Coleman continued, Hall fired, and the mutineer fell, mortally wounded.

Heartbroken, as only a man of Hall's unique temperament could be, he nursed the dying whaler like a grieving mother. But his efforts were futile, and Coleman died shortly after, ending Hall's second expedition.

Returning to the United States in August 1869, the saddened Hall finally resolved upon another goal—the North Pole!

But if he had braved countless dangers in the Arctic with a strong heart, surely he must have wavered when he realized the enormous obstacles

[150]

ahead of him. Once again the bearded explorer made the lecture circuit, eventually descending upon an innocent Washington, D.C., in January 1870. There, he was invited to speak before an influential gathering in Lincoln Hall.

Apparently Charley was quite a talker for, three days after the speech, Ohio Representative Job E. Stevenson introduced a resolution in the House requesting $100,000 to send Hall on his mission. But it was not to be that easy.

The bill had to pass several readings, and was shifted from one committee to another, finally landing in the unhappy lap of the Committee of Foreign Relations.

And now Hall faced his greatest opposition. After all his work, it appeared the bill would pass, but the proposed expedition would be led by Dr. I. I. Hayes, who had tried to reach the Pole 10 years earlier.

It seems the scientific world could not accept the untutored Hall—a bearded bumpkin, they said. Dr. Hayes, on the other hand, was educated, experienced, and able. The situation darkened for poor Charley as support for Hayes grew. Even the stately American Geographical Society joined the fray, endorsing Dr. Hayes as "highly desirable" and pointedly ignoring our homely hero.

The government was confused. On one side, they had Hall, a veteran of seven years in the Arctic; on the other was Dr. Hayes, also an experienced Northern explorer. Unable to decide, the legislators called each candidate before them to state his case—and were stymied. So they passed the buck to President Ulysses S. Grant.

Meanwhile, the $100,000 appropriation was battling its way through the Senate. Finally it was put to a vote, resulting in a draw. The Vice President then cast the deciding ballot—in favor of the bill, although the money was halved.

Days after, Charley received word from President Grant; he *would* head the expedition. The ridiculed printer from New Hampshire was on his way to the North Pole!

Reporting to the Navy, Hall was introduced to his new ship, gunboat USS *Periwinkle*, which he renamed *Polaris*. The ship's sailing master was his old antagonist, Capt. Sydney Buddington of the *George Henry*.

When all was ready, Hall steamed northward to keep a date with immortality.

Polaris' sturdy engine proved its worth, the tiny ship battling north through fog, ice floes, and 'bergs at incredible speed. By late August 1871, Hall had reached the record position of 82° 11′ North.

But Charley's luck had ended; tragedy and disaster lay ahead. That winter, unable to stand shipboard inactivity, Hall completed a two-week sledge journey. While returning to the ship, he found himself exhausted and weak. Upon boarding the *Polaris*, he became seriously ill. Although he continued making plans and dictating notes until the end, his condition rapidly worsened. Two weeks later, on Nov. 8, 1871, he was dead. Apoplexy, said the ship's surgeon and scientist, Dr. Emil Bessels.

Others were not so sure. "Crazy" Charley had protested violently of poisoning on his deathbed. Accordingly, a naval court of inquiry was held, but its verdict was that the explorer had probably died a natural death. Doubts persisted, however, and a number of disturbing questions remained unanswered.

The case was reopened almost a hundred years later by two scholars, Dr. Chauncey Loomis, a Dartmouth College professor, and pathologist Dr. Franklin Paddock of the Berkshire Medical Center in Pittsfield, Massachusetts. Studying the diaries of Hall's crew members and the court testimony stored in the archives of the Smithsonian Institution in Washington, Loomis learned that Hall's insistence on wintering the *Polaris* and her crew in a harbor on the northwest coast of Greenland (which he named Thank God Bay) until the weather relented sufficiently for them to push right on up to the Pole was vehemently opposed by Captain Buddington and Dr. Bessels. Both men resented the aggressive manner and whip-and-spur tactics of Charley Hall—Buddington's dislike of the feisty little explorer dated back ten years. They preferred to winter further south in safer waters.

There had not, of course, been a post-mortem before Hall's body was lowered into his shallow Greenland grave, and Loomis and Paddock determined that there should be. They had no trouble locating the stone cairn still marking the lonely grave and exhuming Hall's body, which, except for the internal organs, was well preserved by ice that had formed in the coffin. Samples of the cadaver's hair and nails were taken and sent for special analysis to Toronto's Center of Forensic Sciences. Neutron-activation analysis showed that Hall had received very high doses of arsenic regularly for two weeks prior to his death, adding up to what would seem to be a fatal amount.

Thus January, 1969, solved one of the questions that have persisted since November, 1871, regarding Charley Hall: he appears indeed to have been poisoned. By whom and why and how are secrets the Arctic has not yet disclosed.

After Hall's death, the *Polaris* was cut to pieces by drifting ice and had to be abandoned. Nineteen members of the expedition, including an Eskimo mother and two-month-old baby, were marooned on an ice floe, on which they drifted for 196 days and 1,500 miles before being rescued by a whaler off the coast of Labrador. The rest struggled to survive for almost a year before they were found, but eventually all but Charley returned safely.

Thousands of words of tribute have been paid Charles Francis Hall over the years. Perhaps the best tribute is a single sentence from a book published in 1876. It reads: ". . . had he lived, it is certain he would have advanced as far to the northward as man is able to go."

And it is strange that this unlikely but dedicated adventurer entered the pages of history to solve the mystery of an Arctic explorer's death—to find Sir John Franklin's grave—only to become himself a strikingly similar riddle to posterity. END

WILLIAM MILLER

The Man Who Drove
a Million People Crazy

by M. Robert Beasley

From Canada to the Gulf of Mexico, from the Atlantic Ocean to the Mississippi River, a million people, clothed in flowing white robes* gathered on hilltops and in cemeteries. While flames from huge bonfires leaped high, they prayed, sang hymns and prostrated themselves, gibbering, muttering, sobbing . . . At midnight all faces turned toward the sky, expecting to see it burst open and all true believers—living and dead—to be called into the Paradise of Heaven. The remaining world and sinners would then be destroyed by fire.

This was the hour of the "Great Reckoning," October 22, 1844. The million fanatics, who had destroyed their homes, thrown their money and jewels into the streets, and now stood waiting entrance into Heaven, were Millerites. This group of feverishly religious people, who gave America of that time its largest and most grotesque display of mass hysteria, was inspired by one man—a self-styled preacher—William Miller.

Miller, born in 1782 into a conservative Massachusetts family, displayed an unusual interest in books and studies from an early age. Upon reaching manhood he turned Atheist, calling all religious rites superstitions and humbug. He later joined the Army and while on active duty suffered a leg injury. Enroute to a hospital he fell from the wagon—landing on his head. He was unconscious for several days, but recovered physically, leaving the service in June, 1815.

During the Battle of Burlington he witnessed so much suffering and death that he converted back to religion. Believing the Lord was trying to convey a message to him, he devoted 14 years exclusively to Biblical research, specifically seeking the secret of death and the hereafter.

Using the periods referred to as 2,300 days, the "seven times" Gentile supremacy, and the 1,335 days in the Book of Daniel as prophetic periods, he concluded that Judgment Day would occur between March 21, 1843, and March 21, 1844.

In 1831 he received his first message, "direct from God."

"Go tell your findings to the world," God told him one Sunday morning.

"I can't," he replied, "for I have no way of meeting people."

---

* The white robes element of the Millerite Saga has been strongly questioned over the years by the Advent Christian Church, the present-day outcome of the Millerite movement. They have marshaled well-documented arguments to prove that the white robes were a figment of the Press's imagination. On the other hand, many letters from persons touched by the movement attest that there were, indeed, white robes—with elastic set in at the ankles of ladies' robes so that the "limbs" needn't show.

"That will be arranged," said the Voice from Heaven.

A half hour later a messenger arrived from Dresden, telling him the local preacher had suddenly been stricken ill, and requesting him to speak from the pulpit that morning.

This was it! A way had been opened to deliver his message.

After informing the congregation that Judgment Day was approaching, he cautioned them that before his prophesy could be fulfilled there first must be four definite signs:

1. Wonders would be seen in the skies;
2. The earth would tremble in various places throughout the world;
3. There was to be war among mankind;
4. Man would show marked intelligence in earthly progress.

As if by divine power, the signs began to appear:

1. On November 13, 1833, thousands of brilliant stars were seen falling from the skies, and balls of fire blazed in the Zenith for 50 minutes.
2. Earthquakes were reported in England, India, West Indies, and various other countries.
3. Numerous revolutions began breaking out in Europe, and the people had but to look around to find martial strife of every kind.
4. Their generation had displayed unprecedented intelligence during the past few years, resulting in an unparalleled inventive and industrial expansion.

This resolved all doubts and the Millerite Cult was born.

Miller personally delivered several thousand speeches throughout the east, while a thousand other preachers joined forces to spread "The Word." Miller's dynamic speaking power was shown in Portland, Maine. After a lecture there in 1841, booksellers sold more Bibles in one month than they had during the previous ten years!

As the critical period approached and the impending cataclysm seemed inevitable, the populace was again roused to feverish mass demonstrations when solar haloes appeared over Danville, Kentucky on January 4, 1843—followed shortly by another fiery display over New York City.

All Hell Broke Loose!

Loved ones who died were not buried, but were carried to camps so

...a woman tried to walk across the river...

they might all ascend into Heaven together. Betrothed girls refused to complete the marital agreement, so they might enter Heaven as virgins. Numerous cases were reported where fanatical devotees killed their entire families, followed by their own suicides, believing the dead would be resurrected into Heaven first. Individual suicides were a daily occurrence, while hospitals and mental institutions accepted capacity loads.

A woman in Windsor, Connecticut, believing she had been in direct communication with the Lord and had acquired supernatural powers, tried to walk across the river—and was immediately drowned. Another enthusiast, saying he possessed celestial powers, drove his horse and buggy over a cliff only to learn he didn't; he was splattered over the hillside along with his horse.

Then came the final straw. The biggest ball of fire ever to approach earth was seen when the Great Comet of 1843 appeared in the sky. Even the confirmed Atheists trembled at this blazing spectacle. This phenomena more than doubled the believers flocking into Millerite Camps.

The day after this fiery display, Miller published a statement in the *New York Herald* that the destruction of the world by fire would take place April 3, 1843. Ironically enough, Miller was stricken ill at a mass meeting on April Fool's Day, 1843. Even while semiconscious he continued babbling: "I shall see Christ this year!"

On April 3rd, at Westford, Massachusetts, a zealous group of Millerites had gathered at the famous Bancroft mansion prior to assembly on the hilltops for ascension. The mansion had been stripped bare of furniture to provide fuel for the bonfires, and thousands of believers were gathered inside fervently praying. Typical of small towns, Westford had a village idiot, this one called Crazy Amos. Because of his obvious mental shortcomings, Amos was not a member of the Millerites, but he was not to be outdone.

As the Bancroft mansion filled to overflowing, he secured a large horn and let out several ear-splitting blasts on the front lawn.

At the sound of the horn, the worshippers tumbled from doors and windows shouting "Hallelujah! Glory to God! The time has come!" thinking the horn was a summons by Gabriel.

"You fools! Go dig your potatoes!" screamed Crazy Amos. "Angel Gabriel won't go a-diggin' 'em for you!"

...he killed his entire family...

April 3, 1843 passed uneventfully, and the earth, instead of being swept by fire, donned garments of spring and burst into leaf and song. The Millerites consoled themselves that the original prophesy stated Judgment Day would come sometime *between* March 1843 and March 1844—so they turned to prayer—still convinced the fiery end was near.

On March 21, 1844, the final date of the expected ending of the world, they again gathered, praying through the night, expecting to be snatched momentarily into Heaven. But again dawn broke as usual and, unmindful of man's prophesy of coming destruction, the earth continued its normal course.

Slowly and silently the groups disbanded, their eyes filled with tears, their hearts heavy. The white robes were soiled and torn, they were hungry and exhausted. But where could they go . . . ? They had no homes or worldly goods and were now faced with the urgency of finding food, clothing and shelter, for the bitter winds of March did not share their fanatical faith.

Miller, who had remained at his Massachusetts home for the crucial hour of Judgment, spent several days checking calculations then announced that the error had been located. He had used the Gregorian calendar instead of the Jewish one, which put him seven months off in his figures. The Great Day was *certain* to take place on October 22nd!

Couriers were sent to his thousand Ministers. "Our faith has been tested! By rechecking calculations, and through spiritual messages, I have received, I humbly announce as a faithful Disciple, that the Second Advent of Christ will occur October 22nd, 1844. Prepare yourself for this Great Day!"

Incredible as it sounds, after two dates had proved failures, Millerites gathered back into the fold with renewed fervor—while *thousands of new converts were added!*

A woman was found in South Coventry, Connecticut, who was said to have died following ten years of illness. After doctors had pronounced her dead, she had returned to life. For the next 120 days she ate no food, only drinking two cups of weak tea daily, and spent all her time loudly singing hymns. At all meetings this women was held before them as an example of miracles being performed on earth, since she is reported to have said she was returned from the dead to await Judgment Day.

At one such meeting in Philadelphia, a group of young men, not under the influence of fanatical fever, surrounded the meeting hall. At a given signal, every window in the building was broken simultaneously and firecrackers were tossed into the room. The wind whistled through the smashed windows, extinguishing the candles and lamps, and the firecrackers began exploding in the dark, Millerite-packed room. Several of them were trampled to death and many others seriously injured in making a mass exodus from what appeared to have been the wrong direction in their Ascension.

On October 22nd, the now familiar pattern was repeated. Every hilltop and cemetery was jammed with white-robed figures huddled around huge bonfires, praying and chanting hymns.

A thrifty farmer in Chester, Vermont, had apparently hired a seamstress to make up "Ascension" robes for six of his best cows. "They'll come in mighty handy up there," he said. "It's a long trip, and the kids will be wanting some milk."

One father in New Haven gathered his family in the living room on that fateful night of October 22nd. Looking out his window he saw the night sky ablaze. Believing the time had finally arrived, he killed his entire family of five, followed by his own suicide. Only the servant girl escaped. He never realized that what caused the sky to be illuminated with fire was—not the coming of Judgment Day—but his neighbor's house and barn burning to the ground.

The night of October 22nd passed without the prophesied destruction. Dawn found pathetic, disillusioned groups, soaked by the rains of the night, cold from October winds, and broken in mind, body and spirit. Not only were they still mortal and earth-bound, but having destroyed their worldly possessions, they were paupers.

The task of beginning life over was too much for many to face. Thousands of suicides and family slaughters occurred. Hospitals and asylums were unable to accommodate the unprecedented number of mental cases.

Through all the agony, poverty, insanity and suicides, Miller reposed comfortably and securely at his luxurious farm. What the fanatical Millerites overlooked was that in April 1843, when Miller first predicted the ending of the world, he had just installed 40 rods of new stone fence on his property. On the October date, when he had positively forecast the destruction of all things worldly, he had a full woodshed and pantry, and his fields and livestock were well tended. Such preparations for the future certainly cast suspicion on the sincerity of a man who prophesied utter oblivion for mankind.

Also overlooked was the fact that at each meeting enormous collections, often diamonds, gold and life savings in cash (which he said would be of no value), were taken in and saved.

During the next five years, Miller lived as a recluse, gradually going blind. Possibly the head injury in 1810 finally caught up with him, for his years of marked mental deterioration developed into complete insanity before his death in 1849 at Low Hampton, New York. With his dying breath, he still tried to incite others with his delusions, crying out: "Victory! At last I see Him!"

Perhaps his million followers could have been spared their poverty, hardship, insanity, and untimely deaths had they studied the same Bible a little further and read the recorded words of St. Matthew, in speaking of Judgment Day: "But of that day and hour knoweth no man, no, not even the Angels in Heaven . . ."   END

Ill-Fated King of the Islands of Refreshment

by Vincent J. Dowdell, Jr.

In October, 1961, the remote South Atlantic island of Tristan da Cunha became front-page news when its supposedly extinct volcano erupted. Its 264 inhabitants hastily evacuated the only home they had ever known; eventually they were resettled 6500 miles away in England. After 150 years, the lonely island was once again uninhabited, just as it always had been until a determined sea captain from Salem, Massachusetts, took absolute possession in 1811, proclaimed himself king, and set out to develop an international refreshment stand for passing whalers and merchantmen plying the trade routes between the Northern Hemisphere and the Indies.

Born in 1772, Jonathan Lambert came from an old Salem seafaring family. As a sailor aboard the second *Grand Turk* under Captain Benjamin Hodges in 1792, Lambert first sighted the island group he was to claim nineteen years later. By 1795, Lambert was master of his father's schooner *Ruth* and his future seemed bright. Then followed a series of financial misfortunes, and he never prospered. While others in similar circumstances sought a fresh start by moving westward, Lambert conceived a bold and fantastic plan: he would colonize and develop the world's most isolated spot, a small island in the middle of the South Atlantic. Discovered in 1506 by the Portuguese admiral for whom the island group and its largest island are named, Tristan da Cunha consists chiefly of the main island and two smaller, uninhabited isles, Nightingale and Inaccessible. "The world's loneliest isle" has been nearly untouched by time and civilization; it rises out of the South Atlantic 1700 miles from Capetown and 2100 miles from Rio de Janeiro. Precipitous cliffs tower

Jonathan Lambert—from a miniature painted on ivory about five years prior to his mysterious death on Tristan da Cunha. (Courtesy of the Essex Institute, Salem, Mass.)

2,000 feet above the sea. There is no harbor; getting a boat ashore or putting it to sea safely is often impossible. The nearest populated place is St. Helena, Napoleon's isle of exile, 1400 miles to the north.

Leaving his childless wife to be supported by the Overseers of the Poor, Lambert left Salem in 1810 and took passage aboard the Boston ship *Baltic*, under Captain Lovell. Arriving at Rio de Janeiro on November 6, 1810, Lambert promptly ran into trouble. Since Napoleon's armies had overrun Portugal, Rio was then the temporary capital of the Portuguese Empire. Because of his French-sounding name, the Portuguese officials suspected Lambert of being a French agent. They seized the ship, placed Captain Lovell under guard, and hustled Lambert and his seven fellow-passengers off to jail. After five days' imprisonment, all were released through the efforts of Thomas Sumter, the American "Minister at the Court of the Prince Regent of Portugal in Brazil," who vouched for Lambert as an American sea captain.

Lambert spent several weeks in Rio waiting for the *Baltic* to sail and tried to interest others in his scheme. Sumter gave Lambert a coffee tree, sugar cane, and a supply of seeds. Benjamin Seaver, master of the British merchant vessel *Charles*, offered to help Lambert and discussed the possibility of eventually joining him. On or about New Year's Day of 1811, the *Baltic* hove to off Tristan. Lambert was rowed ashore in the ship's boat with two other associates: a man named Williams, who for reasons of his own assumed the name "Andrew Millet," and an Italian named Tomaso Currio, who anglicized his name to Thomas Currie. When Captain Seaver looked in on Lambert three weeks later en route to Capetown, the settlers had cleared two acres; radishes, cabbages, potatoes, and pumpkins were already growing well. Lambert and his two associates had also collected seal skins and sea-elephant oil. When he reached Capetown, Seaver wrote to Earl Caledon, who was then Governor of the Cape of Good Hope, on behalf of Lambert and himself, asking the British government and the East India Company for help in colonizing Tristan. In particular, Seaver requested "a small vessel from 50 to 100 tons to carry from this colony such young, industrious families as may be willing to embark, and any other persons that would be useful in tilling the ground, with a few black cattle, goats and sheep, and such other small necessaries as would conduce to the growth and productions of the island." In exchange, Lambert would display the British flag and accept British sovereignty over the island, reserving to himself only the governorship.

But even before Seaver had arrived in the Cape Colony, Lambert had drafted a proclamation taking absolute possession of the Tristan group and renaming them the "Islands of Refreshments." He entrusted the document to his friend, Captain Lovell, who had stopped again on his way homeward, 34 days after leaving Lambert's party ashore. When Lovell eventually reached Boston about six months later, he brought the announcement to the *Boston Gazette*, which published it on July 18, 1811, with this introductory note: "The following communication was handed us by a gentleman who is witness to the facts therein stated, and who thinks notwithstanding the appearance of eccentricity which the narrative gives, that Mr. Lambert and his associates will found an important and highly valuable settlement."

Captain Lovell also observed that after 34 days on the island, Lambert had cleared about 50 acres. The letter eventually appeared in the world's newspapers and periodicals. The *North American Review* commented that, both in sense and style, it "was, to say the least, quite equal to some which have issued from far mightier thrones." The declaration spells out Lambert's claim "on the rational and sure principles of absolute occupancy, and as such, holding and possessing all the rights, titles, and immunities properly belonging to proprietors by usage of nations." He also

declares "that the cause of the said act set forth in this instrument originated in the desire and determination of preparing for myself and family
a home where I can enjoy life without the embarrassments which have
hitherto constantly attended me . . . and remain, if possible, far removed
beyond the reach of chicanery and ordinary misfortune." He invites ships
of all nations to supply themselves at a reasonable price, and concludes by
promising to hold himself and his people, "to be bound on the principles
of hospitality and good fellowship and the laws of nations (if any there
are) as established by the best writers on that subject, and by no other law
whatever, until time may produce particular contracts."

By the end of 1811, Lambert's enterprise seemed ready to pay off. In a
letter dated December 21, 1811, to Captain John Briggs, whom Lambert
had met at Rio, Lambert gives a detailed and glowing account of life on
the island. He also solicits financial help and material support. In addition
to the produce they had raised, the trio had killed about 80 sea elephants
and accumulated about 1000 gallons of oil. Lambert planned to make a
business of collecting oil and skins but needed a ship. He proposed that
Briggs buy a small fishing schooner of about 50 tons and send his brother
to Tristan in her, with ten or twelve men. Lambert also needed a boat or
two badly: "A boat would be victuals and drink to us," he wrote. He asked
for salt to preserve fish which he would ship to the French islands of Mau-
ritius and Reunion. The letter reads like a prospectus, but there were
strings attached to Lambert's proposals: because he couldn't put up any
cash, he could only be the "idea man." But he assures Briggs that the enterprise could not fail and would pay handsome dividends.

The letter was Lambert's last written communication. What happened
to him is still shrouded in mystery. From one to three others had joined
the original trio between December, 1811 and May, 1812. In March of
1813, a British naval vessel, HMS *Semiramis*, paid a routine call. Captain
Richardson reported to his superiors that he found Currie alone on the
island; Currie told him that Lambert and several others had drowned on
May 17, 1812, when their boat overturned in a sudden squall. Although
Richardson doubted Currie's story, he could only speculate as to what had
really happened.

as to what really happened...

News of Lambert's death didn't reach Salem until September, 1814. Dr. William Bentley, the pastor who kept a lively diary of contemporary Salem history for 35 years, made this entry for Sunday, September 11, 1814: "Notes: Prayers for Samuel Lambert and wife. Death of his brother Jonathan. This is the bold adventurer that seized upon an Island in the Great Ocean and collected a few companions to inhabit it, and gave notice that he should supply all circumnavigators. He perished when fishing in his boat with some of his companions. He was a man of real genius and intrepidity. Nothing common could satisfy him and he had acquired all that general knowledge which observation in Men and manners could supply. He had a ready tongue and good pen, an inquiring mind and power to know and possess what circumstances could give him, at the instant they appeared. I knew him intimately well." Nine days later, a brief obituary appeared on the back page of the *Salem Gazette*; it concluded with this comment: "Mr. Lambert was a man of real genius, and had, according to accounts, been successful in bringing forward his little colony, which in times of peace and commerce promised to be of general benefit." A year earlier, Dr. Bentley had noted that the Lambert family "had one son settled on Islands in the South Sea in a very excentric manner. The whole are endowed with talents."

Currie recruited a few others to keep the venture going. Although he had accepted a British flag from Captain Richardson, it offered little protection. During the War of 1812, American whalers and privateers used Tristan as a base and took what they wanted without bothering to pay. In May, 1815, Commander Peter Gordon, of the *Bengal Merchant*, wrote the Colonial Secretary and Registrar of the Cape of Good Hope that Currie "always expressed himself contented with his situation in every respect except one, which was the want of a female companion . . ."

In September, 1815, Richard Cleveland, a Salem sea captain who had been a classmate and friend of Lambert, anchored off Tristan while en route from Salem to Batavia via the Canary Islands. He sent an officer in a boat ashore "to ascertain who were the inhabitants, to procure from them whatever eatables they might have to spare." After four hours, the boat returned with a good supply of potatoes and fish. The officer reported that there were only three men on the island, who appeared to be Italians

[165]

Below: *The Scotsman Glass in front of his Tristan da Cunha residence in 1824.* Right: *This church photographed in May, 1963, was one of the few buildings to survive the 1961 volcanic eruptions. Note the striking resemblance of the portion on the left to Glass's 1824 house.* (U.S. Navy photo by Toby Marquez)

or Portuguese; when asked what had become of Lambert, they said he had drowned with others in attempting to go to Inaccessible Island. Captain Cleveland knew Lambert too well to believe their story. That night he expressed his doubts in his journal:

"Jonathan Lambert was a native of Salem and a school-mate of mine. He was a man of good capacity and much eccentricity. Having been unsuccessful in his endeavors to acquire a competency, and being disgusted with commerce and with the world, he formed the project of establishing himself on this island, which from its healthy climate, virgin soil, and being in the track of vessels bound to India, might be made an object of attraction to such as were in want of supplies. According, with several others of no less desperate fortune than himself, but very inferior in point of education and capacity, he landed on the island; and when they had produced enough for the supply of ships, he caused a notice thereof to be published in the Boston papers, inviting ships to stop and obtain such refreshments as he could supply. Not long after this, it was reported that he had perished in attempting to go to Inaccessible Island, but as he was of an irritable, tyrannical temper, his friends have supposed it to be more

[166]

probable that his comrades, unable to bear with it, had put him out of existence."

Napoleon was exiled to St. Helena in October, 1815; to prevent the possible use of Tristan as a base to rescue Napoleon, the frigate *Falmouth* was dispatched with a garrison force in August, 1816. The long-lonely Currie was glad to have someone to talk to and unburdened himself to the British authorities. "I came under an agreement to remain one year," he reported, "and to have passage found me to the Cape of Good Hope, in case I did not wish to remain. My agreement was twelve Spanish dollars per month, besides the one-third of twenty percent on all produce during the time I might remain." But he complained that he was never paid. "I suffered the greatest distress from want of clothes and provisions. I have been constantly robbed of livestock by the Americans, whether vessels of war or merchantmen." Of Lambert's fate, he asserted that "he [Lambert] remained on the island till the 17th May, 1812, when he and two other companions took the boat and left the island. I never heard of them since . . ." With Currie in 1816 was a man he called his apprentice, a native of Minorca who had agreed to serve two years for wages. The garrison left in

[167]

1817 after a year's occupation, but Corporal William Glass, a Scotsman, elected to settle on Tristan with his wife and family.

A revealing account of Lambert's probable fate is contained in a book written in 1832 by Augustus Earle, a "draughtsman in His Majesty's Surveying Service," who was stranded on Tristan for eight months in 1824. Earle and Glass became good friends and often discussed Currie. According to Earle's journal: "On the arrival of the garrison the only inhabitants they found were an old Italian named Thomas [Currie], and a wretched looking half-caste Portuguese. They said they were the last survivors of the American party settled here under Lambert, who, as their story ran, was lost with a number of men crossing to one of the neighboring islands; but from all the intelligence I obtained from Glass, who described this Italian to be a morose, mysterious person, I suspect he and his comrade knew something more of the fate of poor Lambert and his party than they chose to disclose. A story was easily invented, of all their companions perishing 'at one fell swoop' and, as a matter of course, the survivors became masters of all the property on the island. There was too strong evidence that these two villains dispatched their comrades by some unfair means . . ."

Currie always had plenty of money available, "and, tempted by the easy access his money gave him to the military canteen, he was constantly seen in a state of intoxication; and it was when he used to be half drunk, that he was accustomed to drop ambiguous phrases, and express the greatest horrors respecting Lambert and his companions." Currie told Glass that he had heaps of money buried on the island "and that he would one day show the place where his hoard lay, to that man in the garrison who pleased him most; thus insuring constant good treatment from the men, each hoping to be the favored heir; but one day, after a dose extraordinary, he was taken suddenly ill, and expired before he could explain to his companions where his treasure was concealed, though evidently anxious to do so."

Searching for Currie's hoard has been one of the few recreations on Tristan; it was interrupted only temporarily by the October, 1961, evacuation, despite predictions that Tristan would never again be habitable. When the British Colonial Office announced in August, 1962, that the volcano had quieted down, all but five Tristaners voted to go back. An advance party of about 60 returned in April, 1963, to make the island livable. If Currie's buried treasure is ever found, it may reveal what really happened to the self-made king of the "Islands of Refreshments."   END

Funerals Fit for Pharaohs

by John Mason

Back in 1873, there arrived in the town of Wilmington, Massachusetts, a young doctor and his wife by the name of Hiller—a name that will never be forgotten in Wilmington.

Henry Hiller was born in Mannheim, Germany, whence his grandfather had emigrated from Cape Cod. After obtaining his Doctor's degree in Mannheim, Henry moved to England and married a charming young English girl who had just graduated from a London medical school. They took a honeymoon trip to America and liked it so well they settled on Cape Cod. But after a while Dr. Hiller felt they could better serve humanity and themselves if they were near a big city. So they came up to Boston and looked around for a future home.

The town of Wilmington appealed to them and there they settled, building a big new house of 14 rooms near the railroad station.

Dr. Hiller had invented a patent medicine (or "Elixir"), and he sold a lot of it in his office on Tremont Street in Boston. He got rich very fast and was free with his money. To a *Boston Herald* reporter, Mrs. Hiller said, "Everything we touched turned to gold in our hands. We were as happy as could be save for one thing. Children were born to us, but they did not live. Though we both were vigorous, our little ones pined away and died in early life; so of the 23 darlings I have borne, 14 of whom were twins, not one is alive today to give joy to my heart and add sunshine to my home. It was God's will. Let His will be done."

Besides being interested in art, music, and science, the Hillers were interested in spiritual things and often talked of the hereafter. Mrs. Hiller,

[169]

Detail showing the elaborate carving of the casket.

who loved things costly and elaborate and bizarre, said she wanted a casket such as had never been seen before, and the doctor agreed that they couldn't spend their money in any better way.

Over in Cambridge lived a very famous woodcarver and cabinet maker, James MacGregor—and to MacGregor the Hillers went with their plans and specifications. The grand old Scotsman listened open-mouthed as the doctor and his wife described the two caskets and the inner box that they wanted built and decorated. He figured and figured and finally told them that even with the help of his four expert assistants it would take at least seven years to do the carvings. But, if they would pay him $40 a week, big money in those days, he would go ahead with the job.

The original coffin was to have been for Mrs. Hiller, but it was the doctor who died first—on November 7, 1888, after having been thrown from his carriage.

Just two weeks before his death, one of the neighbors asked him how his casket was coming along. He replied, "Oh, it'll be ready when I need it." But it wasn't half finished when death came; so his body was placed in a vault in nearby Winchester, and the funeral was postponed until the following year.

On the first of September, 1889, MacGregor announced that the first costly coffin had been completed and he was ready to tackle the second one. Mrs. Hiller announced that the doctor's funeral would be held in a few days, on September 4—which it was.

Three and a half years later, MacGregor finished the second casket—an exact duplicate of the doctor's. When it was delivered in Wilmington,

[170]

Frances B. Hiller

Mrs. Hiller was so proud of it she had it set up in the front parlor. When her friends came to call, she would climb in and lie down so they could see "just how splendid she would look when she was all laid out." She even had a wax model of herself made, attired in her fabulous burial robes, and she placed the model in the casket in the parlor.

The outside casket was supported by eight heavy brass lion's paws. They were 17 inches high, cost $100 apiece, and weighed 475 pounds. When the steel hammock was hung inside the inner box (and that was placed in the outside casket), and the lion's paws were put under the whole affair, it stood five feet from the floor and weighed a little over 2,000 pounds! It was said to have cost close to $30,000.

The casket cover had two ivy vines running around its edge, meeting in the center where there was a skull carved in the wood. A lizard was carved creeping out of one of the eye sockets. On the ends and sides of the casket, MacGregor and his assistants had carved angels, cupids, and dragons by the dozen. There were bats flying over serpents and a big owl holding a tiny field mouse in his talons, carved in mahogany four inches thick.

Inside the box, a metal hammock was suspended from the four corners of a second inner chamber, and on the cover of this box were gold and silver plates engraved with portraits of the Doctor and his wife and their 23 children.

In describing the caskets they had ordered, Mrs. Hiller said, "I paid over $1,000 for planks from the giant redwood trees of California but they weren't good enough and I cast them aside. Then I paid $2,000 for some cedars of Lebanon and discarded those."

[171]

Once Mrs. Hiller put the casket on exhibition in Boston's Horticultural Hall, which she had had draped in black for the occasion. Though the casket and the burial robes were well worth the dollar charged for admission (the $20,000 robe was made of corded silk, trimmed with 500 yards of hand made silk lace and hand embroidered in France with over 5000 daisies), the venture was a financial failure.

Mrs. Hiller was no piker when it came to spending her money after the Doctor passed away. She planned a mausoleum 40 feet square and 40 feet high, with plate glass windows behind a bronze grating so that visitors could come and look at the costly coffins and fancy carvings. "Two watchmen," said Mrs. Hiller, "will be on guard day and night and there will be lights burning as long as the world lasts."

Five years after Dr. Hiller died, friends and relatives of Mrs. Hiller were startled when they received bright red invitations printed with gold ink that read as follows:

"You are cordially invited to be present at the renewal of the marriage vows of Frances B. Hiller and Henry Hiller, at their residence at 2 PM, Easter Sunday, April 2nd, 1893."

The townsfolk were flabbergasted. Just how could the comely widow renew her marriage vows with Henry Hiller when he had departed this earth five years before? And why wasn't he referred to on the invitation as Doctor Hiller?

Well, here's what happened—in Mrs. Hiller's own words to the society editors of that day. "Among my servants," she said, "there was Peter Surrette, my coachman. He came from Montreal and he was always a perfect gentleman. One day Peter asked me if it was true that I was going to marry again, and I told him 'no.' He seemed very happy and shortly thereafter he began his lovemaking.

" 'I'm a poor servant without money or friends,' he said, 'but I am a faithful, devoted admirer of your womanly qualities, and, as humble as I am, please consider a proposal from me.'

"I was thunderstruck at first, but the subject attracted my attention, and I said, 'Why not. He is honest, loyal, obedient, and loving.' I remembered how some of the greatest men of our time came from the meek and lowly, and began to make inquiries. Fr. Ryan consulted Peter and told me that Peter did not love my money but me. I then found out that he came from a very good family, and would be a good man to look out for my property. Accordingly I asked him if he was willing to sign the antenuptial settlement, and he wanted to know what that meant. I told him, and again he expostulated that it was not my money he was after, but he loved me as only man can love. I shall have him placed in the hands of a tutor and fitted for Harvard."

The second Mr. Hiller promptly applied himself to the task of educating himself (although the Harvard idea didn't work out) so as to be suited to occupy the place in society to which he had been elevated.

So, in 1893—five years after the death of Dr. Hiller—they got married. But, instead of Mrs. Hiller becoming Mrs. Surrette, she had her husband's name changed (by a special act of the Legislature) to Henry Hiller —and Henry Hiller he was to the end of his life. (He outlived Mrs. Hiller by more than 40 years.)

Mrs. Hiller's romance and wedding were the sole topic of conversation for months, eclipsed only by the funeral that she had so elaborately planned years before her death.

The glamorous Mrs. Hiller died at age 56 on May 18, 1900, after a long illness. Every reporter who could be spared was in Wilmington covering her grandiose funeral.

Early in the morning, workmen took down the wooden casing around the private vault in back of the Hiller homestead and wheeled out the massive sarcophagus and placed it on the lawn. A big crowd gathered, hoping to catch a glimpse of the rich carvings on the costly casket, but only a few reporters and relatives saw the owls, angels, birds, and snakes that had been painstakingly carved in the solid mahogany 12 years before. The warm spring sunshine glistened on the solid brass lion's paws at the four corners of the heavy boxes. A special patented lifting device was brought from Boston to convey the casket into the tomb.

The mammoth funeral car (designed by Mrs. Hiller and specially built long before her death) was too high to go under the trolley wires, so carpenters hastily cut it down 14 inches. It was, in reality, more of a truck than a car and most impressive, completely covered in black velvet with broadcloth draperies sweeping the curbstone. Mr. Charles Nichols of Woburn was seated in a big chair on the truck from which he drove the four coal-black horses caparisoned with black netting.

The *Boston Traveler* reported that on the day of the funeral, May 23, "thousands crammed the trolleys and steam cars—and hundreds of others blocked the side roads with carriages and bicycles."

The procession formed at 9:30—an open landau filled with flowers, then the hacks, all drawn by black horses. It took ten men to lift the

[173]

Top: *Four black horses drew a mammoth funeral car draped in black velvet.* Bottom: *Thousands lined the streets of Wilmington and packed the churchyard, craning their necks for a view of the fabulous funeral.*

casket through the side window and, when they rested the coffin on the veranda railings, the supports buckled. A number of the bearers scrambled down the steps and hastened to the lawn, where they put their shoulders under the case and sustained its weight. After a brief rest, the burden was taken to the rear of the funeral car and one end of the case zigzagged up to the floor of the sombre canopy. As the casket rested upon the car, there was a moment of intense excitement. The canopy on the car, towering 19 feet above the street, swayed alarmingly, and the body of the car settled and lurched as if about to collapse. After a few minutes effort on the part of the bearers, the casket was moved to the center of the car's floor.

During the transferral of the remains from the house to the street, cameras were used on every side. The awed silence was punctured by the heavy breathing of the bearers and the click of the "snap boxes." (As this was one of the first funerals to be covered by news photographers, the accompanying photos are very rare.) Hats were raised, and heads were bowed by a few who stared in wonder as the strange, though much-heralded, exhibition passed as if it were a holiday review. Henry Hiller rode in the first of the eight carriages in the procession.

The fences along the street and in front of houses served as seats for the curious. The highway was blocked with people. Trains whizzed by the little railroad station near at hand, and passengers craned their heads from the car windows. They had evidently planned to catch a glimpse of the spectacle during their flight through the village.

After the service, the sarcophagus was rolled into the tomb beside that of Dr. Hiller, the massive gates were closed, and then everyone thought that the two famous Hillers would always remain in that mausoleum.

But this was not to be. Early in June, 1935, it was agreed that the 10-foot-high tomb at the entrance to Wildwood Cemetery was an eyesore. The town voted to remove the tomb and to bury the caskets in the ground. It was quite a job, and the workmen dug for several hours. When the pick of one of the workmen struck the tomb, there was a loud *whoosh*. The workmen dropped their tools and ran away, frightened. But it was only the air coming out of the sealed vault.

The caskets were in excellent condition, and the carvings were as splendid as they had been 35 years before. Nevertheless, they were lowered into the pit dug for them and buried. There they are today, marked only by two stone urns over simple bronze plaques.   END

He Dreamed of Peace
and Improved His Gun

by Jean Mitchell Boyd

D r. Gatling lived across the street from us in Hartford, Connecticut, when we were young. We spoke of him as Dr. Gatling Gun, because he had invented some kind of a gun with a revolving battery.

Around the corner lived Mrs. Colt, a sweet white-haired lady who wore a black bonnet that sparkled with jet. Her husband had been Colonel Colt, and he had invented a revolver, so we spoke of her as Mrs. Colt Revolver. She rode in a brougham with a fat coachman and thin footman, but Mrs. Gatling Gun rode in a victoria with plum-colored cushions and looked like royalty.

It must have been September when Dr. Gatling gave me the book, and I decided that he was a much finer gentleman than Mr. Lawrence in *Little Women*. I was sitting on the steps of his side door eating a pear with the dew on it, which I had picked up under his pear tree. All the fruit on the street belonged to everyone. When we finished Dr. Gatling's pears, it would be time for General Dwight's plums. After that there would be the apples on the trees which Mr. Gideon Welles planted after he was through being Mr. Lincoln's Secretary of the Navy and came to Hartford to live.

It was pleasant on Dr. Gatling's steps. I wondered why he didn't have a big back yard like Mrs. Colt's where there were deer and peacocks. There were white statues, too, which Colonel Colt had brought over from Europe after his revolver made him rich. Some had no nightgowns or shawls and were not respectable.

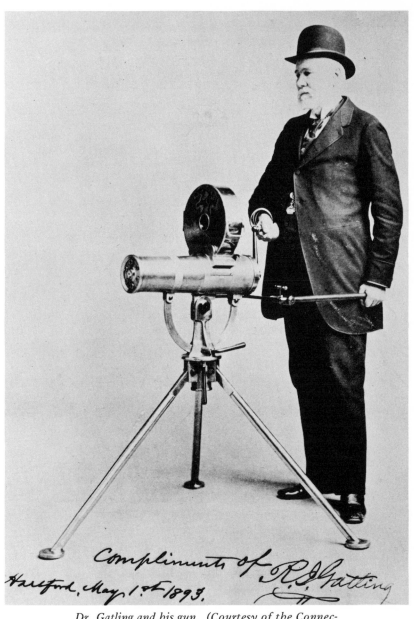

Compliments of R. J. Gatling

Hartford, May 1st 1893.

Dr. Gatling and his gun. (Courtesy of the Connecticut State Library: Colt Collection of Firearms)

I finished the pear and was wiping my hands on the grass when the door opened and Dr. Gatling came out with a book.

"Good morning, my dear," he said.

I stood up straight as children in the Nineties were taught to do when a grown-up appeared.

"Good morning, Dr. Gatling. I ate one of your pears with the dew on it."

"That's the way they taste the best. I have a book that has Rob's name in the front, but it's about a little girl, and I think a little girl might like to have it. Would you like it?"

"Oh yes, I would."

I went up the steps and he gave me the book. There was a little girl's head in gold on the beautiful blue cover, and gold letters which said *The Little People of the Snow* by William Cullen Bryant. That was a name I recognized, I told Dr. Gatling.

"There's one of Mr. Bryant's poems in our spelling book. It begins: 'So live that when thy summons comes.' It's in the *New Graded Speller* that Mr. Graves wrote." We looked across the street where Mr. Graves lived. I thought it would be nice if he came out and recited the poem, but he didn't come.

"This book is a poem, so you might like to sit down on the steps and read it—then have another pear."

"I will. Thank you very much, Dr. Gatling." I felt that I was an extremely polite child at the moment. There were moments when I was not.

He went into the house, and I read the book. It was a poem, longer than "The Village Blacksmith" or "The First Snowfall"—a sad story about a little girl named Eva, who disobeyed her parents and was frozen to death. It must have been a lesson to her. There were pictures and the last one was a grave with little fairy people laying frost wreaths on it by moonlight. A tear fell on the page right beside the grave. I rubbed it with my sleeve, then held the book in the sun, hoping the tear wouldn't leave a mark.

I wondered if all little girls named Eva died young. Little Eva in *Uncle Tom's Cabin* died, but she wasn't frozen. I wondered what made her die. I wished that I had asked Mrs. Stowe before she died herself. I didn't know her except by sight. She hadn't lived on our street in Hartford, but I had seen her in her yard, or walking around the corner past Mark Twain's house. She liked to pick ferns beside Little River. She was sweet and sad like Mrs. Colt Revolver.

...we went to war with Dr. Gatling's gun...

The door behind me opened. I closed the book with the tear inside and stood up.

"Oh, I'm afraid it was a sad story," Dr. Gatling said.

I nodded. "She died."

"I'm sorry," he said. "I had forgotten that she died."

"Her name was Eva like the one Mrs. Stowe wrote about. I cried over her, and over Beth in *Little Women*. I like to read sad stories."

"Come in a minute."

We went into the back parlor where Mrs. Gatling was embroidering forgetmenots on a tray cloth.

"Good morning," she said. "Did you like the book?"

"Yes, I did. I cried a little when Eva died, but only one tear fell on the page beside her grave."

"I would like," said Dr. Gatling to Mrs. Gatling, "to give our young neighbor something that would bring a smile, not a tear."

"I know," she answered.

On the table was a lovely pale lavender satin box with purple violets painted on it. She opened it and there were chocolates and sugared violet leaves in it.

"I wish the box was full of candy, but perhaps you'd like to have it even if it isn't."

"The whole box?"

"The whole box."

"Oh yes! I'll be very choice of it and keep my very best hair ribbons in the box when the candy is gone. Thank you very much. And thank you, sir, for the book. I'll always keep it." And I went smiling home.

When the pears and plums and apples were gone, when the Christmas tree in Mr. Gideon Welles' old library was half forgotten, we went to war with Dr. Gatling's gun. For the Spaniards blew up a battleship called the *Maine* and that's why there was a war. All our lives we had heard about the Civil War. Our own grandfathers had fought in it and told us stories, but they were like stories from a book. This was a real war.

We thought of the Spanish Armada sailing up the Connecticut River to Hartford and landing near Colonel Colt's factory. The Spaniards would wear red sashes with daggers thrust in them, and carry guitars. They might

[179]

sing "Juanita." They would march past the factory, gazing in wonder at the blue dome shaped like an onion with a gold colt on top. Suddenly the windows would open and hands holding Colt revolvers would start shooting at the red sashes and guitars. If any Spaniards escaped and reached our street, guns from Dr. Gatling's attic would be fired at them, probably by our fathers.

It was all very exciting. We saw two parades. We wore buttons that said "Remember the *Maine*." It was our war. It was the war that would test Dr. Gatling's gun, we were told.

Colonel Roosevelt dashed up San Juan hill and the gun worked. In Manila Bay, Admiral Dewey on his ship the *Olympia* said to his mate, "Gridley, you may fire when you are ready."

We imagined Mr. Gridley aiming Dr. Gatling's gun. His aim was good. One shot—and the war was over. We thought of Admiral Dewey climbing up to an object called a crow's nest and firing a shot from Colonel Colt's revolver to celebrate. Maybe he told Mr. Gridley that he could fire one more shot from the Gatling Gun if he didn't hurt anyone. It was a nice war.

Yet through it all we heard that Dr. Gatling was not happy. We thought he should be very proud—and have a monument in Bushnell Park near the lily pond.

It was over a period of time that those of us who were children back at the turn of the century learned the story of Dr. Gatling and all the things he had done, and why war made him unhappy. It seemed to come to us piece by piece as one neighbor told us one thing about him, and another told some other thing.

We learned of a boy in North Carolina, son of an inventor, who helped his father make a machine for sowing cotton seed, followed by a machine for thinning the plants. Later, as a young man, Dr. Gatling invented a machine for planting rice. When he went to Missouri in 1844 he adapted the machine so that it sowed wheat in drills. He studied medicine in Ohio and became a doctor.

It was in 1861 that the idea of a new kind of gun came to him and he had one made. It had a revolving handle, which kept up a steady rifle fire from eight to ten rifle barrels revolving on an axis. It was the first Gatling Gun. It was the first year of the Civil War.

Early in that war, Dr. Gatling saw the first of the wounded soldiers coming home, some never to walk, others never to work or see the stars. There were those who never came home. The pity and the horror of it all touched him deeply. War must end. He thought if there could be a weapon so terrible that man would hesitate to use it against his fellow man, surely there would be peace.

He dreamed of peace and improved his gun. Before the war ended it was in use. In 1865 it was adopted by the United States government and some countries of Europe. He hoped there would be no more war.

In the last years of his life he worked on a motor plow. Someone on our street said he was sorry that he had invented the gun and hoped to be remembered for the plow. He moved away from Hartford and died in New York in 1903.

No one remembers the plow. In the language of the underworld there is a word—"gat." The dictionary says "Gat (slang) Short for Gatling Gun. A gun." The irony of it! In his gentle greatness he wanted to give a smile and not a tear, peace and not war, to be remembered for a plow and not a gun. END

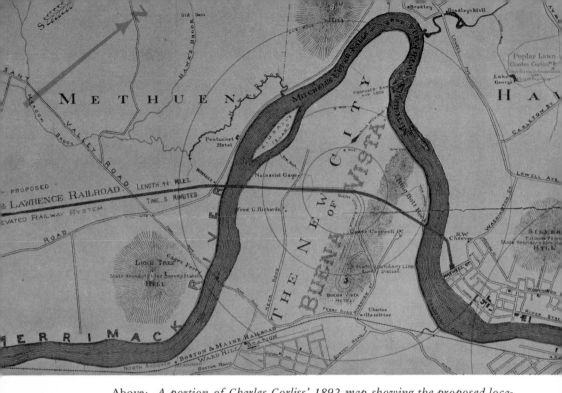

Above: *A portion of Charles Corliss' 1892 map showing the proposed loca-tion of his dream city "Buena Vista" and the route planned for the Haverhill & Lawrence Railway.* Below: *Aerial photograph of the same area looking southwest, taken in 1972. The highway is Interstate Route 495.*

The City That Never Was

by Richard W. O'Donnell

Had not "a northeast storm of no mean proportions" ripped through the Ward Hill section of Haverhill, Massachusetts, on April 3, 1891, Charles Corliss's fantastic dream might have come true. The proud and beautiful city of Buena Vista would be standing today on the 34 square miles of land between Haverhill and Lawrence, on the banks of the Merrimack River. But dreams are fragile things, and the icy winds of that vicious April evening swept away forever all plans for what might then have been the most modern community in the Commonwealth of Massachusetts.

Charles Corliss was a prosperous farmer who owned a splendid old homestead known as Poplar Lawn on Broadway in Haverhill. He was highly respected, possessed a tidy fortune and, by all odds, should have retired to his estate and lived to a ripe old age. However, in 1887, at the age of 59, the dynamic Mr. Corliss decided to build a city.

At the time, Corliss owned a great deal of land on Ward Hill which, back then, was a vast, nearly uninhabited area isolated from the mainland of Haverhill by a long hairpin turn in the Merrimack River. To the majority of Haverhill and Lawrence residents, Ward Hill was a desolate place. But to Charles Corliss it was Buena Vista—the hill with "the sublime view." In a letter to the old *Haverhill Bulletin*, the gentleman farmer described his feelings for the lonely old hill:

"The idea of a community there may seem somewhat extraordinary to those who have not visited the spot, but those who have feasted their eyes on the sublime view which is enjoyed there, a view which embraces the highland and the lowland, and the river and mountain, and city and country, and which, in fact, lays the whole surrounding country open to the gaze, realize that no pleasanter or more beautiful spot could be found in

Charles Corliss

all New England, renowned as it is for beautiful vistas and lovely scenery."

A lot of people laughed out loud when Corliss announced that he planned to build the City of Buena Vista on Ward Hill. Their laughter can be forgiven because it was next to impossible to reach the place on available roads. However, Corliss had an ace up his sleeve!

"We will build a Meigs monorail between Haverhill and Lawrence," he proposed. "And the trains will stop at Buena Vista. Both Haverhill and Lawrence will be only three minutes away from our new city."

Thus it was that Corliss and a group of Merrimack Valley business leaders established the Haverhill and Lawrence Railroad. The gentleman farmer, who was elected president of the railroad line, revealed that the monorail system to be used had been developed by Joseph Meigs of Lowell. Cylindrical cars would be used with drive wheels straddled on a center rail. Corliss claimed that the monorail would transport passengers between Haverhill and Lawrence in about five minutes at speeds then unheard of.

Said the railroad president: "Our trains will depart from Maxwell Street in Haverhill, and stop at Buena Vista so that the residents of that fine city may get off. Our trains will then travel to Prospect Street in Lawrence, and make a return trip after picking up passengers there."

[184]

The monorail would have covered about four and a quarter miles, and for it to become operational a railroad bridge would have to be built across the Merrimack River. This would have been an expensive proposition, but the officers of the Haverhill and Lawrence Railroad were confident funds would become available once their stock went on the market.

More plans for the future city were revealed. There would be a 100-foot-wide boulevard across the Merrimack River for traffic headed into downtown Haverhill. And traffic would be heavy: Buena Vista would be an industrial city with an estimated population of about 10,000 by the start of the 20th century.

Power for the new city and its industries would be supplied by a unique lock and dam system to be built at Mitchell Falls on the Merrimack at a cost of $120,000. Years earlier, army engineers had concluded that the only way to make the Merrimack navigable above Haverhill was to build a lock and dam at Mitchell Falls. Corliss and his associates planned to do just that. The falls would then be harnessed to provide power for Buena Vista.

Next came news which made it seem a certainty that the city of Buena Vista would soon be a reality. A group of Ward Hill landowners announced that they were going to build a brand new hotel at the top of the hill, overlooking the river. The Buena Vista Hotel, it was reasoned, would attract tourists. The tourists, in turn, would fall in love with the great beauty of the place and rush out to buy land there. Houses, schools and civic buildings would spring up. And industries would begin moving into the area, which already had a shoe factory. In no time at all, a thriving city would burst forth where once there had been only dense woodlands.

In 1890, while the hotel was being built, Corliss announced plans for the first public sale of stock in the great Haverhill and Lawrence Railroad. The big sale was scheduled for July 30, 1891. Then to make certain that there would be a small army of stock buyers on hand for the sale, Corliss made what can best be described as a dramatic gesture. In an advertisement published by the *Haverhill Bulletin* on July 8, 1890, he announced: "I, Charles Corliss of Haverhill, Massachusetts have laid out, on my land

Meigs Monorail train

[185]

in Bradford (Ward Hill), twenty-five lots of land, each 50 feet front on the proposed Meigs Avenue, and 120 feet deep to the line of said proposed railway, (for further description see map of my land in Bradford) and will give, free of expense, if the said railway is built within two years from this date, to subscribers for the capital stock of said Haverhill and

The Buena Vista Hotel in the wake of the nor'easter

The Buena Vista Hotel (second version).

Lawrence Railroad. . . ." (Stock shares sold for $100 each. There were 2000 of them for sale. Corliss planned to give the land free to purchasers who bought several shares.)

The stage had been set. All that remained was for the drama to unfold. It was a beautiful dream, a lovely dream; indeed a worthwhile dream. And it came mighty close to coming true.

The Buena Vista Hotel was officially completed on February 21, 1891, though a small crew of workers remained inside to get the interior ready for the grand opening which was scheduled for June. It should be noted that the grand opening was just in time for that first public sale of stock in the Haverhill and Lawrence Railroad. But during the late afternoon of April 3, a Tuesday, the wind began to howl and sleet and hail fell from the sky. Some people claimed it was a cyclone. The *Haverhill Bulletin* next day described what took place as "a northeast storm of no mean proportions."

And up on Buena Vista the winds were meaner and angrier than any place else that fierce day.

"The wind was really blowing," Thomas A. Simmason, who was working on the interior of the hotel, testified at a public hearing a few weeks later. "It rattled the hotel and made it shake. I feared it might collapse on me and I got out of there. It was terrible outside, but I figured I'd be better off outside than inside.

"Then I saw some smoke coming from what was going to be the dining room. Then there was flames, but they didn't last long. That wind did most of the damage. It almost blew that hotel over on its side."

There were public hearings after the soon-to-open hotel collapsed. The official verdict was that the structure of the hotel was sound and that it was a victim of circumstances. It just happened to be standing in the way when the freak storm came along.

The northeaster also wrecked the Haverhill and Lawrence Railroad before it got chugging. Stockholders and future investors lost interest in the project. Still, Charles Corliss was a fighter and he went down swinging.

First off, on the eve of the first public sale of railroad stock it was announced that the Buena Vista Hotel would be rebuilt. But this news didn't inspire any great response. For the record it should be pointed out that the hotel *was* rebuilt and remained in business until torn down in November, 1910.

Next there were advertisements in all Merrimack Valley newspapers announcing that the great stock sale would be held "at three o'clock,

Thursday afternoon, July 30, 1891 at the office of W. M. Bowley, Rooms 16 and 18, Academy of Music, 103 Merrimack Street, Haverhill, Massachusetts."

Corliss also published advertisements reminding Merrimack Valley citizens that he was prepared to give away 25 lots of land up on Ward Hill, and he contacted close friends and urged them to buy a share in what he honestly believed was a potential gold mine.

The railroad stock sale was a flop. Only a handful of people showed up for the big event, and stock sales were few and far between. Despite the lure of free land, Merrimack Valley residents just weren't interested in building that railroad to Buena Vista. Still, there had been some buyers. For this reason, Corliss did not give up. Next, he had a large color map of Buena Vista printed. He thought if people could see what he had in mind for the Haverhill-Lawrence area, then both the railroad and Buena Vista might be saved.

The map came out in 1892. But it was published too late. By then rumors were circulating through the Merrimack Valley about a trolley line the state was planning to build. Corliss journeyed to Boston to speak before a legislative committee which was considering a proposal that the Commonwealth of Massachusetts spend $400,000 to establish the Lowell, Lawrence and Haverhill Electric Railway. His words were ignored and the trolley line became a reality. The great Haverhill and Lawrence Railroad finally went out of business. And the dream city of Buena Vista simply faded away.

Charles Corliss died on February 18, 1897. His various newspaper obituaries referred to him as "one of the best known of local men," and devoted a great deal of space to the fact that it "was well known among his friends that he could recite from memory Scott's long Scottish epic, 'The Lady of the Lake.' " Only casual mention is made of the fact that he was once president of the Haverhill and Lawrence Railroad.

Three days after his death, "strange knockings were heard" and "strange forms were seen" at Poplar Lawn, the old Corliss homestead.

Perhaps Charles Corliss returned to Buena Vista that same night to spend an eternity feasting his eyes "on the sublime view which is enjoyed there. . . ."   END

Empire Builders

SECTION 6

Ice-Cool Ice King

by W. A. Swanberg

In 1805, a pint-sized, bull-headed Bostonian, 22-year-old Frederic Tudor, shipped as supercargo in a vessel carrying freight to Jamaica and other West Indies ports, and had an inspiration that all but floored him.

These islands were of course hot and uncomfortable. Yet the people there were downing hot, uncomfortable food and drink. Think of how much more pleasant it would be for them to sip iced drinks and eat ice cream! Such innovations were unheard of there, since until Tudor came along no one was crazy enough to think of shipping ice into tropical climes. Any sane person knew that the stuff melted in the heat.

Tudor, however, reasoned that with protection ice could be shipped to the Caribbean without disastrous loss. Ice, which was going to waste in New England, was unknown in the islands, and it was just a question of getting the two together. It must be admitted that Tudor was not strictly a humanitarian, thinking only of the boon ice would bring to these sun-baked people. He was figuring on making money on the deal.

Returning to Boston, he got busy on his project, although people gazed at him and significantly tapped their heads. Tudor was not one of those soft souls intimidated by public derision. A rugged individualist of good family, he had refused to go to Harvard where his brothers were educated, saying, "Colleges are places for loafers." In the winter of 1805–06 he cut ice with a couple of helpers at a pond in Saugus. He scraped together enough money to charter a ship, loaded it with ice, and sent an advance man down to St. Pierre, in Martinique, to take orders from merchants for the ice that would soon cool them off.

Worse luck, when Tudor got to St. Pierre in March, 1806, with 150 tons of ice, he found that his advance man had miserably failed. Merchants there who had read about ice said it was nothing more than frozen water, and they were not so foolish as to pay good money for a useless commodity that melted away to nothing. Get out, Yankee!

With his ice melting fast, Tudor went to the proprietor of a large refreshment palace, the Tivoli, and mixed him a drink composed of rum,

*Frederic Tudor—slight of
person, indomitable of will.*

lemon juice, sugar, water, and—ice. The man drank it and was delighted
with the coolness that seemed to trickle down his gullet and spread pleasantly all over. Possibly the rum had something to do with it, but he allowed Tudor to make him a batch of material he had never seen before
—ice cream. He ate it. He smiled. Such coolness and flavor! He would try
it on his customers.

He did, to universal applause. Patrons at the Tivoli howled for more
cool drinks and ice cream. Ice was a whopping success in St. Pierre, and
Tudor scored a propaganda victory too when a local newspaper ran a
story about the marvels of ice. Unfortunately, he suffered a financial loss
of almost $3000 because much of his ice melted before he could sell it.

Undaunted, he returned to Boston, determined to have an ice house
ready for the next cargo. However, Jefferson's embargo on shipping stalled
him for several years, during which he turned his hand to farming. In
1811 he borrowed money to buy a ship, but before he could get under
way the war of 1812 balked him again. Things got so bad that he was
thrown into jail for failing to pay interest on his debt, finally gaining re-
lease by pawning his watch.

The Sheriffs were after him again in 1815 when he embarked for Havana with a cargo of lumber. He built an ice house in Havana in time to
receive his first cargo of ice, meanwhile demonstrating to barkeepers and

Harvesting ice in Massachusetts.

coffee-house proprietors the wonders of iced drinks and ice cream. They all pronounced it *bueno*, and he did a profitable business. He built another ice house at St. Pierre and gladdened the citizens there as well. His insanity was now paying off, but he was still dissatisfied. Even in ice houses, protected by layers of hay, his ice was melting far too fast. He needed better insulation.

Although he was only five feet three and so slight that a stiff breeze would blow him down, Tudor had a quality that was characteristic of Yankee enterprise of that era—an indomitable will and perseverance that regarded a problem not as a defeat but as a challenge. Back home again, he built a model ice house, so devised that the drip from the melting ice collected in a trough that ran into a barrel so that it could be measured. He experimented with various kinds of insulation to replace unsatisfactory hay. He tried cornstalks, wheat straw and tanbark, carefully measuring the run-off with each and finding them wanting.

Then, in a flash of brilliance, he tried plain, ordinary sawdust. It worked wonderfully, and the best part of it was that sawdust was being thrown away as waste by the many sawmills thereabouts and could be had for the asking. Having licked his biggest problem—the quick evaporation of his stock in trade—Tudor hammered away at the others. He built efficient

[192]

ice houses by adjacent ponds. He hired covered wagons to haul the ice from pond to port. He employed an aggressive young man named Nathaniel Wyeth to cut ice for him—a prize move in itself, for Wyeth was another Yankee who was obsessed with the idea of efficiency. Wyeth invented a new machine, a saw operated by horsepower that cut through ice as if it were butter. He developed a conveyor device to swish the blocks from pond to storage house. With Wyeth on the job, Tudor's production snags were solved and all he had to worry about was developing new markets.

"Our biggest problem," he said, "is that people in warm climates are abysmally ignorant of the virtues of ice. I must educate them."

With his West Indies business already thriving, he invaded the South, constructing an ice house in Charleston in 1820 and following with others in Savannah and New Orleans. He wrote advertising handbills to let Southern people know that until they had tasted iced drinks and ice cream, they had not really lived, and giving clear instructions about the use and preservation of ice. He persuaded doctors to write testimonials about the benefits of iced dishes in warm climates, and the virtues of ice in preventing spoilage of perishable foods.

By 1821, when he was still only 38, Tudor had several salesmen covering the South, preaching ice, demonstrating ice, shaving ice to frosty particles for cool drinks, manufacturing ice cream in portable freezers and dishing out free samples. As with any new product, there was often sales resistance, and Tudor's agents were authorized to supply the doubters with a small free shipment along with a special insulated case to hold the ice, also free.

These methods were astonishingly successful. For one thing, Southerners discovered that by mixing shaved ice with whisky and a sprig of mint, a drink could be made that seemed to diminish one's cares and make the whole world brighter. They also took delight in a galaxy of new and pleasant-tasting concoctions—ice creams, sherbets and frappes. Housewives discovered that milk, meats and other foods could be kept wholesome for days if cooled with Mr. Tudor's wonderful ice.

Up in Boston, Mr. Tudor was getting rich fast. He was pleased to note that people who once sneered at him as a crackpot now regarded him with respect. At 50, he married a 19-year-old girl—a romantic triumph that seemed to unhinge his caution a trifle. Instead of sticking to his specialty, in 1834 he mortgaged his properties and took a $150,000 speculative flyer in coffee. He lost his shirt and once more was tossed into jail for debt.

[193]

The man who had won success and riches in comparative youth, faced utter disaster at 51.

But iceman Tudor had ice water in his veins. He told his creditors coolly that if they kept him in jail they would never get a cent out of him, whereas if they turned him loose he would repay them in time. They wisely agreed. Liberated, he resumed the ice business, and although it took him 14 years he paid back every cent, which with interest came to more than $280,000.

Now known as the Ice King, owning several vessels of his own, Tudor was so infernally successful that a batch of imitators sprang up, aiming to cash in on the new bonanza. This fairly made him froth at the mouth, for he reasoned with some logic that it was he who had originated the idea, suffered the misfortunes attendant on the new enterprise and educated the outlanders to love ice. Now these Johnny-come-latelies were out to exploit the market he had created. A hard cuss, he had no mercy on his competitors. He tilled new fields, hiring men to cut ice on ponds and rivers far into Maine. With his efficient methods he was able to operate more cheaply than the others, and in fact was perfectly willing to sell his product at a loss and thereby grind a competitor out of business. Only a few of them survived this onslaught, none of them ever reaching the stature of the Ice King.

The feat that really made him stick out his chest was when in 1833 he sent a cargo of ice through tropic waters clear to Calcutta in *Tuscany*, one of his specially constructed ice ships. After 100 days, the *Tuscany* landed two-thirds of its frigid cargo intact; only the cakes on the outer edges melted. The natives of India, never before having seen ice, believed it some sort of magic material, but they soon became educated to its advantages. One Parsee asked the *Tuscany*'s captain: "How this ice make grow in your country? Him grow on tree?"

In 1849 Tudor hit a new high, shipping 150,000 tons of ice to the West and East Indies, South America and the Southern states. In the spring of 1861 he came near starting the Civil War prematurely when one of his ice vessels, the *Rhoda Shannon*, bound for Savannah, got lost in fog and headed into Charleston harbor.

This was unfortunate, because at that very time Major Anderson and his federal soldiers were holding Fort Sumter, in the harbor, to the rage of the Carolinians. The *Shannon* was flying the American flag. The seceded Carolinians, convinced that she was bringing reinforcements to Anderson, let fly with cannonballs that put holes in the vessel's sails, causing it to turn tail in haste. Major Anderson, indignant at this insult to the flag, came very near opening Sumter's guns on the Confederate batteries, which would have started hostilities between the states on April 3 instead of nine days later.

The Ice King sired six children and kept shipping ice until he died at 80 in 1864, when the business was taken over by a son. There were still those who said that he *did* start the Civil War—in a manner of speaking.

It was those mint juleps, suh, which had become a favorite beverage of the Southland, thanks to Tudor's ice. Some abstemious souls in Massachusetts believed that the julep was the devil's own creation. The way they figured it, the Southerners would drink a julep, which gave them a glow of pride. They would sip another, which filled them with a sense of authority as well as pride. Then still another julep, which had the effect of building up the authority and pride and adding a strong feeling of belligerence. It was after drinking three or even more juleps, these critics declared, that the Southerners said and did the rash things that led to war. If there had been no ice, there would have been no juleps. No juleps, no war.

Now this is a serious charge which, out of respect to the memory of the Ice King, should not be allowed to go unchallenged. For one thing, the Southerners were on good terms with good bourbon long before Tudor added ice to it. For another, the North had its statesmen who enjoyed a warming glass or two, some taking it neat, some with plain water, without benefit of ice.

Frederic Tudor did some strange things in his long career, but he did *not* start the Civil War. Indeed, it could be argued that he did his best to cool it off.   **END**

Model of Tudor's most famous ship, the Ice King *(from a faded old newspaper photo).*

[195]

America's most famous trademark—Lydia Pinkham at age 57.

A Remedy Founded
on True Unicorn

by Patrice Smart

Lydia Pinkham and Lydia Pinkham's Compound are synonymous. One cannot hear the name Lydia Estes Pinkham without thinking of the famous medicine, and one cannot hear of the phenomenally successful multi-million-dollar business without thinking of the woman whose name it bears.

Though Lydia Pinkham is one of the most publicized names in the feminine world, very few people know anything about its owner. Yet Lydia is responsible for giving women more freedom than any other individual, including the great suffragette Susan B. Anthony. For her Compound brought relief from the aches and discomforts of those female ailments which physicians of Lydia's day deemed normal and natural.

Doctors of the early 19th century made no effort to ease the conditions that caused these painful female distresses. These were accepted as the penalties of womanhood, and thus made members of our "gentle" sex frail creatures forever tinged with the handicap of "delicate" health. So it was Lydia Pinkham, with her Herb Compound, who first offered the American woman equality with men—at least in health.

Born in Lynn, Massachusetts on February 9, 1819, Lydia was the tenth of 12 children. Belonging to such a large family did not foist any burden on Lydia or her brothers and sisters because their parents, William and Rebecca Estes, were wealthy as well as socially prominent.

In fact, Lydia's early life was lived blissfully. A healthy, happy child with startling red hair and strikingly beautiful dark eyes, she was tutored for many years by the poet, historian and abolitionist Alonzo Lewis. Later she attended Lynn Academy, graduating with honors. But it was her home life, in the midst of this large, congenial family, where the tall, slender, fragile-appearing Lydia developed her modern and advanced viewpoint on subjects ranging from anti-slavery, politics, temperance, health, to freedom of speech. One sometimes wonders if the quality of greatness found in people has anything to do with the time and place. Oddly enough, three of the most famous American women of the early 19th century lived near each other in Lynn, and were friends. Lydia Estes Pinkham was a year older than Susan B. Anthony and two years younger than Mary Baker Eddy.

The Pinkham family, all 14 members, started out as Quakers, but found the religion of The Friends too restrictive. They could see no evil in singing, and they defended people's right to enjoy the good things of life such as music, dancing, and sports. As all the Estes family were argumentative—there was no such phenomenon as a "meek" member— it can be assumed the Society of Friends heaved a sigh of relief when William, Rebecca, and their brood withdrew from the church.

Both Lydia and her mother were active club women. They joined every organization in Lynn to which "ladies" were eligible. And it was while serving as secretary of a debating society that Lydia Estes met Isaac Pinkham.

Lynn society must have been somewhat amazed when it learned that "things were serious" between Lydia and Isaac, for Mr. Pinkham most definitely lacked "romantic" appeal. He was short, plump and pouchy, and besides, he was a widower with a small daughter named Frances Ellen. But Isaac had a charming personality, was intellectual, kind and considerate, so although Lydia and Isaac went through life the counterpart of "Jack Sprat and his wife," they were a happy, devoted couple.

The Estes-Pinkham nuptials of September 7, 1841, was a social event in Lynn and the 24-year-old bride and 29-year-old groom moved right into their new home—a gift from Lydia's father.

For the next quarter of a century, Lydia's life was that of an intelligent, warm-hearted wife and mother. Isaac, known affectionately as "Squire Pinkham," prospered as a shoe manufacturer and real estate operator. Between the years 1844 and 1857 Lydia presented her "Squire" with four sons (one who died in infancy) and a daughter—Charles, Daniel, William and Aroline. During those years Lydia, with true Estes vim and vigor, kept house, made herb remedies for her family and friends, and kept her children and husband well and happy. The Pinkhams' amazingly fine mental and physical health Lydia attributed to her daily advice —"Eat plenty of roughage and use your brains."

Lydia did one other thing during those happy years—something that

[198]

was to make her famous and wealthy beyond her wildest dreams. She became interested in helping women less fortunate than herself in health. She was shocked at doctors' indifference to "feminine ills" and decided something should be done about it.

She increased the output of her old-fashioned herb remedies that she brewed in her kitchen, bottled them, and offered them freely to those in need. Some of the recipes she found in medical books, others had been handed down by her family, still others came from friends and neighbors. She gave advice willingly and unstintingly, even to strangers. Never was a woman turned away from her door without gaining something, if only a cup of fennel tea. And when children came with their mothers, they would each receive a slice of horehound.

Lydia was not unschooled in medical knowledge. She belonged to the Eclectic Society—a national organization devoted to medical reform. She also spent much time in research, and study of the then popular scientific book *American Dispensatory*, written by the pharmacologist Dr. John King. But it was from her understanding of the Indians' use of herbs that she finally created the formula which was to become the famous Lydia E. Pinkham Vegetable Compound, based on a recipe obtained from machinist George Todd in payment of a debt. This remedy to cure "woman's weaknesses" was founded on True Unicorn—a bitter-root herb which Indian women believed to be both a uterine tonic and a uterine sedative. This is the reason the Compound early got the reputation of being an "Old Indian squaw remedy." Lydia added a dollop of alcohol to the herbal concoction, which only enhanced its salubrious effect.

The American Medical Association had not been established at the time Lydia took on her responsibilities as the American Florence Nightingale (the English nurse was her contemporary, born in 1820). Anyone who carried a black satchel could call himself a doctor. So the woods were full of quacks and charlatans, and Lydia was subject to much criticism by many who didn't know better. But those who had used her Compound were loyal and devoted followers because its remedial qualities were amazingly apparent. And by 1873 everyone, that is everyone in and around Lynn, Massachusetts, was talking about Lydia's magic medicine.

And it might have been that this remarkable cure would have lived and died with only local fame if Fate in the form of the Panic of 1873 had not played its part. Isaac, by then 60, had been ill for some time and the Pinkham savings plus Lydia's share of her family's estate were almost dissipated. The financial crash wiped out the last of their possessions, and the family was practically destitute. Their home was sold and they moved into a small house.

Aroline, 16 years old, was in high school, and the boys were doing odd jobs to help out. Lydia was still giving nursing services and advice without cost. In fact, by this time, she was so respected locally that when she made the statement it was safe to take baths in winter, it was accepted, and—to some extent—practiced.

None of this paid the ever increasing bills. Although her boys were willing to work, there was not much work to be had. Their mother's early advice "use your brains" was to pay dividends, for when the situation got desperate, Dan figured out a solution. "Why not *sell* the Compound? At least to stores!"

Lydia was shocked at the thought of commercializing on her pet, private charity and immediately answered, "I'd just as soon charge a visitor for a cup of tea!"

This silenced Dan for a short period, but the rest of the family realized he had a splendid idea and kept needling their mother until, under their continued pressure—plus dire necessity—she was forced to agree to gamble their few remaining dollars. Thus the great Pinkham venture began.

Working together as a family unit, Lydia, Isaac, Charles and Will soon caught Dan's enthusiasm. So when Dan kept insisting "Advertise! We must advertise!," they agreed to have handbills printed which the three boys would pass from house to house. After covering Lynn, they took the train to Boston and distributed as many as 2,000 a day. In the meantime Lydia wrote copy for the handbills, labels for the medicine, on sale for a dollar a bottle, and a four-page folder. This forerunner of the modern "brochure" was entitled *Guide for Women*. Written in a quaintly intimate and highly emotional style, it did much to increase the demand for the Compound.

One of Dan Pinkham's best advertising ideas was to drop little notes reading: "Try Lydia E. Pinkham's Vegetable Compound and I know it will cure you. It is the best thing there is for female weakness. (Signed) Cousin Mary," in New England cemeteries on Decoration Day.

Sales of the Vegetable Compound were now far-reaching enough to attract the attention of the now extant American Medical Association.

Lydia was questioned about her product and qualifications for producing it. She answered, "I am only a woman who wants nothing more than to do good for other women. However, I do believe that I have a unique formula and a complete medical theory to explain it. And I also believe it is the greatest medicine discovery since the dawn of history."

Lydia's obvious sincerity and the testimonials from her many followers, plus the fact the Federal regulations pronounced "Lydia E. Pinkham's Vegetable Compound for ailing females and all their weaknesses, a great help to generative organs—and for kidney disease," cleared her with the Medical Association.

By the end of 1875 the Compound was really selling. Dan decided it was time to branch out and tackle New York. In May of '76 he reached the city with 20,000 handbills. Before long he was ordering hundreds of thousands of bottles and urging the family to move the business to "Gotham." Lydia was adamant on this. "No," she said, "our work will always be in Lynn."

Dan was never without ideas. "All right." he capitulated, "Then at least let us get a trademark." Dan felt a picture of his Mother would be most appropriate. He finally wore down her resistance. At the age of 57, she had the photograph made which she claimed was a "speaking likeness," and which was to become one of the most famous trademarks of all time. It pictures Lydia in a neat black dress with a tortoise-shell comb in her hair. At her throat is a white lace fichu fastened with a cameo pin. She looks like anybody's dream grandmother, and possesses the same sweetness and appeal that has made Whistler's Mother, in the portrait he called "Arrangement in Gray and Black," so famous.

Business soared. A house was rented next to the Pinkham residence and converted into an office and laboratory. Then the happy family relationship suffered a double tragedy. In 1881 Dan died in October and two months later, Will died also. Both of galloping consumption.

After the boys' deaths, the business was incorporated as the LYDIA E. PINKHAM MEDICINE COMPANY. In spite of her heartbreak, Lydia continued to market the Compound. But she needed help to handle the ever-increasing correspondence. She hired "lady typewriters" and immediately advertised—"Remember—all your letters are opened and read in confidence by women. Only women ever had, or ever will have access to the files. The very office boy is a girl. Even the mailing is done solely by women and girls."

This brought more and more "confidences" and more and more sales.

Lydia's name became so well known it tickled the fancy of humorists and lyric writers, and the famous Lydia E. Pinkham Theme Song was born. Kept alive for years by the continuous addition of new verses it was echoed everywhere and at every type of party:

> Tell me Lydia, of your secrets,
> And the wonders you perform,
> How you take the sick and ailing
> And restore them to the norm.
> Mrs. Jones of Walla Walla,
> Mrs. Smith from Kankakee,
> Mrs. Cohen, Mrs. Murphy,
> Sing your praises lustily.
> Lizzie Smith had tired feelings,
> Terrible pains reduced her weight,
> She began to take the Compound,
> Now she weighs three hundred and eight.
> Elsie W. had no children,
> There was nothing in her blouse,
> So she took some Vegetable Compound
> Now they milk her with the cows.
> Oh there's a baby in every bottle,
> So the old quotation ran
> But the Federal Trade Commission
> Still insists you'll need a man.

Refrain
> Oh-h-h-h we'll sing of Lydia Pinkham
> And her love for the human race,
> How she sells her Vegetable Compound
> And the papers, the papers . . .
> They publish her *face*.

The song amused Lydia. "Fine publicity," she'd laugh. "Let them carry on. Just let me save the human race."

Time was running out for Lydia. After 64 years, an unselfish, gracious,

Lydia Pinkham's residence (right) and laboratory (left), Nos. 233 and 235 Western Avenue, Lynn, Massachusetts, in 1879. Lydia is standing in her doorway.

and kindly life was to come to an end in May of 1883. All the world mourned the loss of a great humanitarian—a great lady who lived almost a century ahead of her time in her thinking on health in general and women's health in particular.

The Lydia E. Pinkham Vegetable Compound is still made today. Of course, the formula has changed somewhat from the original, which, it is interesting to note, has never been patented. Nor was there any secrecy about the formula's ingredients. So if you want to whip up your own cure for "all those painful complaints and weaknesses so common to our best female population," here it is—

(with Licorice added for flavoring)
8 ounces True Unicorn Root
8 ounces False Unicorn Root
6 ounces Life Root
6 ounces Black Cohosh
6 ounces Pleurisy Root
12 ounces Fenugreek Seed.

END

Rapscallion
from Vermont

by W. A. Swanberg

The most side-splitting character in Vermont a century ago was a stocky, genial, quick-witted young smart aleck named James Fisk, Jr. A cut-up as a kid, he kept Brattleboro amused and sometimes a trifle annoyed by pranks that were generally harmless, meaning that nobody got killed. The town was a dull place after he ran off with a circus in his teens, but things perked up right away when he returned a couple of years later, dressed like a ringmaster and wearing a walnut-sized piece of glass in his stickpin. From that time on, Jim Fisk seemed to apply circus standards to just about everything, including his own dress and behavior.

His father, an itinerant peddler who sold yard goods and notions from a wagon in backwater towns in the Brattleboro region, found this out when Jim told him in a nice way that he was an ignoramus business-wise. Why didn't he spruce up his wagon and himself, get some snappy horses and put a little life into his salesmanship? Pop Fisk, nettled, allowed that he knew a thing or two about peddling and maybe Jim was too all-fired big for his britches.

Jim thereupon bought his own wagon, painted it circus red and yellow, acquired four spirited steeds and went out peddling on his own, clad grandly in top hat and checkered jacket. He so quickly outstripped his father in sales that Pop Fisk sold him the business and retired to run the Revere House, a heavily mortgaged temperance hotel he owned on Brattleboro's Main Street.

Within two years Jim was known as the Prince of Peddlers, boss over five circus-painted wagons spreading everything from jerseys to jews-harps

Thomas Nast cartoon of Jim Fisk from Harper's Weekly.

over a large part of New England. His booming laugh and outrageous jokes were familiar in every country tavern from Pittsfield to Rutland and from Nashua to Troy, New Hampshire. The Fisk success was based not so much on high pressure as on his ability to make his wagons and his goods so infernally attractive that few could resist them. A bear for work and a stickler for efficiency, he was shrewd but honest in his dealings, combining a pitchman's smooth patter with humor that was joyful and painless because it hurt nobody. He had a genius for telling yarns about himself that had listeners rolling. What with this and his genuine liking for people, the folks in Brattleboro easily forgave his weakness for gaudy attire, spending money like water, and monopolizing attention generally.

Once again the Connecticut River town lost some of its liveliness when, in 1860, Jim Fisk sold his business and took a city-slicker job with Jordan, Marsh & Company, the big Boston wholesalers. This time he was gone for good, but one thing was sure: wherever he went he would be heard from, not being the shrinking type.

When the Civil War broke out, Fisk went to Washington, took the fanciest suite in Willard's Hotel, and seemed to think it was up to him and Jordan, Marsh to outfit and equip the whole Union army. He did so well in this line that the Boston firm had to expand, buy more mills and take Fisk in as a partner. Never forgetting his old friends from Brattleboro, he got jobs for dozens of them at Jordan, Marsh and managed to give a clear impression that he was running the show. As the war neared its end, this bothered Eben Jordan, the president, enough so that although he liked Fisk personally, he bought out his interest for $65,000 and heaved a sigh of relief.

Fisk's next stop was Wall Street, where he set up shop as a broker with perfect confidence that he would bend the stock market to his will with ease. This did not sit well with other speculators, a group of whom took pleasure in catching him in a bear movement and cleaning him of every penny. Outraged, he borrowed money—his credit was good, for he always paid his debts—and stormed the market again, this time with more caution.

Brattleboro was watching him, wondering what the merry native son would be up to next. He always had a capacity for doing things that made people say, "Gee whiz!" whether in New York or New England. Well, sir, he got together with Jay Gould and several other plungers, was elected a director of the Erie Railway, and did some fast work with watered Erie stock that gave them control of the railroad. Commodore Cornelius Vanderbilt, who was outwitted in the stock transaction to the tune of $8,000,000, howled that it was illegal, which it was, although Vanderbilt himself had never been too finicky about such niceties. Things got so hot that Fisk, Gould and a whole posse of Erie directors had to flee New York law and take refuge across the river in Jersey City.

Pop Fisk's boy was now getting into the New York newspapers, which described him as a jovial fat man with a penchant for aggressive clothing and big diamonds—real ones now—and an endless fund of jokes. By judicious bribery Fisk and Gould managed to coax the New York state assembly to legalize their larcenies, so the pair returned to New York in acknowledged control of Erie. Fisk promptly gave railroad jobs to many of his friends from Brattleboro and elsewhere. He also formed a quiet habit of going abroad in a gilded carriage drawn by two white horses and two black, with two white footmen and two colored ones to add a touch of dignity.

The folks back home didn't know what to make of all this. It was clear that Jim had forsaken the honesty that marked him as the Prince of Peddlers and was hardly an example of Yankee virtue and thrift. On the other hand, it had to be admitted that the business world in general was so slippery in those wild postwar years that a fellow was either a slicker or he was out on his ear. Fisk occasionally visited his home town and won over the doubters with his vast good cheer. He was taking care of his father, who had become a harmless lunatic, and his fondness for his stepmother, who was still running the Revere House, was something to see. Millionaire though he was, pulling strings that manipulated great financial and corporate interests, he never lost the attitude of an irrepressible boy.

But the plain truth was that Fisk cared nothing for convention. There was talk because his wife Lucy continued to live in Boston. In 1869 he and Gould startled the nation by buying the Grand Opera House in New York and installing the Erie offices there in connection with a 2600-seat theater. The theater was Fisk's special plaything. He put on a succession of productions with indifferent success, then hit pay dirt with an extravaganza called *The Twelve Temptations*, which had a cast of hundreds, a wicked cancan, and a stage waterfall using tons of real water. It played to packed houses for months.

Always a big kid seeking new toys, Fisk, now known as Prince Erie, bought the Narragansett Steamship Line and had himself outfitted in a splendid admiral's uniform. A lover of canaries, he put one in every stateroom. He was host to President Grant on a cruise to Fall River, the President's host again in his theater box. The Fisk boy was traveling in big company—but he and Gould raised a national howl when they engineered enormous gold speculations that paralyzed business and ruined many gamblers on Black Friday. It was noted that Boss Tweed, a good friend of Fisk's, was on the Erie board, and that Tweed's judges were unfailingly accommodating to Fisk and Erie.

In fact, it was apparent that Fisk had fallen in with a parcel of plunderers and become one of the foxiest of them all. In the city he was either loved or hated—never viewed dispassionately. Early in 1871, when New York's Ninth Regiment was faced by bankruptcy and dissolution, the outfit saved itself by electing Fisk colonel, whereupon he had himself fitted for a $2000 uniform heavily weighted with gold braid. Brattleborans smiled at that—it was Jim all over—but it had to be admitted that he bought new uniforms for the whole regiment and instilled not only cash but new life into it with a recruiting drive and a series of most unmilitary entertainments, such as blowing the whole crew to a free showing of *The Twelve Temptations*. The men of the Ninth, some of whom had viewed him with disdain as a rich "angel," began to cheer their fat colonel.

Sadly, that same year Fisk became entangled in a scandal from which no ingenuity could save him. With his wife in Boston, he had been sup-

porting a bewitching but profit-minded brunette, Josephine Mansfield, in such queenly style that he had spent a fortune on her. When the ungrateful Josie fell in love with Fisk's good friend, handsome Edward S. Stokes, Josie and Stokes put their heads together and decided they could make a pretty penny by blackmailing Fisk, using as a threat some letters he had written Josie. Incensed at this treachery, Fisk fought back, charging the pair with blackmail. He was sued by Josie. He was sued by Stokes. The affair got into the papers and Fisk, penitent for once, begged his wife's forgiveness.

It was noticed that the New York papers were now selling very well in Brattleboro even though they arrived a day late. People there no longer merely said, "Gee whiz!" Their pride in the home-town boy was taking a worse licking than ever before. There were street-corner arguments, some

disowning Fisk as a disgrace to the town, others defending him on the ground that he would never have got into such straits if his wife had not insisted on living in Boston, and that he was a victim of a nasty conspiracy. Citizens were careful not to discuss the matter in the Revere House, where Ma Fisk, who loved Jim as if he were her own flesh and blood, was looking unhappy but resolutely holding her head high.

The next news reached Brattleboro by telegraph on January 6, 1872, and it convulsed the town as it had never been convulsed before. Ned Stokes, furious because he was losing his lawsuit and was exposed as a conniving blackmailer, had followed Fisk to the ornate Grand Central Hotel and shot him fatally.

Prince Erie met his fate with admirable courage. After he died, age 37, the following day a strange thing happened. It came out that he had been quietly supporting many poor people—a secrecy unusual for the biggest show-off in town. New Yorkers who had sneered at his display and deplored his blunted ethics now recalled warmth and friendliness. Rascal though he was, he had never been hypocritical about it, and the sad truth was that rascality, fully equipped with hypocrisy, was the rule rather than the exception in the Tweed era. Fisk was given a military funeral, the most magnificent since Lincoln's. Then his body was shipped home to Brattleboro.

A change had likewise come over citizens there, who reflected that Fisk had been as big in his goodness as in his sins, and they would never see his like again. The snow-covered streets were jammed with sleighs as people who knew Jim as a harum-scarum kid came from miles around to see him off. The Rev. William Jenkins prayed like sixty for a full half hour, doubtlessly hoping to steer a slightly tarnished soul upward instead of downward. Fisk was buried in the Protestant Cemetery, and it wasn't long before the people of Brattleboro raised $25,000 and commissioned the sculptor Larkin Mead to execute a proper monument. Mead hewed a tall marble shaft with four lightly-clad young women around it representing the career of Fisk in railroading, commerce, steamboating and the stage.

It's there today. Some of the young ladies' fingers and toes have been taken by souvenir hunters, but it is still the most impressive monument in town, a reminder of one of the most picturesque characters New England has ever produced. END

Little, Brown Was Doubtful

by Gladys N. Hoover

Though Fannie Farmer died way back in January, 1915, her famous cookbook goes marching on, and her name remains a household word —"Look it up in Fannie Farmer."

Little, Brown & Company of Boston published the first edition of The Boston Cooking School Cook Book in 1896, and the tenth revised edition in 1959 has had three printings. The eleventh edition, published by Little, Brown in 1965, had its eleventh printing in June, 1973.

"Fannie Farmer" has become the world's best-selling cookbook, indeed a bestseller of all time. Like the Bible, year in and year out it maintains its steady sales. Known as the "Bride's Bible" or "Housewife's Bible," it has been translated into foreign languages and even into Braille. This New England spinster schoolma'am taught millions of women "the way to a man's heart."

Since the first edition, which gave explicit directions as to how to build a fire and clean lamps, and mentions tomatoes at $1.25 a pound and eggs at 25¢ a dozen, new illustrations and chapters have been added and revisions made to keep up with such innovations as frozen foods and prepared mixes.

Millions of copies have been printed to date, yet when Miss Farmer first took her book to Little, Brown & Company, they turned it down, flatly saying they were not interested in it and did not believe women would buy still another book of recipes.

However, with typical Yankee determination and belief in her brainchild, Miss Farmer offered to pay the printing costs of the first 3,000

[211]

Fannie Farmer

copies. The book has been a gold mine through the years for its publishers, their bestseller of all time, as they now blushingly admit.

Before her book was offered to the publisher, every recipe in it was tried out either by Miss Farmer herself or her sister Cora.

Little, Brown owns a first edition of this famous book, guarded jealously as few others are still in existence. (Librarians report that cookbooks are in such demand that they wear out fast.)

Fannie Merritt Farmer was born in Boston, March 23, 1857, eldest of four daughters of John Franklin Farmer, printer, and Mary Watson Farmer. When she was quite young, the family moved to Medford, Massachusetts, occupying half of a double house at the corner of Paris and Salem Streets. She received her early schooling in Medford.

During her teens, while attending Medford High School (some authorities say she was 17, but her playmate of Medford days and life-long friend, the late Miss Emma A. J. Law, who lived in the other half of the double house, has insisted she was 13), she suffered a paralytic stroke—perhaps polio—which confined her to bed for many months, leaving her finally with one leg which swung a little.

Fannie was a pretty little girl with red hair, which she did not like, and twinkly gray eyes, according to Miss Law. In later years her hair turned white on each side, as her best-known portrait shows. She was of medium height and pleasant expression, with a charming personality, boundless energy, and original ideas.

The Farmer girls and their friends lived the normal lives of young New England girls in the latter half of the 19th century. Dancing school, sleigh rides, skating, taffy pulls, and card parties were their regular amusements. The Farmers were also fond of singing to piano accompaniments.

After her formal schooling was cut short by her illness and the family had moved back to Boston, Fannie helped her mother with the cooking for their boarding house. First they lived in West Rutland Square and later at The Ilkley, an apartment house on Huntington Avenue.

Because of her skill and ingenuity in cooking, probably inherited from her mother who liked to swap "receipts" and copy them down in notebooks, Fannie entered the Boston Cooking School and, upon her graduation at the age of 32, was asked to continue there as assistant director, then director. This school aimed to train teachers of cooking.

In 1902 she started her own school, Miss Farmer's School of Cookery, on Huntington Avenue, whose aim was to educate homemakers to become expert cooks. At her school, Miss Farmer gave lectures and demonstrations carried on with the help of maids.

She made frequent trips to the best hotels to try various foods. Often she was accompanied by her brother-in-law and sister, Mr. and Mrs. Herbert Perkins. They would all order different dishes from the menu and try to figure out how they were made. If they could not, Miss Farmer paid the chef to give her the recipe.

In middle age she began to lose the use of her legs entirely and was confined to a wheelchair for the rest of her life, but she still got around. Once, accompanied by a maid, Miss Farmer made a lecture tour from the East Coast to California, with many side excursions and stopovers to collect ideas and information. During her frequent lectures in later years, she sat in a wheelchair and had a maid bring materials for her demonstrations.

"Miss Farmer's outstanding contribution to the art of cookery was an insistence on exact measurements. She taught her students to use 'level' measurements to achieve precise and uniform results." Only thus, she reasoned, could uniformly good results be obtained.

She made a great deal of money and was the main support of her family for many years, especially after her father's printing business declined. Many anecdotes told by Miss Law illustrate her generosity.

Once a family living in the Medford house, which her father had made over to her, could not pay their rent for six months. She not only did not press them, but sent them a Thanksgiving dinner. When her friends remonstrated, she exclaimed, "Why, they would pay if they could."

For a number of years at the School, she cooked turkeys with all the fixings at Thanksgiving and sent her father around to find poor families to whom to give them.

Once Miss Fannie bought a beautiful light astrakhan cape for her younger sister. At church Mr. Farmer looked at Fannie and said, "Why don't you get yourself something pretty, too?" "Why," said she, surprised, "this coat is perfectly good."

Her sister once told her she should dress more fashionably when she lectured before women's clubs and was invited to rich houses. "If you will do my shopping for me, I will gladly pay for anything you want me to wear," Fannie replied.

Though extremely generous always, she left an estate of $165,000—a goodly sum at that time.

Despite changes in administration and ownership, Miss Farmer's School of Cookery was carried on for years under the same name at 40 Hereford Street, Boston—in later years primarily a training school for chefs, cooks, caterers, and others engaged in trades relating to food.

In 1919 the Fanny (note spelling) Farmer Candy Shops were incorporated in Rochester, New York, by a Canadian group, and after some litigation have been operated by an agreement in which the name could be used but with different spelling. Miss Farmer's picture is used on the box covers together with a picture called "The Homestead," which is of no particular place. The candy stores have no connection with the School or the book publishers.

Besides her celebrated cookbook, Fannie Farmer wrote several other books which never attained such popularity. They were on specialized subjects such as *Chafing Dish Possibilities, Food Cookery for the Sick and Convalescent* (a subject dear to her heart), *What to Have for Dinner* (recently republished), *Catering for Special Occasions,* and *A New Book of Cookery.* For ten years before her death, she conducted a regular column on cookery in the *Woman's Home Companion.*

Very little biographical material concerning Fannie Farmer exists. Little, Brown knows of no biography, and *Books in Print,* a compilation of all published American books by R. R. Bowker, New York, lists nothing published about her through 1963. Miss Farmer shunned all personal publicity, never allowing her publishers to use her picture in the cookbooks.

But then she never needed such publicity. Her fame rests solidly on her book—the mainstay of millions of American kitchens. The eleventh edition of the Boston Cooking School Cook Book was revised by Wilma Lord Perkins (Mrs. Dexter Perkins), wife of Miss Farmer's nephew. This is the seventh edition edited by Mrs. Perkins.

As Baedeker is to the traveler, as Blackstone is to the lawyer, so is Fannie Farmer to the housewife. END

George Francis ("Express") Train.

(Courtesy Culver Pictures)

[216]

Space Age Victorian

by Dawn Anderson

"Fire, fire, you miserable cowards! Fire upon the flags of France and America wrapped around the body of an American citizen—if you have the courage!"

So cried out George Francis Train, who had taken time off from his trip around the world to get himself involved with the Communards in a revolution against France's Third Republic. Mistaking the gathering below the balcony of his Marseilles hotel as friendly Communards eagerly anticipating one of his impromptu, spirited speeches, Train had shouted out such revolutionary sentiments as "Vive la République!" and "Vive la Commune!" before he realized that a good part of his audience consisted of troops loyal to Gambetta's Third Republic.

The officers, who had noted with displeasure the flag of the Commune flying along with the flags of France and America on the balcony, ordered a firing squad to kneel and take aim.

Realizing that he was their target, Train dramatically wrapped his body in both the Tricolor and Old Glory, then stepped forward, knelt, and shrieked out his dare in French. It worked. The rifles were turned away, and the troops marched off.

After 13 days in the Lyons Bastille, Train was granted permission to state his case before Gambetta. Instead of pleading for clemency, the Boston-born prisoner, completely self-possessed, began the interview himself by berating Gambetta for not offering him a chair, then boldly stated this proposition: "M. Gambetta, you are the head of France, and I intend to be President of the United States. You can assist me, and I can assist you.

"Send me to America, and I can help you get munitions of war, and win over the sympathy and assistance of the Americans."

Luckily Gambetta realized that Train was an unconventional man with the unique penchant of finding himself irresistibly drawn to the causes of the underdog throughout the world. He had arrived in France with no intention of becoming a champion of the Communards, was no more than superficially connected with them, and no real threat to the Republic; he was merely acting out his life-long role of spectacular advocate of whatever cause had momentarily captured his fancy.

The Frenchman refused to consider Train's proposed deal and expelled him from France.

On returning to New York, Train boasted that his 'round-the-world trip had taken only 80 days, a remarkable achievement in 1870—though he neglected to count the month he had lost dabbling in the French Revolution.

The purpose of the record-breaking trip had been to publicize the way travel time across America had been shortened by the completion of the Union Pacific Railroad, which Train had promoted, as well as to publicize the self-proclaimed future President of the United States. A side result was that, two years later, Jules Verne's *The Tour of the World in Eighty Days* was published. George Francis Train had doubtless been the inspiration for the creation of Phileas Fogg, the main character of that famous book.

"Express" Train, as he had been appropriately dubbed because of the breakneck speed at which he raced from one social, political, or business venture to another, had very nearly been permanently derailed, right at the start of his life.

Born at 21 High Street, Boston, on March 24, 1829, he was taken as a baby to New Orleans, where his father opened a store. By 1833, the year of the yellow fever, New Orleans had become a city of the dead. Among its victims, the plague had claimed in rapid succession George's three sisters, his mother, and his nurse.

"Send on some one of the family, before they are all dead. Send George," wrote an alarmed Grandmother Pickering from her Waltham, Massachusetts, farm to her son-in-law in New Orleans.

George's father wisely heeded his mother-in-law's request, booked ship passage to Boston for his son, and attached a card to the boy's coat reading:

> This is my little son George Francis Train. Four years old. Consigned on board the ship *Henry* to John Clarke, Jr., Dock Square, Boston; to be sent to his Grandmother Pickering, at Waltham, ten miles from Boston. Take good care of the Little Fellow, as he is the only one left of eleven of us in the house, including the servants. I will come on as soon as I can arrange my Business.

George's father never reached Boston; he too presumably fell victim to the pestilence since no further trace of him could ever be found.

In writing for George, Grandmother Pickering had not only saved that branch of the Train family from complete extinction, she had rescued for the world a boy who was to become the best-known American on the face of the globe, a social and business phenomenon, who set three 'round-the-world travel records, promoted the building of railroads in the United States, introduced street railways to England, and was to boot a candidate for President of the United States, an advocate for Women's Suffrage and Freedom of the Press, the owner of a splendid Newport, Rhode Island, mansion, and the self-proclaimed Great American Crank.

The four-year-old made the 23-day, 2,000-mile boat trip from New Orleans to Boston with no guardian to look after him, not once washed himself nor changed his clothes, learned from the sailors to curse as coarsely as they, and exhibited an independence of spirit that was to amaze the Pickerings' strict Methodist household.

The lad was little burden to his grandparents since he was extremely self-reliant, dressed and cared for himself, ran errands, and soon learned to set the table as well as to prepare meals.

By age 10, he was rising at four in the morning to sell the farm's produce at Boston's Quincy Market. At 14, he was working 18 hours a day for a Cambridgeport grocer. After two years, he was champing at the bit, complaining that he had learned all there was to know about the grocery business in six months and wanted "a wider field of labor."

One day in 1845, Colonel Enoch Train, the cousin of George's father and the owner of Train and Company, a shipping house at 37 Lewis

[219]

Wharf, Boston, called at the grocery store to see George. After believing for many years that the whole New Orleans-based branch of the Train family had been wiped out by the plague, the colonel had presumably heard a rumor concerning the lone survivor and so had sought him out.

The merchant caught up on the boy's history, and no doubt tucked away in a corner of his mind the thought that the boy might very well, in a couple of years' time, add some new blood to his business. But if he did, he was careful not to mention it.

Therefore the elder Train must have been greatly surprised by a visit from his newly found young relative the very next day, and flabbergasted by the boy's direct approach concerning the shipping house.

"Where do I come in?" bluntly yet confidently demanded the 16-year-old, to Enoch's amazement.

"Come in? Why, people don't come into a big house like this in that way. You are too young." If that was Yankee "push," this young man surely had more than his share, Enoch must have thought.

Not to be disheartened at so quick a brush-off, George Train persisted, "I am growing older every day. That is the reason I am here. I want to make my way in the world."

"Well, you come to see me when you are 17 years old." The Colonel was leaving the door slightly ajar. No use discouraging the boy.

"That will be next year. I am 16 now. I might just as well begin this year—right away. . . . I will come in tomorrow."

Enoch's vigorous protests might just as well have been left unstated since nothing he could have said would have dissuaded the single-minded George Francis Train from showing up ready for work the next morning.

From the very beginning George Train's remarkable agile mind "thought big," revitalizing and updating the respectable old firm, urging the conservative Colonel Train on to commission the big new clipper ships that were to revolutionize the shipping industry.

"I want a big ship, one that will be larger than the *Ocean Monarch*," young Train told Donald McKay, who built the Train Company ships in East Boston. (The *Ocean Monarch*, at 800 tons, had been considered a veritable monster of the seas.)

"Two hundred tons bigger?" asked McKay.

"No," said Train, "I want a ship of two thousand tons!"

That was the origin of the world-famous *Flying Cloud*. Before she had made even one voyage for the Trains, they sold her for $90,000, which represented almost a hundred per cent profit!

[220]

The mighty clipper, Flying Cloud.

By age 20, George Train was a partner in Train and Company; his yearly income of $10,000 was phenomenal in 1849. At 21 he was manager of Train and Company's Liverpool office. "Express" Train was rolling and looking for a new challenge.

The young human dynamo found his challenge in 1853 in Australia—that raw and backward land where gold had been discovered just two years before. With a partner, he established a shipping company in Melbourne that was said to have made $95,000 in commissions the first year, and organized a fleet of ships to California; he vigorously introduced "Yankee notions" to the country.

"They would fight hard against everything that was new or American, but I took a delight in overcoming their bias, and forcing them to accept our ideas," he bragged. The Boston-type chaise like Holmes' "Wonderful one-horse shay that ran a hundred years to the day," the Concord wagon, canned goods, bowling, and tenpins are just a few of the American innovations Train brought to the Australians.

But he was never one to stick completely to business when any social or business crisis was flaring up; so it is not surprising that when the discontented gold miners began a revolt against the Australian government, they offered the substantial young business man the presidency of their proposed "Five-Star Republic." Luckily Train refused, for the insurrection was quickly put down.

For the next 12 years after his Australian adventures, "Express" Train raced around the world on a frantic schedule.

In Italy, he was for a short while courted by the Italian Carbonari, who had probably heard exaggerated accounts of his part in the Australian miners' revolution. Nevertheless the enthusiastic American briefly reveled in the romance of being called "Liberator" and "Citizen Train."

In America, he was a "coupling-chain" for joining Spanish Queen Maria Cristina's money to the effort of building a 400-mile stretch of railroad connecting the Erie ports with the Ohio and Mississippi. Later he was the ballyhoo artist who promoted construction of the Pacific Railroad, and he organized one of the first American trusts, the Credit Mobilier of America, to finance it. In all his undertakings, Train was content to take a quick profit and get out, and was out of the Credit Mobilier when it later collapsed in scandal.

In England, he pioneered in establishing horse-drawn street railway lines for cheap transportation while serving as unofficial ambassador there for the Union cause in the Civil War at home. He also claimed credit for suggesting the following practical improvements to the backward English: pouring spouts for inkwells, steps for carriages, the perforation of postage stamp sheets, erasers on pencils, and coal delivery by chute instead of in bags.

Always a celebrity hunter, he went to Russia for the single purpose of delivering a letter to the Grand Duke Constantine and was rewarded for his efforts by having the Grand Duke arrange a visit for him to the Nijni Novgorod commercial fair!

This respected though flamboyant business man had begun to associate himself more and more with the spectacular and the sensational. By 1868, Train was in a Dublin jail cell, one of 15 he was to occupy during his lifetime as a result of his support of controversial issues.

He boasted, "My prison experience has been more varied than that of the most confirmed and hardened criminal; and yet I have never committed a crime, cheated a human being, or told a lie . . . I have used prisons well. They have been as schools to me, where I have reflected, and learned more about myself . . . and from them have launched many of my most startling and useful projects and innovations."

What project had he decided upon in the Irish prison? That he should be the next President of the United States! The thought actually had been brewing within him for nearly a decade before.

His qualifications: "I am that wonderful, eccentric, independent, extraordinary genius and political reformer of America, who is sweeping off all the politicians before him like a hurricane, your modest, diffident, unassuming friend, the future President of America—George Francis Train!" The voters' unassuming friend charged them admission to his presidential campaign speeches, an unprecedented practice, and collected $90,000 from people in three years of barnstorming.

Although they got more than their money's worth in entertainment from his bombastic oratory, most of his audiences by this time regarded him as a harmless eccentric, but one step removed from a madman. While much of what he said made a great deal of sense, much also was wild and rambling, a theatrical display that momentarily amused and held a crowd, but, as he himself admitted, "the moment they got out of my reach they got away from me, and slipped back again to the sway of the political bosses." When election day arrived, no votes were recorded for George Francis Train.

"Express" Train hardly noticed his defeat, since three days before the election he had thrown himself into the Woodhull-Claflin affair in New York City. The sisters Victoria Woodhull and Tennessee Claflin had been jailed on an obscenity charge following their published attack on the love life of The Reverend Henry Ward Beecher.

Train succeeded in getting himself jailed, too, when he printed three columns of verses from the Bible in a newspaper he had started, with the claim that nothing the women had published was any worse than his Bible quotations. The result was that, after five months' imprisonment in the Tombs, he legally was declared a lunatic and was released. (The verdict of lunacy was later set aside, following Train's appeal.)

After two more record-breaking trips around the world—one in 67½ days, the last in 60 days, an involvement in promoting the Chicago-based World's Columbian Exposition, and noisy but ineffective participation in the presidential campaign of 1896, "Express" Train was coasting into the last station. Although he was making fewer speeches, he wrote almost incessantly, bombarding the newspaper editors with his thoughts. He usually used a double colored pencil, red on one end, and blue on the other, to produce startling effects on a stream of penny postcards.

Train had separated himself almost completely from his wife—probably to her relief since she had always preferred obscurity to the publicity in

[223]

which her husband had gloried—and his three children, choosing to live out his days alone. During his days of wealth, he had wisely set up trust funds to care for both his wife and his children, and had seen to it that his daughter and two sons had had good educations.

In his prosperous times he had constructed Train Villa, one of the most luxurious of the Newport homes in its day, and had lived there at a cost of about $2,000 a week. In his last years his cost of living was three dollars a week at the Mills Hotel in New York City. He had spent the money he had formerly made in tremendous amounts lavishly, but he now claimed that he had no need for money and that, if he had more than three dollars a week, he would only have to give it away.

Train had become a vegetarian believing that, with proper diet, a man was capable of reaching the age of 150 years. He spent his time sitting on a Madison Square bench, talking to little children and feeding peanuts to the squirrels and pigeons. He often wore a red ribbon across his chest and liked to be called "Citizen Train," pleasant reminders of his Communard adventures and the glorious days gone by.

At the age of 74 he dictated a 100,000-word, 340-page amazingly accurate autobiography in 35 hours without the use of notes to refresh his memory! His mind was still razor-sharp.

"I have lived fast. I have ever been an advocate of speed," he reminisced. "I was born into a slow world, and I wished to oil the wheels and gear, so that the machine would spin faster and, withal, to better purposes."

After Train's death a year later, the doctors who examined the brain of the ingenious eccentric found it to weigh 53.8 ounces—six ounces greater than average, and ranked it 26th in a list of the brain weights of 106 famous men.

Tagged as he was by contemporaries with labels such as "megalomaniac," "mountebank," and "peripatetic humbug," many could not decide whether Train was in fact a genius or just plain mad. Yet with all his tomfoolery, he had combined an honest enjoyment of living with a long list of solid accomplishments in a kaleidoscopic career that would make us wish that Boston could produce another such phenomenal "Express" Train. He would undoubtedly find the giddy pace of the 1970s most congenial!　　　　　　　　　　　　　　　　　　　　　　　　　END

New England Granite

SECTION 7

Victorious Army of Two

by Alton Hall Blackington

There are several versions of this story and the girls' ages are given all the way from 14 to 22. One widely published picture of the Bates sisters shows them to be of equal height and apparently about 10 or 12 years old. But if the *Salem Gazette* of 1886 had its dates correct, Abigail was 16 and Rebecca 22 on that late summer day when they fooled the British.

Scituate harbor down on the South Shore had been a favorite rendezvous for British ships during the War of 1812. Barge loads of "Lobsterbacks" were always coming ashore to demand food, vegetables, and other supplies from the farmers and fishermen and threatening to burn the Town if the stuff wasn't handed over.

On the morning of June 11, 1814, several barges from the warship *Bulwark* landed at Scituate and set fire to ten of the fishing vessels. The townspeople organized a company of militia under the direction of Colonel John Barstow, who had come down from Boston with some troops. Pretty soon the *Bulwark* hauled up anchor and sailed to Maine to harass the citizens of Thomaston and Warren (then called St. George) on the river of the same name.

Much relieved at the departure of the big British man-of-war, the Scituate fishermen turned to rebuilding their fleet, and the farmers tended to long-neglected fields and gardens. Even the lighthouse keeper, Reuben Bates, went inland to help gather the summer's last crop of hay and the fall's first red-ripening apples.

[226]

" . . . the first of the five barges halted . . . "

Mother Bates remained at the Light to look after the children. Her boys played in the woods and around the wharf and went fishing, while the girls (Abigail and Rebecca) helped with the housework and polished the big reflector in the light tower. For diversion they practiced "Yankee Doodle" on a big drum and on an old cracked fife their father kept in the top bureau drawer of the living room.

On the morning of September 1, 1814, Rebecca Bates was up in the tower cleaning the light when she noticed a big ship maneuvering in the mist just off shore. It was the 74-gun British warship *La Hogue*, and Rebecca lost no time in dashing down the steep stairs to send her two younger brothers to the village to warn the citizens.

For nearly two hours the big warship tacked and stood off to sea, then tacked again and came back. Men and women gathered on the hills, and

"One, and two, and three!"

the children climbed trees to watch the enemy ship. When it was seen that boats were being made ready and the anchors splashed, the towns-people panicked. Valuables were tied up in bed sheets, children were bundled in blankets, and, along with chickens, cooking pans, dishes and spinning wheels, the old and young were packed into carts and other conveyances for evacuation. All the small boats, canoes, and even scows scurried out to the vessels in the cove to bring ashore nets and fishing gear before they could be captured by the British and burned as before.

Shortly after 2 P.M. the American spyglasses showed great activity aboard the *La Hogue*. The sound of drums rolled in from the ship, as "quarters" sounded. Guns glistened, and bayonets sparkled as the red-coated Marines climbed into the waiting barges.

Up in the light tower, the two Bates girls watched breathlessly as the oars moved in rhythmic precision, and the officer in each boat barked out his orders. In a few minutes the enemy would land and in all probability lay the fair town of Scituate in ashes.

Abbie said, "I wish I were a man, I'd show them," and Rebecca answered forlornly, "What do you think you could do against so many?"

"I'd fight, that's what I'd do, with Father's old musket. Say! Wait a minute, I've got an idea. Come on, Rebecca! Quick!"

Down the narrow stairs they tumbled pell-mell, Abigail wishing she didn't have on a bright red dress (but there was no time to change), and little Becky still wearing her apron.

Grabbing the drum, Abbie slipped the straps over her shoulders, say-ing "Fetch Father's fife from the bureau, Becky, and be careful of that crack. Hurry up! Out the back door! Don't worry, Mother, we won't be gone long."

Scootching along under the sand hills, they reached some chokecherry bushes and then ran like the wind toward a big sand hill where they would be unobserved. Rebecca moistened her finger and held it up to the breeze, "Off-shore, thank heaven," and she played a few low notes on the old cracked fife.

Abigail tightened the straps, gave a few light taps, and nodded to her sister, "One, and two, and three!" And from that sandy hollow, the stirring notes of "Yankee Doodle" rolled out over the water. Shoulder to

[228]

shoulder marched the sisters, in and around the grass-covered hummocks, the shrill notes of the fife and the beat of the drum becoming louder and louder as they approached the beach.

Suddenly they heard shouting from the village, a few guns barked, then more cheering. Abigail began to laugh, but Rebecca silenced her, whispering, "Stop it! If you make me laugh I won't be able to pucker up."

Just beyond their heads, hidden from sight by the sand hills, the first of the five barges had halted. Dripping oars resting mid-air, the Marines sat motionless while the officer shouted an order back to the other boats.

The two excited girls put everything they had into that spine-tingling tune the British had heard so many times.

Another cheer from the village and more shots, and then a second fife and drum corps struck up "Yankee Doodle." Unable to stand the suspense any longer, Rebecca (who needed to catch her breath anyway) crept to the top of the dune and peeked thru the waving beach grass.

Every officer on the enemy barges was staring, not at the village of Scituate, but at the *La Hogue* riding majestically at anchor. As they stared, a signal flag fluttered in the September sun, and a puff of white smoke floated up the deck. The boom which followed was a second signal for the barges to return to the ship, and in the excitement to obey that order, three of the boats bumped together, and one young Britisher fell overboard.

Elated that their ruse had worked an apparent miracle, the excited daughters of the lightkeeper went back to their blowing and beating, the off-shore breeze wafting the hated Yankee tune to the retreating Red Coats, who scrambled aboard their warship and sailed away.

In one last, departing gesture of defiance, the *La Hogue* fired a round shot at the Lighthouse, but it splashed harmlessly into the sea 100 yards from shore.

Naturally the Bates girls were hailed as heroines, and all thru their long and useful lives they were called upon times without number to tell and re-tell how they scared off a big British war vessel with their father's old fife and drum. There is no doubt about it that their quick thinking and brave action saved the town of Scituate from British vengeance that day.

END

The Vermont Version

by Leon W. Dean

Illustrations by Austin N. Stevens

In scanning the pages of Vermont history, I have been intrigued by the ways in which people have gained for themselves the immortality of print. Far from being the exclusive domain of the great, these pages abound in the deeds of the humble. Captains of industry and generals of armies there may be, scholars and inventors, statesmen and writers, but along with these big fish are many lesser fry. In fact, one may say that such immortality is within the reach of almost anyone if he can do something unusual enough.

An Indian squaw, for instance, is said to have been the first recorded person to go over the falls at Bellows Falls and live. The account appeared in print in 1781. Caught in the current and faced with death, so the tale goes, she downed a bottle of rum that she was taking to her thirsty spouse and lay down in the bottom of the canoe to await her fate. Later she was fished out below the falls quite safe—and quite drunk.

Thus in one fell swoop, as it were, did an unknown Indian squaw plunge to a place in history.

Or take General Brownson of Sunderland. The general was a veteran of the Revolutionary War and carried in his body eighteen different pieces of lead. In addition to his wartime service, he was a man of consequence in the community, but if he had not carried so much lead weight, it is doubtful that he would have been considered worthy of historical note.

Clearly, a slug of rum or a charge of buckshot may be all that is needed to insure one a niche in the hall of fame.

In Calais lived a queer one by the name of Pardon Jones. As a young man he is said to have been highly intelligent, a gifted speaker. At one time he represented his town in the State Legislature. Then he went haywire, and it made him famous. For many years he went about his affairs with a short pitchfork attached to his wrist so that he need not touch anything that his fellow men had touched. When making purchases, he carried his money in a tin pail at the end of the fork, and the clerks made change for him.

Or consider the case of Frank Rice. Frankie was born April 12, 1854, in Sutton. When five years of age, he weighed 105 pounds on anybody's steelyards. At the mature age of three, he could lift a bushel of potatoes. As a senior citizen of eight, he weighed in at 130 pounds. Then he rested on his laurels, settling down to a more normal way of life; but he had already put his birth date on the calendar of events.

In fact, all one need do to get into the record books is to pitch a hitless baseball game or to be like Andrew Blair of Goshen Gore, who once ran down and captured a fox. Then, fearing that he had taken an unfair advantage of the animal, he informed it that they would try again. Off went the fox, quite agreeable to the idea, having been given a few rods' start. Then off went Andy in pursuit. Over hill and fence, through brush and briar they tore until the man once more came off the victor, assuring himself of honorable mention in the category of unclassified sports.

History reveals Vermonters to have been a versatile and original lot. Not all of them won recognition by chasing foxes. Joseph Smith of Sharon attained glory by establishing the Mormon Church. In Burlington was born William H. Russell, originator of the famous pony express. Bennington lays claim to John F. Winslow, builder of the *Monitor*, Civil War hero ship in the first battle of ironclads. Another Bennington notable was Daniel W. Harmon, one of the giant figures of the western fur trade. William B. Clapp, born in Montgomery, was the first man in the United States to can meat; and Walter Colton, Rutland, made the first public announcement of the discovery of gold on the Pacific Coast.

Other Vermonters have done remarkable things of lesser import but nevertheless gained renown. A certain eccentric individual set out one day for St. Johnsbury with a bag of potatoes that he had bought. Two

18 pieces of lead overweight.　　　*Touch not anything with thy bare hand.*

or three men had helped him settle the heavy sack on his back. On his homeward way, one of the potatoes worked its way through a small rent in the bottom. Knowing that he would not be able to reshoulder the bag if he set it down, yet loath to part with such a precious article of diet, he kicked the fractious tuber all the way home. If you can't organize a fur trade, just boot a spud.

We read in the history of Woodstock of one who was known as a mighty apple-tree man. He experimented for some years in trying to make apple trees grow wrong side up on the assumption that such a method would produce fruit without cores or seeds. Once he set two scions in which he had great faith. The two did not bear fruit for years. Finally, however, they blossomed, and a few apples matured. They were long and slim, with two cores instead of none.

Barnet produced a human phenomenon by the name of McCulloch who was a living almanac. Although he never created the sensation of Zerah Colburn of Cabot (see p. 110), he apparently knew his stuff. It is reported that he could tell at once the day of the month, the day of the year and what kind of a day it was on which an event occurred. He could tell whom he had heard preach on a given date, the text, the psalm and the tune to which the psalm was sung.

If you can't become famous in any other way, try living it up for an unreasonable length of time. A French Canadian named Shovah died in Milton in 1857 at the age of 103. When 100 years old, he shouldered

Not everyone can catch a fox—twice.

half a bushel of grain, carried it on foot two miles to mill and returned with the flour the same day, having enough gumption left to live three more years.

'Way back about 1803 was when a man in Charlotte had a vision. The incident occurred in an open field in broad daylight. In the vision, he foresaw the anti-Masonic troubles that are now history, the Civil War and the abolition of slavery. After that, according to the vision, a monarchial power would arise and take over the government of the United States. So perhaps Vermont has given us something to look forward to as well as look back upon. END

Plunging into history.

The World's Greatest
Single Rescue Feat

by Edward Rowe Snow

"Now shove . . . for God's sake, shove!"

What is the world's greatest single rescue feat? Is it the spectacular accomplishment of Grace Darling of Northumberland, England, or the remarkable act of Captain Elmer Mayo when he saved Surfman Ellis? Should it be the rescue by Joshua James and his crew of the sailors aboard the *Anita Owen* in 1885 at Nantasket, Massachusetts?

In my mind, when George Bloomer's crew brought in the sailors aboard the schooner *Grecian*—off the shores of Chatham, Massachusetts, in 1885 —it became the most dramatic rescue in New England's history. Unfortunately, according to historian Virginia Harding McGrath of Chatham,

[234]

there are several stories of what happened that day and how the rescue was effected.

Many years have elapsed since "Crazy" George Bloomer and I had our Chatham meeting in the twenties, but I'll never forget it. We were standing in the shadow of the Light watching a four-masted schooner sailing up the coast when I decided to ask him about himself. We ended up by spending the next three hours together as I wrote and wrote and wrote.

✻   ✻   ✻   ✻   ✻

My first question concerned the nickname by which many people knew him, "Crazy George Bloomer."

"Well," he began, "they call me 'Crazy George' because of the many times I have been the only one *crazy* enough to attempt a rescue. Quite often I tell some tall stories for the enjoyment of the summer visitors and that might have added a little to my reputation. Let's forget all that.

"If you really wish to record what I consider was our greatest, luckiest rescue, why, we'll have to go back to the year 1885 and the *Grecian*. I'll tell it to you exactly as I remember it.

"We then lived in the southernmost house on the Massachusetts mainland," he began. "Down by James' Head, there on the shore of the old Inner Channel at the cut-thru, as we called it, was an old saltbox house with a gable roof—Down East style.

"At one o'clock on the morning of December 6, 1885, an overwhelming squall came out of the east-southeast. In an hour's time it had set in to blow a living gale to the beach. My 21-year-old brother, Billy, and Uncle Francisco, father's youngest brother, asked me to lend a hand in making ready one of the seven village pilot boats, a strong 22-foot craft built double-ended like a whaleboat, for work in a seaway.

"We launched at once and as we pulled down the channel, Francisco at the sweep, steering, other lights showed along the shore. Francisco hailed and waved our lantern in the air, for we were the first boat out. The channel of the cut-thru ran in by the high land of Monomoy, known as Morris Island, on the low knolls, on the seaward side of which was Chatham Station of the United States Lifesaving Service.

"Landing at the head of the channel, we started walking down the beach headed for that station, against the wind, like men fallen to earth, heads bowed to keep the flying sand and spray out of our eyes."

I might mention that at the point across from where Bloomer and his men were walking, the Outer Bar lay almost half a mile offshore.

"A vessel on the Outer Bar!"

"We went far along the beach and could tell the bars were boiling cauldrons of mad sea. By dawn, the wind worsened so that a strong man in seaboots could scarcely stand unless he leaned forward.

" 'A vessel, a vessel on the Outer Bar!' someone shouted.

"Slightly to the northward we saw a two-masted schooner, headed in, her sails in rags and frozen, their ribands threshing about the spars. The breakers were burying her hull from sight, driving spray over her mastheads. Through the glasses, when the seas receded from her, we could make out five men on her afterhouse, clinging desperately to the main peak halliards. Then another sea began to climb over her, and they vanished in the surf.

"That she was well built, and the masts securely stopped and stayed, was apparent. We judged her coal-laden, there being no evident lift of her hull.

"We struggled up the beach to a point inshore from her. It was to be a gray day with scud driving over the sea like smoke. One of the old-timers, who had saved shipwrecked sailors long before the Civil War, stood just clear of the upwash from the breakers and stared off at her, his chin jammed into the neck strap of his oil coat. His name was Captain Nat."

On that day in 1885, George Bloomer stepped up beside the captain and waited. "The Captain," Bloomer went on to say, "finally turned to shout in my ear: 'No boat can go today, George,' he said. 'She may wash on to the Inner Bar when the tide comes. Get them then with the breeches buoy.'

"We all waited. Seas climbed up, burying her like an outlying rock. She was bilged, and she could never drive over the Outer Bar other than as wreckage when the seas had had their fill of her. A boat *must* go!

" 'Cap'n Nat!' I yelled. 'I'm calling volunteers!'

"Captain Nat spoke: 'Are you crazy, George? No boat can get off the beach, much less live in that sea!'

" 'No!' I cried. 'Not crazy, Nat, just the same as ever, Crazy George Bloomer, and I'm going!' "

Bloomer then acted. He called out: "Volunteers! Volunteers! To man a boat!"

The response to that call was never forgotten by others who witnessed the scene. Men stepped up—over 50 of them. Four were chosen. They stripped down—no hats, coats, boots—only shirt, trousers, and stockings in spite of the cold. If unencumbered their chances were better should the boat overturn.

They set the craft down just clear of the backwash and laid the oars, placing the sweep in its socket with the pintle well inboard. The chosen few, Francisco, the Bearse boys, and Billy, took their places in the thwarts, and made ready. As many of the onlookers as possible laid hold of the gunwale on either side and, with Bloomer at the stern post, they awaited the right sea.

Eight great billows came roaring in at them before one looked right. "Ready!" Bloomer shouted. They ran her into the flood. "Twenty feet more; run with her."

The launching group were now up to their waists in the outgoing sea. The undertow was dragging dangerously at them before they dropped back. As the boys strained at the oars, Bloomer still pushed at the stern post until the water reached his armpits. Then he climbed in. Now came the struggle. Out of the wash a great sea rose under them, casting the boat up toward the heavens like a chip.

"I struggled at the sweep as hard as the others to hold her into it, but it broke too soon. We went over in the midst of the breaking, seething crest.

"Engulfed in a tangle of oars and boat, we were hurled at the shore. We fought the undertow, and we were driven about like so much flotsam, but a dozen men rushed in and dragged us to safety.

"Captain Nat came over as I stood digging sand out of my eyes and ears, wind cutting through me like a knife, the wet woolens dragging at my limbs.

" 'Her larboard's split,' he said, pointing at the boat which they had rescued and dragged up the beach, 'split wide open! They're bringing up another boat,' he finally said, 'if you want it.'

" 'If the boys will go,' I said, and they nodded in agreement."

They brought the second boat for the volunteers. This time they waited longer for the best sea. It came. Bloomer and his men ran her in.

"Again the water came to my armpits," said Bloomer. "I climbed in. As before, we were cast up, up, and up on a great sea, until it appeared as though it would never be done. Then, just as it seemed we would slide over the crest and down the board back of the wave, as we hoped, the billow broke too soon! Like lightning we broached to. Our craft pitchpoled. Luckily we managed to get clear from the boat, for it crashed high

[237]

"They're bringing up another boat—if you want it . . . "

on the beach, planking and ribs smashed into kindling wood."

George Bloomer now decided to wait, as the seas were getting longer. Indeed the tide was making all the time, giving more water on the bars, but they dared not wait too long. They'd be sure of their chance this time.

The boat arrived. Francisco, Billy, and the Bearse boys took their places. As before, the crowd laid hold of the gunwales. Eleven great seas thundered on the beach, and the twelfth loomed at them.

"This one," came the shout.

"Ready." Bloomer yelled, "Now shove! For God's sake, shove!" Out on the backwash they ran her, until all the helpers were beyond their shoulders in spume.

Like a rocket they went, then up and up. Would the billow break? Higher and higher went the peak, and then it began to separate. The battle was won. The boat was on the back of the wave, the men rowing for the next crest. The task, however, had only begun. Outside of that line of breakers a troubled sea was running, so tall they feared it might again pitch-pole the boat.

By sheer strength they gained, foot after foot. In one full hour they barely made 200 yards out toward the Inner Bar. But could any boat ever built go through what was ahead?

One possible hope remained. George pointed to a small gap in the Northeast Bar.

"Try it!" the others cried.

[238]

Bloomer's object was to reach the open Atlantic, row off dead to windward of the schooner, come about, and ride the sea in past her. It was dangerous—but their only chance.

"We changed our course," George told me. "We crabbed off to northeast. It was a ticklish business."

They passed through the breach in the Inner Bar, and then worked off to a point inside the Outer Bar, some 500 yards north of the schooner. For 40 yards the sea was in a frenzy, making it doubtful whether they could cross. For a time they held on the bars, headed to the wind, and watched. Then came a relatively smooth period.

"Now!" shouted George.

They drove ahead. A great cross-sea rose up on the starboard bow and came racing at them, threatening to break. It was an anxious instant. Then, another rose under the boat to port and lifted them clear. Down the back of that great hill of water the boat drove to meet the next sea over deeper soundings. They had jumped the Bar.

"This was the open Atlantic, no bars to ease the onslaught of giant waves 15 feet over our heads when we slid down off their great shoulders. Terror clutched at us. Off to the southeast we struggled, weary from the killing effort of oars. Numbness began to sap our strength and with it our courage. We got to windward of the schooner. The wind seemed bent on snatching us, boat and all, out of the water, when we rode on a crest into the teeth of the gale."

When close enough to be heard by the survivors, Bloomer turned in the stern sheets of the boat. He yelled three times as they rushed by, "Jump, jump, jump!" They made no sign, but the lifesavers thought they had understood.

Now came the test. To get about in the sea, Bloomer would have to start at the right time. A moment too soon, or too late, and they were done. If the crest was close behind, it would engulf them. If just ahead, it would throw them off at the mercy of the next sea. They must ride the breaker itself.

Experience, vigilance, luck, all worked with the crew. Between two great seas they pivoted the boat like a top with both the oars and the sweep, which hung half balanced in air on the mounting crest. Then came the mad rush.

"Forward we shot," said Bloomer, "the roaring sea hurling us with terrific impetus at the schooner. Francisco and Andrew Bearse stood up, facing forward, aiding me to steer with their oars over either side, riding

[239]

fairly on the crest, our bow high, the sea dropping steeply away behind. I saw the schooner's stern coming at us out of a breaking sea, as though over the ridge of a hill, so steep was the cant of our boat.

"In the first breaker that outran the Bay, our speed slacked for an instant, then the great sea mounted up, with us still on the crest, and we surged steadily ahead aimed fairly at the schooner's amidships.

" 'Port oar,' I yelled, 'Port oar!' For an instant, I thought we would charge clear over her between the masts, but she sheered off and swept past the vessel's counter as we emerged from the sea going 20, possibly 30, knots.

" 'Jump!' I yelled, 'God's sake, jump!'

"Not a man moved. There was a blur of forms clinging to the halliards, half buried in the sea, out of which stared scared faces. We shot on into the mad water between the Bars, terribly disappointed.

" 'Hold her!' I shouted; 'Hold her! We'll hit the beach!'

"With frantic effort on the oars astern, we managed to stop her just clear of the shore breakers and bring her about again.

" 'What d'ye think?' I shouted, the boys holding her on the oars; 'Shall we try it again?'

" 'Aye, again!' was the response.

"We maneuvered as before; pulled off to the smoothest place in the Outer Bar that I could find. There seemed to be more sea running now, sharper in the crest. The tide had turned and was going out. The water on the Bars was shoaling. It would not do to linger.

" 'What d'ye think, boys?'

"And again: 'Aye, try it!'

"They were weary with the strain and numbing cold, soaked to the skin with spray that constantly drove over the boat. Well, we jumped the bar, again struggled to the southeast in the full sweep of the open Atlantic. This time we did not go so far out. We could not, there wasn't time.

"Again I turned round on the stern sheets of the boat and shouted down wind, 'Jump for your lives as we rush by. No more attempts—your last chance!' "

Again they reversed the boat. Another great sea came at them, larger and longer running than before, a grandfather of a sea. Fairly at the vessel's counter she chopped, shaving it by inches. Would the crew jump?

In a group the men deserted the halliard. Four of them fell into the stern sheets, nearly knocking Bloomer off his feet, but their Captain missed the boat altogether.

[240]

Chatham's Lifesavers. "Crazy George" is believed to be seated second from the right.

Bloomer took his right hand off the pintle of the oar to reach out and grab the Captain's clothes. George caught him, holding him on the gunwale, the man's body dragging overboard.

"For God's sake, steady," Bloomer yelled at Francisco, "hold her steady!"

Francisco couldn't help, the Captain was too weak, and so it was up to "Crazy George." He worked him slowly, little by little over the side, steering with one hand, finally tumbling him in with the others, who sat where they had fallen, staring at the gunwales as though doped.

Through the gap in the Inner Bar the boat rushed. On the edge of shoal water with the crest beginning to form, Bloomer realized that there was almost half a ton of weight in the loaded boat.

"Forrard of the thwart there, two of you!" Bloomer yelled. "Trim her!" The billow mounted up again, up and up to gather itself for that last 350-yard plunge to shore.

"That single sea" Bloomer told me, "carried us—boat, human cargo, and all—like an alighting gull, so far up the beach at the feet of the spectators that the backwash hardly pulled at her keel. Never in all the years on salt water have I seen a boat run on a sea so far. Indeed, it was our lucky day." END

Around Cape Horn
to Find a Husband

by Harold Helfer

Did you ever hear of the Mercer Girls? Probably not . . . and yet they were undoubtedly the most remarkable class of young women in our country's history. And while, as it so happened, they were all from New England, they could have been from anywhere and it wouldn't have made any difference. For what made them true sisters-under-the-skin, not only among themselves but with those of the female species the world over, is that they had one firm objective in mind transcending all others: to latch on to husbands.

The curtain on their story opens not in their native Yankeeland but at the other extreme—on the West Coast, in Seattle, Washington Territory. The whole fabulous saga began with a simple ad in a Seattle journal, the *Puget Sound Herald*. This called for a meeting of bachelors to devise "ways and means" for procuring a much-needed immigration of the fair sex to Western shores.

There is no question of the interest this advertisement aroused. Not

ON DECK

Asa Mercer and his "girls" enroute to Washington Territory. Illustration "Women were scarce on the frontier" from Harper's Weekly *(1866-8) (Harper & Row, Publishers).*

only was the rendezvous site mentioned in the ad jammed with lonely fellows, but the meeting, as they discussed their pathetic, female-less situation, lasted all night.

Shortly after this meeting another ad appeared in a Seattle journal. It was in the form of a contract and went like this:

"I, Asa Mercer, of Seattle, Washington Territory, hereby agree to bring a suitable wife, of good moral character and reputation, from the East to Seattle, on or before September, 1865, for each of the parties whose signatures are hereunto attached; they first paying me the sum of $300 with which to pay the passage of said ladies from the East, and to compensate me for my trouble."

Within a few days Mr. Asa Mercer had all the "bride orders" he could handle—some 500 of them, by actual count! Probably never before or since has there been such mass concerted action on the part of lonely-heart males in this country for "mail-order" sight-unseen brides. So delighted were the miners, prospectors and other assorted bachelors of the Washington territory at the prospect that their unconnubial state might change, they staked a farewell band recital and parade for Asa Mercer. This was on the day he departed for the East for his brides.

Imagine the chagrin and pique, not to mention the mounting frustration of his clients when weeks went by and the weeks turned into months— and still no word from Mercer! The mounting suspense and growing anger was finally terminated with a letter from Asa to his "connubialless constituents." It seemed that it just took a little time to round up a boatload of brides. But he was making progress.

One thing was for sure: he certainly was stirring up staid New England as it had been stirred up few times before. As the word got out that he was seeking a cargo of young ladies to accompany him West as brides-to-be for a mass of women-hungry men, it created a controversy that was heard all the way from rock-ribbed Maine to the more genteel-like parts of Connecticut. It became the number one topic of discussion, not only in the street and in pubs and over backyard fences but at town hall meetings, in the press, and even in the pulpit.

Nevertheless, the girls were signing up, and that was the important thing. Brave ladies, they were too, who could sign on, in the face of public uproar, for just about as strange a cruise as ever took place. This "boatload of brides" was heading for an area and menfolks totally strange to them. Some were frankly a bit terrified at the prospect of life with some wild, bushybearded rough-hewn Westerner, others appeared ready

[244]

to take it all blithely and in stride.

The one thing these "Mercer Girls," as they were called, all had in common was that they vigorously denied they were going West "after a husband." As this appeared to have unladylike connotations, they made it clear they were merely going out West to see what it was like there.

It turned out that the Western men had no such inhibitions about their motives. When the boat temporarily stopped in at San Francisco, the crew had to fight a pitched battle to keep the male element of *that* city from kidnapping the whole shipload of girls for themselves. However, Asa Mercer had promised his "boatload of brides" for the men of the Washington Territory. And it was in Seattle, after a 7000-mile trip, that the ship finally docked.

Needless to say, the girls were treated royally. Even the most be-whiskered characters were suddenly clean-shaven. Taverns were closed. All the Seattle buildings had been whitewashed. The streets were as neat and trim as they could be. The men were so polite to the girls that they appeared to be downright bumbling and bashful.

This being a free country, the girls were actually under no obligation to marry anybody in particular, or from any kind of group, but nature just naturally took its course. A week later the ice was broken, and the first marriage took place. From then on marriage followed marriage, until virtually all, if not all, those "boat brides" were brides in actuality.

The people were by no means ungrateful to Asa Mercer for bringing in his "Boatload of Brides." They showed how much they thought of him by electing him to the Legislative Assembly. One of the girls he brought over indeed honored him more. She became Mrs. Mercer!   END

WARREN B. JOHNSON

A Yankee Who
Went Home...
The Hard Way

by Laura Page

Warren B. Johnson with the horse, wagon, dog, and cow he took 4500 miles home to New England.

History is full of Yankees who refused to cry quits or say die. If it couldn't be done, they did it. When road barriers went up, they took a detour. And if that wasn't possible, they tunneled under like moles until they got there.

In the year 1882, a Massachusetts man began a curious 4500-mile journey across the nation. Other men had done it, but he was the first to do it with a cow, a horse, a dog and a wagon and in an easterly direction.

A Civil War drum major whose E-flat cornet helped pierce the path of Sherman's march from Atlanta to the Sea, Warren B. Johnson was a six-footer with florid complexion. Weighing about 170, he was "a true type of Eastern Yankee." An army pensioner because of a disability incurred during service in the Civil War, Johnson was urged by friends and relatives to go to California to recuperate. In 1880 he made the trip by train.

The golden West may have been golden even then, but Johnson missed New England. He decided to return home. Had he the money, he would have shipped the cow, horse, dog and wagon he had acquired out West home to New England by rail, but he couldn't scrape up the necessary fare.

There was only one way. He would do it himself.

"On the morning of the first of June, 1882, I started on my proposed journey from Eureka City, Humboldt Bay, California, for Massachusetts, with my outfit, comprising myself, horse, wagon, dog and cow, with all necessary articles for the long journey—making the first day the town of Hydesville, distance 25 miles."

So begins the saga, as told in his own words.

Not long after, Johnson was assailed by his first serious doubts. He had come to the Vandozen River. A teamster had told him that the large, broad river was deep, but had a good, hard bottom.

"My thoughts were covering a large space—from the Pacific to the Atlantic," Johnson wrote. "Can this be done? I had struck out on a long, rough and dangerous journey with a horse and wagon, cow and dog. Can it be done, can this be accomplished, all alone, no one with me? Let happen what will, I decided to try it. I approached the ford; the water was deep; I was not able to see the bottom, with a strong, swift current. There I must decide, go on or go back. If I return back I should never be satisfied. If I go on and make a success, then I have accomplished a wonderful undertaking. I there decided to go on and I did . . ."

Three days later, while working inland east of the coastal range, Fanny, the horse, ran into blister trouble at the small town of Blocksburg. Johnson decided to spend five days there.

Blocksburg was made up of a handful of people, a hotel, two stores, blacksmith, wheelright shop, a few houses and two saloons.

"Saloons are well patronized," wrote Johnson. "I counted 22 horses at one (outside, that is). Their riders were inside drinking and gambling. I asked what business they followed. I was told that they were wool growers, but their main business was drinking and gambling.

"Those that follow this business, and they are many, have nothing but gold. I have seen piles of gold on the tables. They do not appear to be afraid of each other. They do not count out their money—it is laid in piles; they go by the height. Their money consists of five, ten and twenty dollar pieces. I have seen heaps four inches high of twenties. Their money lays on the table until they get through, with their revolvers beside them."

Cold water applied for 36 hours to his horse's shoulders cured the blisters, but Johnson was faced with another problem—the feet of his cow. Nature hadn't designed cows to travel 4500 miles across the continent and Bessie's feet were getting sore. Johnson wanted to put horse shoes on her, but could find no blacksmith expert enough. The Blocksburg authority, however, suggested that he could shoe her as the Spaniards do.

"How do they shoe them?" Johnson asked.

"They sear their feet," the blacksmith replied.

"I concluded to do so and had her shod that way.

"It proved a wise precaution. I traveled more than 600 miles before I could get her shod with iron shoes."

Johnson now began running into difficult country, a succession of hard and hilly roads; cliffs, mountains and canyons. He found that travelers did not go over the mountains, but around them, and that no money was spent improving roads, a complaint frequently heard even today.

One of the most difficult rivers he had to ford was the Eel River. Johnson had dreaded it from the beginning. But he mounted his horse, crossed without incident, returned and repeated it with the wagon and cow.

Feeling jubilant, he began ascending a mountain which began about

two miles further. There he met the mail stage, a heavy wagon drawn by two horses. "It was not a bad place to pass and I gave him right of way," described Johnson.

"The driver sang out for the road and stopped. I told him he had ample room to pass. He had but two passengers aboard. The driver said that he would teach me to get out of the way for the mail driver. With that he started up and came down on the rear wheel of my carriage, crushing it down. He did not stop to see what damage he had done, but went on his own way.

"I was vexed and felt badly, being all alone."

Fortunately, a man Johnson had previously met at the Eel River came along and helped him make temporary repairs until he could get to a wheelwright shop, 16 miles away.

Continuing some 35 miles further, Johnson reached another mountain with dark canyons, one of them "a noted place to stop a stage for plunder." He continued and at a turnout met two Indian half-breeds who tried to grab Johnson's dog, Bert. At that moment a mail stage happened along.

"They saw it also; one of them caught the dog by its head and was pulling him out of the carriage. At that moment I grabbed a long knife that lay beside me and made a lunge at the man holding the dog and told him to let go. Both left and plunged into the canyon."

Johnson followed the stage to the next town of Belle Springs. There he found that Fanny had wrenched off one of her front shoes, and had torn the hoof badly on two sides.

"This seemed to put me in another bad fix; I became blue and despondent. What can I do, what can be done?"

The nearest blacksmith was 26 miles away. Pondering his troubles, he put up at the nearest hotel and found that the landlord (named Aldrich) hailed from Pomfret, Connecticut, and was quite familiar with Johnson's home town of Webster, Massachusetts.

Johnson was tempted to sell the horse and wagon after a fair offer, but

[249]

decided to make one more try to have the horse fixed up. He put a boot on Fanny's hoof and walked her to the blacksmith.

A typical day's travel would cover between 25 and 30 miles. During the late afternoon or early evening Johnson would pull into the best available spot for camping. Frequently he chose a large wheat field.

"I took some of the wheat, as if it were my own, and fed my animals," he wrote. "There was no one around. I could not see a house and had not passed one since leaving Latonville. I tied my animals fast to my wagon after their supper, and got my own supper, eating some cold roast elk venison, after which I prepared my bed for the night."

Now and then he was roused by the snorting of his horse. "My horse's ears were perched straight over her head as if in fear. I looked down the road and became convinced that there were some of those fellows around who are known as 'Infernals.' "

No one appeared, however, and Johnson continued his long journey. When possible, he followed the course of the Central Pacific Railroad—just in case anything happened to him "of a serious nature."

Bessie was milked twice a day and Johnson traded or sold the milk, often to thirsty train passengers at a railroad stop, or to a hotel. He steadily refused offers for the cow.

Most people thought he was insane to travel such a distance. After a while Johnson became used to hearing the same reactions. But the hospitality of people was something to marvel at. He was dined and often wined, and Bessie, Fanny and Bert were given the best available food.

Now and then Johnson ran into a genuine Easterner, and there was a reunion. Experience in travel taught him a few wise tricks. He estimated mileage by distance covered. In 10 hours he covered 25 miles. When going down a steep hill he blocked his wheels with a rope, giving him a measure of braking effect. He was impressed with seeing 16 horses harnessed to one wagon and three other wagons attached to that one, "a common mode of transportation."

Bessie was finally shod in Reno, Nevada. This relieved Johnson of that headache. He had four times used the Spanish method of heating a flat piece of iron and rubbing it over the hoof, but it had been only a temporary substitute for iron shoes.

In Reno, Johnson was interviewed by a reporter, who said after the interview: "Well, stranger, I hope you will succeed, if you do, you will stand on the top ladder of fame."

Wherever Johnson went he was recognized as The Man From the

West Who Was Traveling to the East. Hospitality was more bountiful than ever. Despite the offer of comfortable beds, Johnson stuck with his horse, cow and dog, in the same stable.

Finally, after stopping in Keene and Marlow, New Hampshire, to visit sisters, the weary traveler arrived in Worcester County on May 6, 1884. It had taken him nearly two years, and he had traveled more than 4500 miles.

Two miles from Webster, an escort of carriages met him and, farther on, a crowd on foot. Johnson was hailed as a hero in the town. The suggestion of writing a book was made and he decided to continue his trip to the ocean so he could call his work "From the Pacific to the Atlantic."

On June 14 he ducked into the water at Lynn. He had completed his incredible journey.

Later Johnson opened a meat market in Webster. He delivered orders with the same horse and wagon he used on his transcontinental trip.

He died on November 18, 1896, at 76.   END

Russia Paid Up

by Albert P. Hout

There is a Biblical proverb which teaches that much may be gained by practicing patience. And there are many who can testify to the truth of this beautiful old adage. But it took a stubborn New Englander, the Russian government, and ten long years of waiting to prove what a powerful force patience can actually be.

It all started on the morning of September 10, 1892, when Captain Scullum, Master of the whaleship *Cape Horn Pidgeon*, cruising for right whales in the Okhotsk Sea, was awakened by his first mate and told that the officer in charge of an armed party of Russian sailors had boarded his ship and was impatiently waiting on deck to see him.

The whaling skipper left his bunk and went on deck. While he rubbed the sleep from his eyes, he was rudely informed in broken English that he and his ship were unlawfully cruising in Russian waters.

Captain Scullum knew better. He had been hunting whales in the Okhotsk Sea for three years, and he was certain that his ship was well beyond the three-mile limit. He also knew that the Russians themselves had admitted to a British whaling captain 17 years before that their jurisdiction did not extend beyond that limit.

But when he tried to impart this information to the Russian officer, he was cut short and was told that he would have to set sail immediately for Vladivostok Harbor, where he could argue his case with the officials there.

Scullum, with typical American dislike for being pushed around, alerted his crew and started to arbitrate his case right there on deck. Then his native New England shrewdness took over, and he meekly followed the Russian ship to Vladivostok.

For nine long and weary days, the captain listened patiently as the Russians remonstrated with him about defiling their territorial waters. Then an admiral suddenly made his appearance and informed Scullum that he was free to go.

This is what Captain Scullum had been waiting for. The Russians had been very punctilious about foreigners invading their waters, and now they were freeing them without punishment. This, as Scullum saw it, was an admission on their part that the *Pidgeon* had not been hunting in Russian territorial waters at all.

Thanking the admiral for his kindness, the New Englander pointed out that, as he had respected the Russian's position by bringing his ship into Vladivostok at their request, it would only be fair for the Russians to respect his rights, too, and allow him to submit a bill for the expense he had incurred by staying in the harbor while his case was being adjudicated.

The admiral, feeling that he had nothing to lose, smilingly replied that if the captain would give the admiral an itemized bill, the admiral would see that it was submitted to his government.

Captain Scullum returned to his ship and made out the bill. The actual expense was really very little. But what made it so large was the reason the cagey New Englander had in mind when he submitted to the Russian officer's demands to accompany him to Vladivostok in the first place. His enforced delay had made it impossible for his ship to go north, complete his season's cruise, and get out before the ice set in.

There was no way of knowing what his catch would have been had he not been delayed. But instead of cluttering up the bill with a long list of estimates, Scullum simply figured up the value of what a good season's catch would have been and added it to the other expenses. At the bottom of the page, he wrote in large letters: *Payable in United States gold—* $49,500.

After placing the bill in the admiral's hands, Scullum returned to his ship and set sail for home. When the Russian admiral received the bill, he couldn't help noticing the figure at the bottom of the column; but he just smiled, filed the bill away, and promptly forgot it. Captain Scullum, however, did not.

Upon his return home, the whaling skipper allowed a reasonable length of time to elapse; then he referred the matter of the unpaid bill to the United States Minister to Russia. The Russians immediately started procrastinating. This was exactly what Scullum wanted them to do. For by doing so, they were admitting that the bill was legitimate, and that it would be paid at some future date.

Captain Scullum let a whole year slip by before asking the American Minister to remind the Russians again of their obligation. This time the Minister's prompting brought forth the reply that a committee had been appointed to look into the matter.

[253]

Another long silence followed, and Scullum needled them again. The Russians were happy to report that the committee had completed its investigation and that the *Cape Horn Pidgeon* had been released. Fine! answered Scullum. And now how about the bill? Another delay.

Scullum then let the Russians know that he was in no hurry, but he would never quit reminding them. Learning this, the Russians sent a note stating that after serious consideration, $25,000 seemed a more realistic figure than $49,500. Captain Scullum nonchalantly replied that he had not submitted a bargaining figure, but a legitimate bill. Please remit.

The Russians resumed their waiting game again. And Scullum, meanwhile, kept reminding them of their obligation. Two years later the Russians asked for expense vouchers. Scullum replied that vouchers had not been called for at the time of his detainment and that they were not available now. They retreated again.

Four more long years slipped by while the Russians tried to prove that they could be more stubborn than Scullum. They might have succeeded, too, had the captain hailed from some other part of the country. But the Russians—like Old Scratch before them when he crossed swords with Daniel Webster over the ownership of the soul of Jabez Stone—had to learn the hard way that God Almighty just didn't make men any more stubborn than New Englanders. And when this strategy failed, they tossed in the towel and agreed to arbitrate.

They were going down swinging, however, for the hearing was to be held in the Netherlands. This meant, of course, that counsel and witnesses would have to travel all the way from New England. The Russians should have known better by now; but they didn't, and counsel and witnesses were sent.

Finally, after 24 months of deliberation, more than ten years since the incident, the arbitrator decided in favor of Captain Scullum and ordered the Russians to pay the bill in full.

The Russians accepted the decision, but they let out a howl that could be heard all the way to Siberia when they found out that the final tab was $56,674.63, or $7,175.63 more than the original bill.

When they discovered the reason for the increase, they also found out why their opponent had been such a patient man. With true New England sagacity, Captain Scullum had been charging interest on the money all the time. END

One-Woman
Coast Guard Station

by Harriet Crowley

A while back, Madaket, the little community on the west end of Nantucket Island, was nothing but a Coast Guard station and a scattering of tiny houses. But the building boom finally reached it and now it has some large estates, lots of new shingled houses, some small cottages which rent by the week, and even a complex of cubist houses ironically called "Tristram's Landing."

The oldest part of the Island—Tristram Coffin landed Nantucket's first white settlers there in 1659—Madaket looks the newest in 1972. Everything is newly painted, newly shingled, clipped and tidy—everything, that is, except one tiny house and even tinier scallop shanty on the banks of Hither Creek near Madaket Harbor. The surrounding yard suggests the devastation left in the wake of a major hurricane. Boats of varying sizes, shapes and seaworthiness lie around, some upright, some on their sides. A big hunk of rusting metal is part of the fuselage of the Constellation which plunged into the sea off Madaket a few years ago, killing all twenty of the Air Force men aboard. The rickety fence is patched with packing cases, old planks, and whatever the sea may have washed up on the Madaket beaches. A gigantic pile of empty scallop shells takes up a good portion of the yard, and old, blackened bushel baskets are everywhere.

This is the home of Mildred Jewett, more often called Madaket Millie, and the closest to a Coast Guard station that Madaket has had since 1947. Though the official station was closed down in January of that year, anywhere Millie has happened to be has been, in effect, local headquarters of the United States Coast Guard.

Millie was so opposed to the closing of the station that when the *Kotor*, a Cunard-White Star freighter under Panamanian registry, went aground in a fog a few days later, Millie saw it as a sign from on high that the

Coast Guard should never have left Madaket. Paradoxically, the Coast Guard was so impressed with Millie's performance that it was more than ever convinced that no station was necessary with her around. The captain of the *Kotor* had erroneously reported that he was aground on Davis Shoal, 40 miles from Nantucket, and a fruitless search was going on in that area. The first the Coast Guard heard that the *Kotor* was aground right off Madaket was from Millie. Five rescue ships were dispatched to Madaket, and the freighter was soon pulled off the reef.

Commanding officers of the Brant Point Coast Guard Station in the town of Nantucket show their appreciation for Millie's unswerving devotion and vigilance by conducting ceremonies, writing letters, and bestowing rank. She is an honorary warrant officer. Millie has no car, but when she wants to go to town to market, two Coast Guardsmen in an official car come to get her, an event for which, instead of her usual wool stocking cap and hair in ponytail, she wears her officer's hat and lets her thick, curly brown hair streaked with gray hang loose.

"It has been a great comfort to know that you at all times were on the job for our common interests and safety of all the boatmen in the Madaket area," former commander A. B. Griggs wrote in a letter that Millie keeps in a double frame along with a picture of General Douglas MacArthur.

Frederick C. Coffin, Jr., another commander, wrote, "You are truly the eyes and ears of the Coast Guard at your West End Command."

Carl F. Josephson, now in command of the Nantucket station, says, "I don't have to worry about the West End of the Island with Millie there. Ninety-nine times out of a hundred when there's some sort of a situation out there that bears watching, we just call Millie and find that she's already got it under control. Recently a 30-foot cabin cruiser was reported missing. We had made the first preliminary checks and were about to embark on the active search with airplanes, ships, the whole bit, when Millie located it on Esther's Island. She does a great job."

Millie is a celebrity's celebrity. Many of the famous people who come to the Island find that the quickest way to get in tune with the simpler life is to visit Millie. She's as salty as that codfish packed in little wooden boxes. A few feet above high water mark is about as far from the sea as she ever strays. She's been off-Island three times in her whole life and not at all in the last quarter of a century. She's quiet and gentle with animals and children, loud and boisterous with adults; the more world famous they are, the more Millie enjoys brutal frankness and telling them that it

[256]

Mildred Jewett, otherwise known as Madaket Millie, in front of her scallop shanty. Note the gigantic pile of scallop shells. (Photo by C. W. Folger)

doesn't make any difference to her who they are. She made such a hit with Bea Lillie that every time the famous comedienne, in private life Lady Peel, comes to Nantucket, she goes out to Madaket for a visit with Millie. Millie's TV set was a gift from her.

Though Millie is intensely proud of her Coast Guard rank, she thinks of herself first of all as a dog trainer. After she had been turned down by all the services because of an eye weakness during World War II, she read of the Army's need for trained dogs. Starting with a chow-shepherd puppy, Millie trained around 20 dogs both for the Army and for the Coast Guard to use on beach patrol, and all at her own expense. In most cases, she even paid to ship her animals to Dogs for Defense in Dedham. She

"She can pick up wasps in her bare hands..."

successfully trained dogs that were considered too vicious to be taught anything. Millie gave up meat herself, as all her ration stamps were needed to get meat for the dogs. To pay for it, she worked at anything she could find. She dug wells and worked as a plumber, among other things.

Millie's way with animals and birds is so well known around Nantucket that strays are automatically brought to her. Fishermen who find an orphaned gray seal pup unhesitatingly rush it to Millie, knowing that she can save it if anyone can. (She has never yet succeeded because of the difficulty of obtaining as much pure whipping cream as it takes to nourish a baby seal.)

Children also take to her instinctively. Charles Folger, who took this picture of Millie, tells me that his friendship with Millie goes back to his toddler days. His mother used to take him out to Madaket to the little store Millie ran for ice cream or a soft drink—the tonic always came in a bottle with a ring of rust around it. Millie was his fast friend from the moment he met her.

Millie's uncanny relationship with animals as well as her prodigious strength and buoyant health have for years fascinated a St. Louis doctor who keeps his boat tied up at her place. Dr. Solley believes that she exerts some mysterious tranquilizing effect on animals. "Even on insects," he says. "She can pick up angry bees and wasps in her bare hands. They quiet down and never sting her."

He also thinks there is something exceptional about Millie's central heating system. "She walks around in a light cotton skirt and blouse even when the wind is blowing a cold blast off the water. When I say, 'Millie, you must be freezing,' she says, 'Hell no! I'm always too hot. That's my trouble.' I've seen her plunge her hands into the icy water of the creek, and when she brings them out they're steaming."

Dr. Solley has known Millie to leap into one of her boats and row across the harbor and back if she saw that someone was in trouble. Seeing a 300-pound blue nose shark foundering on a reef at low tide not far from where children were swimming, Millie grabbed a rake and a pitchwork, rowed out and killed the monster in a bloody battle. Her strength is legendary. There's the time she threw two men at once out of her store. Another time she relieved two Coast Guardsmen of a 283-pound log they were trying to shift, hoisted it onto her shoulders and carried it home.

She supports herself by opening scallops throughout the season, which lasts from the first of November through March. The Island tradition that she opens them so fast that three scallops are still in the air while she inserts the knife into a fourth is slightly exaggerated. But she is the undisputed queen.

She opened her first scallop at the age of seven after she and her father and older brother had come to Madaket from the town of Nantucket, where Millie was born in 1907. Millie's mother had left the Island never to return, and they lived with her Grandmother Jewett in Madaket. Her father was a fisherman, a scalloper, and a scallop opener. Much of Millie's education came from the books her grandmother used to read aloud while the men and the little girl opened scallops. School was in the town about eight miles away. When her father had the time, he would drive her there in the horse-drawn wagon.

In the mid-'30s her brother went to Alaska. In 1955 her father died. Millie lived alone in her father's house until new houses began to spring up, and buyers showed interest in her property. A builder, Elmore Taylor, dickered with Millie until finally a deal was made. In exchange for the land Millie owned, Taylor agreed to build her a house which she could live in for the rest of her life.

The snug little cottage that Mr. Taylor turned over to her was the first presentable home Millie had ever had. It was full of new, expensive furniture donated by friends and neighbors, who all rejoiced to see Millie with a decent home at last. There were new curtains at the windows, a $200 arm chair, a new bed, and a lot of other things, including the TV presented by Lady Peel.

Millie, however, was in no hurry to move in. The only thing she cared about was her ducks and what was going to happen to them. As they didn't fit into the new scheme of things on Hither Creek, Mr. Taylor said they had to go. He recalls that there were 125 of them and probably another 50–100 that weren't around when he counted. They were the progeny of a black duck and a mallard that Millie had befriended. When they finally were disposed of to people all over the Island, Mr. Taylor figured that not having to feed them the great quantities of grain that she had constantly lavished on them would leave her a nice hunk of cash to spend on her new house and herself. He and other Nantucketers expected Millie's new living arrangement to bring about revolutionary changes in her outlook and habits. They looked for her to become house proud. They even expected her to learn to treat money with due respect. Mr. Taylor and his workmen had been appalled when getting ready to tear down Millie's store (that had been vacant ever since the health authorities had made her close it because it didn't have running water). Millie would wander in and pick up a dusty envelope that had been lying on a shelf, along with others like it, for God knows how many years. She'd casually extract some money—perhaps a ten-dollar bill or two—and toss the envelope back on the shelf. All that would change, they thought, once Millie got the hang of her new way of life. With the income from opening scallops going up steadily as it has for the past few years (Island authorities estimate that she probably makes about $30 a day now), it was expected that Millie could have security, a bank account, and put something away for her old age. They looked for her to emerge as a sort of suburban business woman type.

People who come to Nantucket looking for local color and people like Charlie Folger who learned to love Millie as little children feel that her story has a happy ending. She never changed one iota. Respectability didn't even begin to take. She resisted moving into the house until Mr. Taylor threatened to cart her possessions that had been lying on the ground for two weeks off to the dump. Once in, Millie embarked on a successful campaign to age the property as fast as possible. Mr. Taylor now shakes his head and says it's hard to believe how new and fresh and pretty it was just a short time ago.

"That living room that goes clear across the front, why, all it is now is just a narrow aisle you can hardly slither through. It's that full of junk!"

They say that she keeps an anchor in the bathtub. But the things that really mean something to Millie are in perfect health or working order and in no danger of ever suffering from neglect. They are the scallop shanty and all the tools used in the trade, her five big dogs, including the 150-pound Newfoundland pup, whose silky black coat glistens with health, and the radio transmitter that keeps her in touch with the Coast Guard and therefore makes it safer for everyone in or on the water in the vicinity of Madaket. END

Legends
in Their
Own Time

SECTION
8

ROBERT ROGERS

Major Robert Rogers (Courtesy of the Vermont Historical Society)

Wabo Madahondo, The White Devil

by Simon Cameron

Atop the granite ridge the panther screamed just once—its cry in the cold December night was a banshee wail, the cry of a woman undergoing indescribable horror. Its effect upon the French sentinel at Fort Carillon (Ticonderoga) below was electric; he shuddered as he gazed nervously up into the blackness. He was newly arrived, this Parisian, handy in the lore of the old world and not the new. He knew he was frightened in the savage wilderness. He did not know he was about to join his ancestors.

The transition was simple.

A muscular, green-clad arm slithered wickedly out of the night. It encircled his throat, choking off his outcry. A knife ended his earthly connections, and this was fortunate indeed, for thus he did not feel his scalp being removed. Minutes later the indignant bawl of a cow was heard near the shore of Lake Champlain. Then silence, broken by a sudden rush and shouts of armed men within the fort.

Gloomily, the commanding officer looked at his dead sentinel. With equal gloom he heard of the disappearance of two others. But his anger exploded when he heard that a dozen cows had been stolen and butchered. Men were expendable—but food! He became apoplectic when he read the note found tied to the horn of a surviving cow: "I am obliged to you, sir, for the rest you have allowed me to take and the fresh meat you have sent me. I shall take good care of my prisoners. My compliments to the Marquis of Montcalm."

Naturally the signature was recognized. It was that of an ex-counterfeiter who two short years before had been threatened with the noose or the cropping of his ears as a common criminal in New Hampshire.

His name? "Major" Robert Rogers, the stalwart and wilderness-wise leader of Rogers' Rangers, a corps of hard-bitten commandoes formed during the French and Indian War to terrorize those supreme terrorists, the French and Indians of the north, and keep them back from the New England and New York frontiers.

Rogers did his job well; with but a handful of men, mostly of New Hampshire stock like himself, he kept the northern hordes in line, operating from his base in New York State, Fort William Henry at Lake George, where the Rangers first began writing history in blood.

His arrival at the fort in 1755 was not auspicious. Only months before he had been arrested on counterfeiting charges, placed under heavy bond and scheduled for trial at Portsmouth, New Hampshire. He escaped punishment when he was admitted as King's evidence—and when he gave valuable assistance in recruiting manpower for a regiment being formed by New Hampshire's Governor Wentworth, but it was a close shave, this brush with the noose. Thus when he came to New York State in his early twenties, with 50 men—part of the New Hampshire Provincial Regiment —he had not only lost a reputation but was faced with the difficult task of building one. Although called from the first "Rogers' Rangers," his men had volunteered for only a single campaign—against the French-held Crown Point, 43 miles to the north, on Lake Champlain. John Stark, a close friend of New Hampshire hunting days in the Goffstown and Merrimack River area, was Rogers' lieutenant, Abraham Perry his ensign, and Hugh Sterling his clerk. Later, when his corps became a distinct unit, his brother Richard joined and fought as a lieutenant.

The emergency of the times helped Rogers. The Crown Point campaign fizzled dismally. The French moved their southern frontier from Crown Point ten miles southward where they constructed Fort Carillon, later rechristened Fort Ticonderoga by the British.

Thirty-three miles to the south, at the head of Lake George, stood Fort William Henry, Britain's northernmost outpost in New York State. The troubled British needed scouts badly here, to furnish them with authentic reports on French activity. Since the enemy had noted bushrangers of their own, the man who was to lead British partisans had to be as bold, daring and ruthless. Who else but Rogers?

For a total salary of $7.75 a month, the Rangers dared more than the French. They faced brutal winter campaigns, the constant threat of injury without help, death in lonely places. And before them always loomed the threat of smallpox, scourge of the frontier.

A party of enemy Indians fell victim to the dread disease while in the vicinity of Fort William Henry. Wondering why these Indians made no attempt to drive off an attacking wolf pack, Joshua Goodenough and Shanks Shankland, New Hampshire Ranger privates, fired into the pack to disperse it, then realized why the Indians couldn't fight. With their teeth chattering in fear, they ran back to the fort with the chilling news. Rogers had it and survived. His brother had it and didn't; he is buried in the fort's cemetery, one of hundreds who succumbed to the smallpox. Captain Hobbs of Rogers' corps died. Taciturn John Stark, who also became a captain in the corps, contracted the disease and lived. Massachusetts-born Israel Putnam survived. Hundreds of regulars at the fort suffered over a period of time. The disease hovered ever near.

Throughout his first year at the fort, Rogers was busy recruiting, organizing and training. Sometimes there was rugged play. Wrestling was a popular sport, encouraged by the muscular Rogers, himself the New Hampshire champion, but was finally forbidden on the Sabbath. At first Rogers had mostly New Hampshire men to work with, many of them friends from his days of hunting, fishing, and trapping, but the corps also included Scotch-Irish, Irish, Germans, Dutchmen, Stockbridge (and later Mohegan) Indians, Spaniards, and a Negro. The preponderance of New Hampshire men was because Rogers constantly had recruiters busy in those home areas he knew so well. By dint of sheer personal dominance Rogers molded these Catawampus timber wolves into a solid fighting unit that dressed as it pleased and was not noted for discipline. (A year later

The Battle of Roger's Rock—the fight on snowshoes that nearly annihilated the Rangers. Rogers is shown right center. From a painting by J.L.G. Ferris. (Courtesy of the Glens Falls Insurance Co., a member of the Continental Insurance Companies)

*Abercrombie's 10,000 men crossing Lake George
before his futile assault against Ticonderoga.*

the Rangers proudly assumed their forest green uniform. Not until the
corps numbered in the hundreds was a Ranger ever lashed for disobedi-
ence.)

The British were of two minds about Rogers. Some liked him, some
didn't; his autocratic, aggressive bearing was balanced only by his abilities.
Sir William Johnson of Mohawk Valley fame, who built Fort William
Henry, admired him during those early years and used him often. George
Augustus, Lord Howe, a brilliant young British officer, learned the art of
forest fighting under Rogers and trained his well regimented army to fight
like Rogers' men. General James Abercrombie, Britain's pompous prize
bumbler, brought Rogers along in his 10,000-man, futile assault against
Ticonderoga. Lord Jeffrey Amherst, the great disciplinarian who believed
in the whip and the firing squad, used Rogers in his successful assault
against the French at Ticonderoga but coldly forbade the Rangers the
"pleasures" of scalping.

One of Rogers' most fabulous scouts took place in June, 1756. The
weather was hot and sticky. Fifty-one men rowed five heavy whaleboats
several miles northward from Fort William Henry. Landing at the base
of the mountain ridge, they shouldered their craft and for four days
played mountain goats with boats on their backs! They sweated, cursed
and floundered. But they moved the boats and their own war equipment

over an entire range, 3,000 feet up, and six miles across, to the South Bay of Lake Champlain, which at this point runs parallel to Lake George.

On Champlain's surface the going was smooth; the men rowed with hearty strokes, and the miles drifted behind. The Rangers saw a 100-boat flotilla bound for Ticonderoga, with General Montcalm, the most capable French soldier in America at any time, aboard. Once the Rangers were so near an enemy party that a sneeze would have ruffled French hair—and probably cost them their own. They scouted as far north as Buttonmould Bay, near the spot where 20 years later a Connecticut-born admiral named Benedict Arnold was to sink part of the first organized American Navy to keep it out of British hands.

They captured two armed bateaux, scaring the daylights out of the French by their sudden, ferocious appearance. Three of the French were killed, and two wounded, one badly. Rogers shook his head sympathetically and ordered him shot. Rice, flour, wheat and wine and brandy were found to constitute the bateau cargo. With their usual judgment in such cases, the Rangers sank the staples and the bateaux, sampled the beverages with considerable enjoyment, then cached the remainder with their whaleboats and returned to Fort William Henry on foot, 18 days after they had left, with four scalps, eight prisoners and, presumably, coated tongues. The French found the whaleboats months later and jumped immediately to the conclusion that Rogers had found a new, navigable channel into Champlain, which they then spent weeks trying to find.

Operation Whaleboat-over-the-Mountains meant much to Rogers. He was given the title of major, although he was not formally commissioned a Major of Rangers in His Majesty's Service until two years later.

Now the major was cutting a wide path. Glowing accounts of his scouts were circulating. His "criminal" background was forgotten. His tall, thick-nosed, black-browed figure drew stares from fascinated women as he stalked along the streets of Albany and New York City, and he drew the envy of fops. He drew grudging admiration from generals. He became the idol of British regulars and American provincials. His own men fought each other to join his scouting expeditions.

The French shared none of these feelings. By now Governor General Vaudreuil of Canada was furious at the depredations of the Rangers against Ticonderoga and Crown Point. He was losing too many supply trains, too many cattle, too many men. He ordered his brother, Rigaud, to attack the Fort William Henry hornets' nest, skimpily garrisoned then by 346 Irish regulars. The French were not unaware of Irish enthusiasm

The Binge that Backfired was

for their patron saint and planned a St. Patrick's Day battle. The Irish had their celebration through the night of March 17, 1757, staggered glassily through the 18th, and still sodden, flopped into bed the 19th.

(Thousands of rum bottle fragments found today in the fort area attest to the remarkable absorptive abilities of those who served.)

Rigaud, backed by 1,600 men, planned everything well, including his conduct at the surrender. He missed only one thing. While the Irish were intoxicated, Captain Stark of the Rangers refused his men liquid rations. Hence they were raging but cold sober when they spotted the French advance and prepared a suitable reception. They poured into the fort from their picket camp after saving a considerable amount of their "possessions," mostly rum. They dunked the Irish regulars into snow and sopped them sober. The French, expecting drunken snores, met the whine of lead instead. Rangers crawled from hospital beds, sick from scurvy and fever, to shoot crazily into enemy ranks. The bewildered French never did get to use their scaling ladders. Rigaud laid aside his dreams of surrender, ordered the Ranger camp outside burned, set fire to some beached boats, and retreated.

But the Binge that Backfired was humorous prelude to tragedy.

Five months later, Rogers was not present (he was busy fighting Britain's battle in Nova Scotia) when the infuriated but determined Montcalm fell upon Fort William Henry again, this time with 7,500 men—French regulars, Canadians, Hurons, Ottawas, Abnakis, and Praying Mohawks. Rangers, however, were at the stockade in force; others were at Fort Edward to the south, where the corps had a second encampment, for by this time it had grown into a sizable body. Twice during the battle the Rangers ran head-on against the French lines. Twice they were repulsed. The New Hampshire Provincials, many sick with smallpox, many wounded, suffered heavily. Ammunition ran out, cannon and mortars burst. The end was inevitable. When Montcalm offered "safe conduct" for disarmed survivors to Fort Edward, Colonel George Munro, the British commander, surrendered.

At the garrison, as the hundreds of men, women and children filed out, there was a sudden and horror-laden silence; the Indians, drunk on rum, were watching them like predatory hawks. The English noted that Montcalm had assigned Canadians, *not* French regulars, to guard the column.

It didn't take long. The Indians pounced, and the butchering began. The hospital was invaded, the patients killed. Indians chased survivors into the woods, running men and screaming women down like panthers. (Skeletons are still unearthed a half mile from the fort.)

Wise in Indian ways, the weaponless Rangers moved fast when the first whoop sounded. But when a New Hampshire giant, Ben Richards, saw an Indian snatch a small boy, he knocked the savage senseless, grabbed the youngster and ran to safety. John McKean of Amoskeag was not so fortunate; he was captured and tortured.

The Indians went to grisly extremes. Disturbing fresh graves, they scalped those within for the bounty. For this defilement they paid heavily; they contracted smallpox and carried the disease to Canada. One nation was almost wiped out by this macabre uppercut from the dead.

When Rogers returned from the Cape Breton area in Nova Scotia, and heard of the tragedy, he became a man possessed. Four months later, with only 150 Rangers, he halted 600 yards from the great gray stone fortress of Ticonderoga. With unparalleled daring he defied the entire garrison to come out and fight, but his challenge failed. So did his attempt to ambush. The French were not to be drawn. A few prisoners were captured, some cows—that was all.

Four months later, this incredible New Hampshire man returned to the French lines on orders from Colonel William Haviland, Fort Edward commander whom Rogers had reason to believe hated him. There must have been something to this, because when Rogers asked for more men for the foray, Haviland refused to supply them. So with 180 of his green-clad companions, Rogers marched into one of the most vicious battles of his career. On March 13, 1758, after scouting on skates, the Rangers took to snowshoes along a mountain ridge on Lake George's west side.

With animal instinct, Rogers smelled danger. The first contact with the enemy ended victoriously; the Rangers savagely routed 100 Canadians and Indians in four feet of snow. But moments later they collided with 600 more. For ferocity, the Battle on Snowshoes has seldom been equalled; men rolled in the snow, growling animal noises, shouting commands, loading and firing guns, and when these were useless, splintering them in tremendous blows. Isolated Rangers who surrendered were tied to trees and hacked to death. Only Rogers and a few others escaped. Montcalm was presented with 144 scalps.

Shaken and battered, Rogers left the hellish scene and made his way to the top of the precipice known today as Rogers Rock, 1,000 feet above Lake George. He tossed his pack down the steep incline. Reversing himself on his snowshoes he backtracked his own trail a distance, grabbed an overhanging limb and swung into a gully. Then he descended to the lake below. When the superstitious Indians arrived at the edge of the cliff, they saw the pathway cut by the skidding pack. In the twilight, they saw Rogers far below. Assuming that only a man protected by a higher power could have survived that precipitous descent, they abandoned the chase. Rogers was safe.

Four months later he returned to Ticonderoga with Abercrombie's 10,000. Of that number, 2,000 were killed in the inept British attack against the fort. The Black Watch Regiment was almost wiped out. Lord Howe, second in command, died in Rogers' arms. Abercrombie, in retreating down the lake in hundreds of boats, lost enough equipment to literally pattern the bottom. Divers are still bringing up cannon, anchors and other equipment, heaved frantically overboard to lighten loads as the men made their way back to their muster point—the ruins of Fort William Henry.

The astonishing saga of Rogers' early years does not end here. One year later he fought once again at Ticonderoga, this time under Lord Amherst. The British lion was roaring. The coldly efficient British nobleman had welded his forces into unity with lashings and executions. Moving swiftly, Amherst took Ticonderoga and moved on to Crown Point; again the French retreated, this time into their Canadian sanctuary. The French dream of empire in America collapsed.

Robert Rogers' most daring expedition is generally considered to be the raid on the Abnaki Indian village at St. Francis. After capturing Fort Ticonderoga and sending the French scurrying back to their stronghold at Isle-aux-Noix on the Richelieu River about ten miles north of Lake Champlain, Lord Amherst sent a party headed by Captains Kennedy and Hamilton to propose a truce to the St. Francis tribe of Abnakis. This tribe had been inflicting grievous wounds on English settlements for 50 years and was known for the savage deeds of its warriors. It was the Ab-

The massacre at Fort William Henry in 1757.
"The Indians went to grisly extremes ..."

nakis who had burned Rogers' own family cabin to the ground when he was a child, and he cordially hated them.

Instead of discussing a truce, the Abnakis made prisoners of Amherst's emissaries. Enraged, Amherst dispatched Rogers and 200 of his Rangers to destroy the Indian village.

The band left Crown Point by boat September 13, 1759, traveling up Lake Champlain by night to avoid the French patrol boats. After ten days, they reached the northern end of the lake, and abandoned their boats, leaving them camouflaged in the custody of two trusted Stockbridge Indians at Missisquoi Bay. The Stockbridge Indians caught up with the Rangers again just two days later with the news that a strong force of French and Indians had found the boats and supplies and were hotfoot on Rogers' trail.

Major Rogers, never one to turn back, merely increased his pace, reaching St. Francis on October 4, to find 600 Abnaki Indians wildly celebrating the safe return of a war party. After scuttling the Abnaki canoes, the Rangers lay hidden until dawn, when they attacked with savagery equal to the Abnakis' own. Despite Lord Amherst's explicit directions, not even women and children were spared once the Rangers caught sight of the hundreds of bloody English scalps drying on racks before the Indian tents.

As the merciless battle waned, so the legend goes, a voice rose from a heap of voiceless Indian bodies, saying: "The Great Spirit of the Abnakis

[271]

will scatter darkness in the path of the accursed Palefaces! Hunger walks before, and Death strikes their trail! Their wives weep for warriors that do not return! Manitou is angry when the dead speak! The dead have spoken!"*

Much of this prophecy was fulfilled by the dreadful hardships encountered by the band of Rangers on their way back to Crown Point, so well described by Kenneth Roberts in his *Northwest Passage*. Yet this was undoubtedly the high point of Rogers' active career. With only 142 of the original party of 200 Rangers at his back, Wabo Madahondo (Rogers' Indian title—the White Devil) had carried out his orders "to disgrace the enemy" despite odds of more than two to one.

Feted as a popular hero at the end of the French and Indian War, Rogers' fortunes were from then on to take a downward course. By the time of the Revolution, he was well on his way to becoming a sodden and useless wreck. He did little, even for the British, to whom he offered his services during that war.

A man is best remembered for his finest. Few now recall Robert Rogers' decline and fall. His image is based on those brilliant early years, when he helped lay the foundations of what was to become America, cementing them in blood and courage as the intrepid leader of America's Goliaths in Green—Rogers' Rangers!   END

* Drake in *Heart of the White Mountains*, quoted in Robert E. Pike, "The Lost Treasure of St. Francis" in *A Treasury of Vermont Life*, Stephen Greene, Arthur W. Peach, Ralph N. Hill, Walter Hard, Jr., eds., Woodstock, Vermont. The Countryman Press, 1956, pp. 170–172.

Alias Captain Thunderbolt

by W. A. Swanberg

When Dr. John Wilson arrived in Dummerston, Vermont, in 1818, he immediately became a fascinating local mystery. This was partly because no one knew anything of his background except that he had come from England, and he did not choose to discuss that matter. An equally compelling reason was his handsomeness and distinction. He was about 35, a six-footer, straight as a ramrod, elegantly attired, and polished but kindly in address. "He was decidedly the finest looking man I ever saw," a neighbor later recalled, "and this, joined to his gentlemanly bearing, suavity of manners, extensive knowledge, ease and grace in conversation, mingled with his Scottish brogue, rendered him utterly charming."

The question was, why did such a man, who could have built a thriving practice in Boston or London, come to remote Dummerston?

Wilson resided in the village at the home of Peter Wellman. He was simultaneously a joy and a torment to the Wellmans—a joy because of his charm and a torment because they were dying to know more about him. He talked wonderfully about English society and politics, but never a word about his own history, and there was something in his manner that forbade questioning on this point. His patients swore by him, not only because he always knew the right medicines for them but also because he could simply *talk* to an ailing person in such a warm, kindly way that it made him feel better instantly. But Dummerston's population was so small and so generally healthy that he had to fill out his income by teaching school during the winter months.

The doctor had a few puzzling eccentricities. When someone knocked at the door, he would leave the room at once until he made sure who was calling. He was never seen without a silk scarf around his neck, although this was not then in vogue, and he was a man of fashion in every other respect. He was not averse to a toddy, and indeed there were a few occasions when he came home very late at night and had quite a bit of difficulty negotiating the stairs to his room.

"There was a mystery hanging about the man," a chronicler wrote. "Many supposed that he was *constrained* to leave his native country; but why or wherefore no one could tell."

For all that, such was his attraction that several local belles set their caps for him. He was invited to every quilting bee in the neighborhood. It was observed that "the ladies would persuade him (though he was always very reluctant) to dance; and it almost always happened that he would fall to the floor before he got through the twistings and turnings of a contra dance." Even this did not disturb his aplomb, for he always arose and dusted himself off with a jest at his own clumsiness. Accomplished though he was in every other way, he was a bit stiff-legged and awkward at dancing.

Several feminine hearts were saddened when Dr. Wilson left Dummerston about 1823 and hung out his shingle a few miles north in Newfane. Here he was said to have done very well as a physician despite his increasing predilection for the "ardent." It appears that on some occasions he made his calls in a condition so unsteady as to bring uneasiness to his patients. Still, he was widely admired, and there was general regret when he moved on to Brattleboro in 1835, a much larger center, where he could expect a handsome practice if he could keep the cork from parting company too often with the bottle.

In Brattleboro it was the same story all over again—the story of a man of marvelous magnetism and ability who was yet so little known that he became the town's ranking mystery. He said never a word about his own personal history, or what it was that caused him to leave his homeland. He still wore the neck scarf, winter and summer. As always, he fascinated women, and when he married a Miss Chamberlain a year later there were a number of other young ladies who felt they would have made him a much better mate.

The Wilsons had a son, after which the cork began squeaking again. Whether it was the drinking that caused unpleasantness between the

[274]

"A six-footer, straight as a ramrod."

couple, or unpleasantness that caused the drinking, the result was that Mrs. Wilson left the doctor, taking the little boy with her. A year or so later, she died, after which Wilson took over his son and cared for him with great affection, doing his own cooking. Now and then he could be heard playing the bagpipes in his sitting room. It was known that for a time he had a mistress, a pretty young woman who lived alone on the west side of town.

In his sixties, Wilson was still a fine figure of a man, meticulously dressed, distinguished in every word he spoke and every movement of his tall frame. Although he was at times somewhat the worse for rum, his gentility never deserted him, and his practice, if not wealthy, was at least considerable. There were those who said they would rather trust Dr. Wilson drunk than any other physician sober. Had any other doctor carried on the way he did, he would doubtless have been ostracized. Wilson had become a Brattleboro institution, discussed over every dinner table. The truth was, the town was proud of harboring such an accomplished eccentric, a man who would have been perfectly at home in Harley Street or the Back Bay. But what—oh, what?—was the reason for his abandonment of

[275]

such urban centers and his flight into the remoteness of Vermont? Was he perhaps stricken by some personal tragedy? Or had he become involved in some scandal or crime?

In mid-May of 1847, Dr. Wilson, then believed to be in his late sixties, came down with an ailment that is not recorded. He summoned another doctor and a friend. Strangely, they found him fully clothed in bed, *even to his shoes*. Instead of a nightgown, he was clad in a suit made by Brattleboro's best tailor, and his neck was covered by the usual silk scarf.

Despite their ministrations, it soon became apparent to Wilson himself that he was not long for this world.

"I know it may seem somewhat notional," he said to his two friends, "but I believe a man should be humored in his last request. I wish to be buried as I am now, fully clothed, scarf, shoes and all. I am insistent on the point that my clothing not be removed. I rely on you both to see that this stipulation be followed to the letter."

After he died, however, it was pointed out that he could not be washed, embalmed and given a Christian burial if his clothes were left on. Also, if the truth were known, the citizens were almighty anxious to know *why* he was so set on this matter, and whether he had something to conceal. He was undressed by a local undertaker.

On the side of his neck, which had been covered by the scarf, was a long, livid scar, apparently from a sword or knife wound suffered years earlier. It was discovered that his left leg was withered, the result of some childhood paralysis. The calf of the same leg bore the scar of a bullet wound. Dr. Wilson had concealed the shrunken condition of the leg by wrapping it with paper wadding, which was tied in place with two silk handkerchiefs. Part of the left heel was gone, also the result of a bullet wound. To compensate for the missing part of the heel, he had worn a thick wedge of cork in his shoe.

This explained why he had occasionally fallen down while dancing. Indeed, the doctor was quite lame, the amazing thing being that he had been able to hide his lameness, betraying not the slightest limp—a feat he could have accomplished only by stern will power and constant effort.

More puzzling yet was why he had gone to such lengths to conceal his lameness and also the wound on his neck. In view of his refusal to discuss his past, there was a feeling that these identifying marks might connect

[276]

John Doherty, alias Captain Thunderbolt.

him with some crime committed earlier in his career.

The local sheriff, on going over old descriptions of wanted men, made an amazing discovery. Dr. Wilson—right down to the neck scar, withered leg and cork heel—answered perfectly the description of the notorious Captain Thunderbolt, the most feared highwayman in the United Kingdom earlier in the century.

Born John Doherty in Scotland, he had made Ireland the scene of his most daring exploits. A lone brigand, he was famous not only for his depredations but also for his handsomeness and eccentricities. When he held up a coach, for example, he would treat his victims with the greatest courtesy, rob only the gentlemen, kiss the women, and then be off, riding his horse like a centaur. His name being unknown, he came to be called Captain Thunderbolt because of his lightning raids. He seemed to like the title, for he adopted it, never failing to tell his victims that they had the distinction of being robbed by Captain Thunderbolt.

Something of a Robin Hood, he often gave his profits to the poor. Although his description was posted at every inn in the south of Ireland, he led a charmed life. In 1808, in a tavern near Dublin, he met Michael Martin, a young rascal from Kilkenny. He took a liking to Martin, who thereafter became his associate in crime. Thunderbolt, who regarded robbery as an adventurous and honorable career, was so impressed by his younger colleague that he adopted him as partner in a peculiar ceremony. He dashed a glassful of brandy in Martin's face, saying, "Henceforth you shall be known as Captain Lightfoot."

[277]

Michael Martin, alias Captain Lightfoot.

The pair became noted for their reckless and ingenious methods of crime. On one occasion, near Kilkenny, they held up a coach, forcing each passenger to come out and clapping handcuffs on each of them in turn before robbing them individually. The constabulary and soldiery were hot on their heels, thirsting for the reward. But while Thunderbolt and Lightfoot were being hunted on the highways, they were busy robbing the till at a tavern, and when pursuers arrived at the tavern the two villains were busy looting the mansion and purse of a nearby country squire.

There were many narrow escapes. Thunderbolt sometimes wore the garb of a priest to escape detection, and he could discuss religion like a professor. During one period when pursuit was warm, the pair fled to the north of Ireland, where Thunderbolt set up in practice as a physician. Lightfoot noted that although he had no medical training, he cared for the sick with the skill and assurance of the most practiced sawbones.

But the lure of adventure soon took the two pistoleers back to their lawless ways. Once, Captain Thunderbolt was shot in the leg as he and Lightfoot fled the police. Later, in hiding, Thunderbolt showed himself almost immune to pain as Lightfoot, with a penknife, removed the ball from the wounded leg. Not once did the pair use their guns for anything more than a threat. Yet, so enraged were the authorities at their incessant crimes that they would have been speedily hanged had they been caught.

The robberies continued until 1817, when, for reasons unknown, they stopped. It was theorized that one or both of the highwaymen had been killed or died of disease.

[278]

The hanging of Captain Lightfoot in Cambridge, Massachusetts.

This was not the case. After a robbery in Dublin, the two desperadoes became separated as they fled. Lightfoot, or Martin, searched for his mentor vainly for days. Ultimately he gave up, took passage for America, and resumed his larcenous career. Skillful as he was, he lacked the finesse of Thunderbolt. In 1821, he robbed one Major Bray in his carriage near Dedham, Massachusetts. Going on to Springfield, Martin was recognized and arrested. Returned to Cambridge for trial, he was soon convicted and hanged—but not before he had told the whole story of his career of crime with Captain Thunderbolt, alias John Doherty.

Now, in Brattleboro, it was seen that Martin's description of Thunderbolt tallied in every way with that of Dr. John Wilson. Even the scar on the late doctor's leg was identical with the one described by Martin, who had cut the ball out with a penknife. Dr. Wilson had arrived in America in 1818, not long after the depredations in Ireland ceased.

The citizens of Brattleboro were willing to lay a pound against a shilling that Dr. Wilson was none other than Captain Thunderbolt. Without a medical degree, he had tended the sick in three Vermont towns for 29 years with what they still regarded as great skill.

What had caused his reformation? No one could answer that question. "But truly," as a local newspaper said with admirable restraint, "there is much romance in real life."   END

Larry Lajoie, Babe Ruth's choice as second baseman for his all-time, all-star team. (*Courtesy of the National Baseball Hall of Fame*)

New England's Greatest Baseball Player

by John U. Ayotte

Napoleon Lajoie was the greatest baseball player born in New England. There have been greater ballplayers—at most three or four—but they were not natives of the Northeast. Lajoie was both an outstanding batter and a superb fielder; with. one possible exception, the best second baseman ever to step on the diamond. But he first came to my attention, not because of his power hitting or uncanny fielding skill, but because he had published a book.

At the time, I was 12 years old and attending a country school. In those far-off days, long before the advent of the Little Leaguers, our low-echelon baseball was conducted without benefit of coaching or adult supervision. Occasionally, we met outside teams, but mostly our games were "choose up" affairs within the school. Our shallow outfield was bounded by a strip of woods, where the ground was always a tangle of dead leaves. Whenever a drive landed in the leafy jungle, the game was automatically halted while all hands searched for the missing ball. Another frequent source of delayed games stemmed from disputes over baseball rules; rules none of us had ever read. Thus it was, one April afternoon when I had a few coins in pocket, that I went to buy a copy of the rules. These I had learned could be found in a book called a baseball "guide," an annual publication, on sale for ten cents at the nearest drugstore.

As I remember, the standard baseball guide of the day was a publication of the A. J. Reach Company, but that spring (1906) a rival guide had appeared, and it was a copy of the newcomer that I bought: a paperback of some 150 pages, small enough to fit a fair-sized pocket. The blue cover featured a tall, handsome player in uniform, with the word CLEVELAND emblazoned on his shirt front. He grasped a formidable bat, and beneath the photograph was the modest caption: "Napoleon Lajoie, Champion Batter of the World."

The rules section of the book was more detailed than I had expected. It seemed to contain everything from instructions for laying out a playing field to the startling information that the home team should have at least two dozen baseballs on hand at the beginning of a game. But the rules section proved to be only a small part of a fascinating volume. The co-authors were Napoleon Lajoie, manager and second baseman of the Cleveland American League Club, and M. A. Bobrick, who was, I believe, a Cleveland sports writer.

Hitherto I had paid scant attention to the sports section of the daily paper. The names of players, whatever their team or league, meant nothing to me. Now the Lajoie-Bobrick pages opened my eyes to a new and exciting vista, the world of professional baseball.

The volume began with a short biography of Napoleon Lajoie—"Larry" to his friends and associates—born in Woonsocket, Rhode Island, September 5, 1875. At the age of 20, while playing with Fall River in the New England League, he had been purchased by the Philadelphia National League Club. Although the league sparkled with star ballplayers, among them Hugh Duffy, Ed Delehanty, Jesse Burkett and Willie Keeler, the recruit from Fall River soon acquired an outstanding reputation. In 1901, the American League achieved equality with the National as a major league and, in a two-year baseball "war," set up rival teams in five cities formerly the exclusive territory of the older league. Higher pay lured many National League players into the ranks of the American; among them was Lajoie, who "jumped" to Connie Mack's Philadelphia Athletics for a salary of $4000, nearly twice the highest amount ($2400) then paid to any National League player. That season Lajoie led his league with a batting average of .422, making 220 hits in 521 times at bat. His former owners next secured an injunction against his playing with any other team than the Philadelphia Nationals, but as the court had no jurisdiction outside of Pennsylvania, the American League transferred its star second baseman to Cleveland, where he received a four-year contract at $7500 a season, and also acquired a citation for contempt of court, of which he was later purged when the National League made peace with its American rival.

At Cleveland, the New England-born ballplayer won two more batting championships in 1903–04, and at the opening of the 1905 season became team manager. In 1906, his baseball guide fresh on the market, Lajoie sought a pennant for his club and another batting title for himself. Both

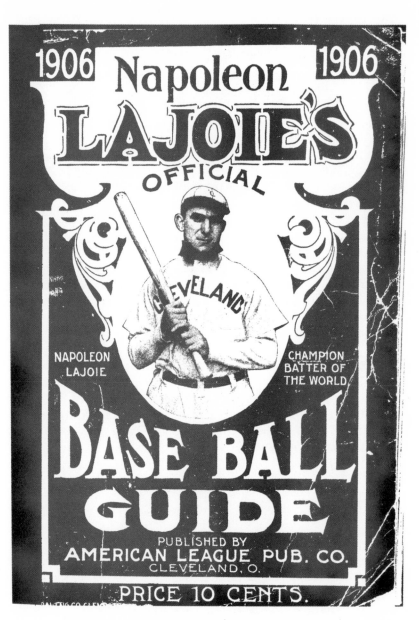

*Lajoie's "little blue book," published in 1906.
(Courtesy of the National Baseball Hall of Fame)*

[283]

had eluded him the previous year when, with his team in first place and his average topping all batters in the league, he had been forced to quit the game in mid-season due to a spike wound.

From the Lajoie biography, the authors went on to give detailed accounts of the 1905 pennant races and the ensuing World Series, when McGraw's New York Giants had beaten the Philadelphia Athletics, four games to one. This was the only World Series from 1903 to this writing (1968) in which every game was a shut-out, and no batter made a longer hit than for two bases. As Bob Gibson and Mickey Lolich dominated the scene in the autumn encounters of '67 and '68, so did Christy Mathewson stand out in the 1905 Series, blanking the Mackmen in three games.

There were also many pages of statistics, including the batting and fielding averages of every big leaguer, and a long array of photographs.

Four sections of the guide gave advice to aspiring ballplayers. "How to Bat," by Lajoie, laid down eight, or it may have been nine, rules for the hitter to follow. Study and attempted application of these rules failed to transform me into a boy batting wonder, but they did make me less vulnerable when I came to the plate. Some years later, when I first saw Lajoie, I had already seen several of the era's best hitters, and I have seen many more great batters since, but none had the easy grace, the timing and the coordination of the boy from Rhode Island, then Cleveland's second baseman, and none could hit so hard with so little apparent effort.

Grantland Rice, a rising young sports writer, was represented by various bits of poetry (using the term in its broadest sense) scattered throughout the guide. Overexposed to the verse of John Greenleaf Whittier, Rice's catchy, slangy idiom had its peculiar appeal in stanzas such as this from "The Alphabet of Balldom:"

> L for Larry Lajoie must stand,
> The kingpin of the nation's greatest game;
> In Balldom's vast brigade,
> He's the star of the decade,
> His prowess with the bludgeon brought him fame.

Having mastered the contents of the guide, I fancied myself an expert on the current major league races. Primarily, I wanted a pennant for Cleveland and another batting championship for Lajoie, but neither hope was realized. Each year Cleveland made a gallant fight, but always lost out in the closing weeks of the season, usually because of injuries to key players. I recall my indignation in 1907 when Unglaub, a dastardly Red

...none could hit a ball so hard...

Sox infielder, collided with Lajoie and put him out of action for several weeks. Unglaub's spikes did not prevent the Cleveland leader from hitting the American League's only grand-slam homer of the year, but they probably did ruin his team's chances for the pennant. In 1909, after Cleveland had finished second, half a game behind Detroit, the previous season, he resigned as manager.

In 1906, Lajoie lost the league batting championship to George Stone by three points. The next year, Tyrus Raymond Cobb, Detroit's 20-year-old outfielder, won the first of his 12 batting titles, nine of them in succession. Managerial worries had not helped Lajoie's play, but in 1910 he battled the Georgia Peach to a sensational finish. More than the championship was at stake; the Chalmers Company had promised an automobile to the winning batter in each major league. An outcry rose from the Cobb partisans when, in a double-header at St. Louis on the last day of the season, Lajoie bunted safely six times. It was alleged that the St. Louis manager had ordered rookie third baseman "Red" Corriden to play deep against the right-handed Lajoie, thus allowing him to bunt with impunity. The clamor subsided when Cobb was found to have won by a fraction of a point, .385 to .384 plus, and that the Chalmers Company would give a prize car to each of the rivals.

The circumstances at St. Louis were suspicious, but the Browns' manager may well have done nothing more than protect his inexperienced third baseman. Infielders and pitchers were particularly careful when facing Lajoie; only those who saw him in action can appreciate the force of his line drives and grounders; the ball came off his bat as if shot from a cannon.

On the one occasion when I talked at some length with Napoleon Lajoie, the St. Louis episode was fairly recent history, and I did not presume to ask for his version of the incident, nor did I venture to inquire how he had liked the bitterly-fought-over Chalmers.

Although he continued to hit well, the aging Lajoie never came close again to wresting the batting title from Cobb. After 13 seasons at Cleveland, the Rhode Islander went back to the Athletics for the last two of his 21 major league years. In 1917 he played with Toronto in the International League and closed his baseball career the next year with Indianapolis in the American Association.

Lajoie's big league lifetime batting average was .339. Cobb ended with

[285]

a .367 average, Hornsby with .358, and Ted Williams with .344. All three, however, had the advantage of playing under conditions more favorable to the batter than obtained during Lajoie's best baseball years. The man from Woonsocket scored a ten-point higher average than his contemporary, Wagner, but "The Flying Dutchman" won eight batting championships, second only to Ty Cobb in this respect. As a matter of comparison, at the beginning of the 1968 season, three of today's veteran hitters had the following lifetime averages: Hank Aaron, .316, Willie Mays, .309, and Mickey Mantle, .302.

Lajoie won three batting titles and missed two others by very narrow margins. No American League hitter has equalled his .422 average of 1901, and since that year, only Rogers Hornsby has done better in the National League with .424 in 1924. Lajoie is one of nine men in the history of baseball who have made 3000 or more hits; the first of these was Adrian (Cap) Anson, the Chicago star of the 1880s and '90s, and the latest (as of 1973), Roberto Clemente of the Pirates. Hitters of the stature of Ruth, Hornsby, and Ted Williams failed to qualify for this exclusive "club," although in justice to Williams it must be said that his batting record would have been even more outstanding had he not sacrificed four of his best playing years in the military service of his country.

Baseball is, however, a game nicely balanced between offense and defense, and very few of the greatest wielders of the bat—including Cobb, Hornsby, and Williams—have been equally good with glove or mitt. Lajoie was a shining exception. Although he played at times in the outfield and at first base, he was primarily a second baseman. A big man, he moved on the diamond with the smooth agility of a cat, and handled the hardest fielding chances with consummate ease. He usually fielded ground balls hit to his left with one hand; a technique which, at least in his case, made for quicker and smoother action than if he had played the grounder with both hands.

Among the great second basemen, only one can be considered a close rival of Lajoie. Eddie Collins, a faster man, covered more ground; whether he covered it as well as Lajoie is a moot question. Connie Mack and Ty Cobb considered Collins the better baseman; John J. McGraw gave him a slight edge. Babe Ruth, on the other hand, picked Lajoie as second baseman for his all-time, all-star team.

Lajoie was never with a major league pennant winner. Had he been purchased by Boston, instead of Philadelphia, in 1896, he would have played on the 1897–98 Boston championship team. Then in all likelihood he would have "jumped" with Jimmie Collins and Edward Lewis (later President of the University of New Hampshire), in 1901, to the newly organized Boston Red Sox. There he would have helped to win five pennants and four World Series. On the other hand, if the ill-advised legal action of the owners of the Phillies had not driven him from the Athletics to Cleveland, he could have played on six championship teams and in five World Series.

*   *   *   *   *

The 1906 baseball guide—that happy creation of Napoleon Lajoie and M. A. Bobrick—eventually broke apart and disappeared. Gradually the players, whose pictures had graced its pages, dropped from team rosters, and then began to vanish from life itself. In the 1950s, several of the more illustrious died: "Cy" Young, victor of 511 major league pitching duels; Hans Wagner of the eight batting championships; and Connie Mack, winner of nine pennants, and manager of the Philadelphia Athletics for 50 years. On February 7, 1959, the "Bonaparte of Batsmen" passed from the scene. Apparently on the way to recovery from an attack of pneumonia, Lajoie died suddenly in a Daytona Beach hospital in his 84th year.

Among the thousands who have worn big league uniforms, from the time of A. G. Spalding and Ross Barnes to the day of Mickey Mantle and Carl Yastrzemski, where does Lajoie rank? There have been, in my opinion, only three players who were greater, and none of these by any very marked degree of superiority. Ty Cobb, one of the greatest of baserunners, played in the American League for 24 years and wound up with an average of .367. Babe Ruth, one of the greatest of hitters, set a home-run mark which probably will never be equalled, was an outstanding defensive player, and in his first years with the Red Sox a very capable pitcher. Wagner, the game's greatest shortstop, was Lajoie's peer at bat and in the field, and was a faster and better baserunner. Pitchers I have not considered; they are specialists who must be rated within their own class. There is no common yardstick to measure the achievements of Lajoie and Walter Johnson, of Ted Williams and Robert Feller, of Willie Mays and Bob Gibson. Nor can we ever know how Ruth the homerun hitter would have fared against Ruth the southpaw.

If New England's greatest native-born baseball player were alive today and active in the game, there would be less talk about the supremacy of the pitcher and the decadence of modern batting. For as Ty Cobb wrote, not long before his death, with the lively ball Larry Lajoie would have been a .450 hitter!   END

[287]

Chess Tyro Who
Beat the Masters

by Bartlett Gould

It was somehow fitting that 1972, the year Bobby Fischer finally squared off against Boris Spassky for the world's chess championship, marked the 100th anniversary of the birth of an imperturbable New England genius who blazed across the chess world like a supernova and like a supernova went into early and tragic decline. But for a few short years his light was the brightest of all.

Harry Nelson Pillsbury was born in Somerville, Massachusetts, on December 5, 1872. His parents were ordinary middle-class citizens with no wild talents lurking in the family tree. Harry was to all appearances a normal boy, perhaps a bit brighter than average but not enough to occasion comment. With no special predilection for any profession, he planned to attend business school to fit himself for a commercial career.

Then on Thanksgiving Day, 1888, someone introduced him to chess. It was like the first taste of honey to a young bear; within a few hours, the world of stocks and bonds had lost him forever.

When Pillsbury enrolled in a Boston business school, his first act was to join the Deschapelles, one of the city's livelier chess clubs. Then, hearing that they played a lot of chess at the Y.M.C.U., he began dropping in there. The rest of his spare time was spent at Van Doren's Chess Divan. The club experts beat him easily at first, but the enthusiastic tyro improved with incredible rapidity. Soon he was beating *them.*

These successes simply whetted Pillsbury's appetite and, in 1892, he decided to challenge John Barry, for many years New England's No. 1 player.

Although it was obvious that Pillsbury fairly oozed talent, the experts considered him still too inexperienced to be a serious threat. The opinion seemed justified when Barry won the first four games; but then Pillsbury overcame his stage fright and proceeded to pulverize the astonished Barry five straight to win the match.

It was at about this time that the world champion, Wilhelm Steinitz, paid a visit to Boston.

Steinitz was a short, heavy-set, near-sighted man with a flowing beard and a talent for invective that had earned him a reputation for being difficult. He wrote much on chess and loved a fight; when lesser lights ventured to criticize his style of play he took great satisfaction in lambasting them on the printed page.

Actually, although he kept it pretty well concealed, Steinitz had a large fund of kindness and good nature. He agreed to play a three-game match with the eager young Pillsbury, giving him the odds of a pawn. As Steinitz was capable of giving most experts greater odds than this with impunity, it was a feather in Pillsbury's cap when he won the match.

The World Champion was impressed, and predicted a brilliant future for his youthful antagonist.

This was all the encouragement Pillsbury needed. He dropped any vague plans he might have had for a business career with as much alacrity as he would have dropped a live cobra, and went into chess full time.

The life of a chess professional cannot be recommended as a quick route to wealth, and in Pillsbury's day it was even less lucrative. There were a handful of celebrated masters who received appearance money for playing in tournaments, gave lessons, wrote articles about chess and would, for a fee, visit a club and put on a simultaneous exhibition against the members.

Pillsbury, only 20 years old and with no tournament reputation, would have been taking a short cut to the poorhouse were it not for a special talent he possessed: he was able to play without looking at the board at all.

Pillsbury could sit off in a corner of the room and, as his opponent's moves were announced to him, picture the situation on the board easily. Moreover, he could handle several games at once and have not the slightest difficulty in recalling the position on each board. He would even remember every move of each game the next day.

Many chess masters can play a game or two "blindfold," but the ability to do it wholesale is something else again. It requires phenomenal visual-

The inset photograph of Harry Pillsbury well illustrates both his remarkable, composed manner and his eternal cigar. (Courtesy of Pillsbury's Chess Career, 2nd Edition, David McKay, 1937) Chess set photographed by Stephen A. Whitney courtesy of the Prentis Collection, New Hampshire Historical Society, Concord, N.H.

ization plus a memory that would shame an IBM computer. Pillsbury included it as part of his regular show.

His ability to put on this extraordinary exhibition as a matter of course created a constant demand for his services, especially as he was also blessed with an amiable disposition, pleasing appearance and warm personality. His only vice was a passion for large black cigars powerful enough to fumigate a factory.

Although he made a decent living and enjoyed the work, Pillsbury knew he could go on giving blindfold exhibitions the rest of his life and still be only a second-rater. He had set his sights on something higher and wanted the toughest competition he could get. He took part in every tournament he was able to squeeze into his schedule.

At first his results were not spectacular. In 1893 he finished seventh out of 14 players in New York. He then played a couple of short matches against two visiting German masters. He beat them, but they were about as far from world championship caliber as a minor league outfielder is from Willie Mays.

Pillsbury kept working, studying, playing. Next year in New York he climbed to fifth place. The following tournament saw him finish second. Finally, in 1894, he wound up in the top spot. Now a group of admirers got together and raised a fund to send Pillsbury to England as America's representative to the Hastings Tournament.

Hastings 1895 is still rated as one of the greatest tournaments ever held. The list of 22 entries was headed by the new world champion, Dr. Lasker;

ex-champion Steinitz and two outstanding challengers—fiery Michael Tchigorin of Russia and prim and dogmatic Dr. Siegbert Tarrasch of Germany. After this quartet of superstars came the champions of France, Britain, Italy and Austria.

There had been some grumbling about admitting a 22-year-old newcomer to this august assemblage, but it seemed only sporting to let in someone from America. Pillsbury's entry was accepted.

When he arrived, Pillsbury was offered rooms in a fashionable hotel noted for its gaiety. He politely refused.

"I want to be quiet," he explained. "I mean to win this tournament."

Which was taken as seriously as would be the announcement of a high school pitcher that he intended to strike out the entire Red Sox lineup.

In the first round, Pillsbury was paired against Tchigorin, a black-bearded, blazing-eyed bundle of nerves who could attack like a demon. They must have afforded a startling contrast. A contemporary account reads: "Mr. Pillsbury is decidedly pleasant and unassuming in manner, a perfect type of American and a tremendous smoker. Remarkably composed, he sits at the chess table in comfortable style with a self-confident look on his face."

Self-confidence wasn't enough. Pillsbury lost.

Undismayed, Pillsbury next faced the grand master, whom experts picked to be the next world champion.

Dr. Tarrasch was neat, always immaculately dressed, and supremely confident of his superiority. Across the board sat Pillsbury, meditatively smoking one of his black cigars and showing no emotion whatever except for an occasional nervous blink of the eyes. The spectators wondered how long it would take Tarrasch to make mincemeat of the American.

The game Pillsbury produced on this occasion has been ranked as one of the most magnificent ever played. Tarrasch was checkmated on the 52nd move, and from then on Pillsbury was taken seriously.

As the tournament progressed Pillsbury continued on his unruffled way, winning game after game. True, he did not complete the remainder of the schedule unscathed; he lost to Lasker and Schlecter, and in three other games had to be content with a draw. But his 15 wins put him on top, and when he beat his last-round opponent, thus assuring himself of first place, the spectators forgot all about the amenities of chess and turned the auditorium into a bedlam with shouts and cheers.

The youngster from Boston had proved beyond doubt that he was the equal of any player on earth. He returned home to be greeted as a champion should be.

For the next seven years Pillsbury was constantly on the move, with hardly a chess club of importance in Europe or on the American continent failing to scrape out its treasury every year or so to arrange for a Pillsbury visit. Old chess books and magazines abound with accounts of his blindfold demonstrations, for those who witnessed one could never forget it.

He would take a seat in a comfortable armchair, light one of his omnipresent cigars and take on 16 opponents at once. No matter how difficult the position on the chessboard, Pillsbury never seemed in the least perplexed and would anounce his moves without hesitation. He usually won all the games, but when he did lose was the first to offer congratulations. Chess writers never wearied of praising his brilliance and graciousness.

In one respect he was unique. Instead of taking on soft touches, Pillsbury operated on the theory that the tougher the opposition, the better. Upon one occasion in Germany he was playing in a tournament with an uneven number of contestants, and it was his turn to have the day off. Perhaps he was bored. At any rate, to fill in the time he decided to give a blindfold simultaneous exhibition.

No other master, during a tournament, would dream of playing a series of blindfold games, even against rank amateurs. Pillsbury challenged 21 *masters!* To make it easier for his opponents he allowed them to consult with each other, and announced his own moves in German notation.

This is still ranked as the most impressive feat of blindfold chess ever attempted. The session lasted 12 hours and the last game was not finished till after 2:00 a.m. When the next game of the tournament got under way a few hours later, there was Pillsbury with his customary cigar, fresh as a daisy and impatient to get started.

Nor did he confine himself to chess. One of his favorite pastimes was to conduct 12 games of chess and six games of checkers simultaneously. To make sure he did not suffer from ennui, he would play a few rubbers of whist at the same time. Afterward, if he had been given a list of words to memorize, he would reel those off.

Pillsbury himself did not take this memorizing very seriously. It was too easy. However, there came a time when two learned gentlemen deter-

mined to give him a *real* test. Before his customary chess/checker exhibition he was handed a slip of paper with the following words on it:

Antiphlogistine, periosteum, takadiastase, plasmon, ambrosia, Threlkeld, streptococcus, staphylococcus, micrococcus, plasmodium, Mississippi, Freiheit, Philadelphia, Cincinnati, athletics, no war, Etchenberg, American, Russian, philosophy, Piet Potgelter's Rost, Salamagundi, Oomisillecootsi, Bangmamvate, Schlechter's Neck, Manzinyama, theosophy, catechism, Madjesoomalops.

Pillsbury glanced over the list and went on with the show. Afterward he repeated the words in order from memory, then recited the same list backward! Next day, when he encountered the two men at the club, he went over the list again, just so they wouldn't think he was forgetful.

The exhibitions brought in money but were, to Pillsbury, of minor importance. He was after nothing less than the world championship. In 1897, and again in 1898, he beat Showalter, the United States champion, in matches, but took little interest in the honor.

"I'm after only *one* title," he declared.

In those days there was no international chess organization to assure that every contestant got his chance. Matches were personally arranged, and took money. Who could blame the world champion for not being eager to risk his title without adequate compensation, especially against an opponent who might take it away?

In January, 1901, Pillsbury married Mary Bush of Chicago. For the remainder of the year the couple stayed in the United States. The exhibitions went on as usual but he played in only one tournament, finishing first at Buffalo.

In 1902 he was back in Europe and took second place in tournaments at Monte Carlo and Hanover.

Pillsbury had not given up on the world championship, and had he been able to arrange a match a few years earlier would likely have made it. Now it was too late. His health declined with tragic swiftness.

In 1903 he came in third at Monte Carlo, and it was beginning to be evident that he was far from the Pillsbury of a few years back. Two months later at Vienna, where he finished fourth, it was obvious that Pillsbury was a sick man.

For many years his life had been one of constant traveling, late hours, irregular eating, and the mental strain of frequent blindfold exhibitions, topped off with a steady diet of at least 20 cigars a day. All of this must have taken its toll.

Under medical treatment, he was advised to discontinue the blindfold demonstrations, but this he could not bring himself to do. His manner remained cheerful, and, although often feeling wretched, he never complained and calmly assured his friends he would soon be as well as ever. He may have believed this himself; certainly no one could have realized the end was so near.

Deathly ill, he played his last tournament at Cambridge Springs in 1904. Plagued by constant insomnia and general misery, a shadow of the old Pillsbury, he finished eighth in a field of 16. Yet even now, although most of his games were only a pale reflection of the smashing attacks he used to handle so brilliantly, he somehow managed to summon up what was left of his waning resources to overcome the world champion, Dr. Lasker, in the last game they would ever play together.

For the remaining months left to him Pillsbury rested and tried to recover his health, but it was not to be. Early in 1906 he suffered an apoplectic stroke and died on June 17 of the same year. He was buried in the family lot at Laurel Hill Cemetery, Reading, Massachusetts.

Pillsbury was only 33 years old when he died, but as long as chess is played the world will never cease to feel a sense of awe at the accomplishments of this cool and resolute New England Yankee who may deserve to be rated as the greatest of them all. END

Lightning from His Eyes, Thunder from His Mouth

by Eric Kelly

Between the 12th and 20th of July, 1852, a tired old man was driving with his secretary among the Seven Hills of his native Salisbury, New Hampshire. It was too late for the apple blossoms, but the crops were well on their way and the smell of worked earth still lingered. Of mornings, the mists hung white in the lowlands, while off and about, the hills of the Kearsarge Range stood green in their eternal primal strength. This was the country that had given him birth, he was from it and of it, and he had carried its vigorous power among men and nations for a half-century.

Dan'l Webster, riding with Charles Lanman, would stop the horse near almost every farm. A word with a woman from the kitchen, a word with the toiler with his shovel or rake or hoe, questions of crops, livestocks, how-do-you-do's, and even politics. The word he left with them was imperishable. It was retained in memory decades after Black Dan had gone to his rest in the Marshfield Cemetery.

But Dan'l at this moment was not the Dan'l of the Dartmouth College Case, or the Reply to Hayne, or the Plymouth and Bunker Hill Orations. He had suffered physically from a bad fall from his carriage in May, and his spirit had encountered an attack of excruciating bitterness ever since his Seventh of March speech two years earlier in which he had attempted to settle the question of whether new states should be allowed to have slavery. Old Dan'l, anxious to preserve the Union had advocated adoption of Henry Clay's "comprehensive scheme of adjustment." He was no

Daniel Webster, 1850 (Dartmouth News Photo)

Webster as a young man, ca. 1801.

longer the Steam Engine in Trousers, the Man Cathedral. He was however still the Godlike One—he would always be that, and the "Great
Stone Face" as well, and men would never know just how deep his sorrow
was.

Already a legend, an unfathomable mystery, with a mind that seemed
superhuman behind those dark, deep-set eyes, a man about whom stories
sprang up by scores all over New England. Everything he did was notable.
Every appearance he made was a sensation. He had taken New England's
stand against the southern separatists in his Reply to Hayne, he had defied the northern separatists in his Seventh of March speech. He had
preserved the Union with all the power of his mind and body, and by so
doing through this last Compromise he had become the target of the
Abolitionists' fury. Excoriated, denounced as a traitor by half of New
England, he had been likened to Ichabod by the Quaker poet, Whittier.

Now, he was a broken old man. Yet he never breathed a word of complaint. A mantle of dark mystery cloaks him, a mystery such as epics are
made from. Three times the Presidency was near him, three times it was
denied and given to lesser men. When Faneuil Hall was denied him in
which to make an explanation of that Seventh of March speech, it must
have been a terrible blow.

He was back briefly in the lovely Salisbury Hills, back to the Old Elm
Farm in that part which had been set off as Franklin in 1825—an old man
visiting the scenes of his youth. This was his land, his valley, his farm.

Birthplace of Daniel Webster, Salisbury (now Franklin), New Hampshire

Even the beautiful home in Marshfield, Massachusetts, with the throb of the sea so near to it was not so typical of him as this. He carried a power of mind and body that comes seldom to those born amidst a softer civilization.

Dan'l's life was in itself a succession of miracles. He won over the Supreme Court in the Dartmouth College Case when the lower courts were against him; he attacked the South when it was strong; and he defended the North against its own weaknesses. He broke a great rule of Grammar which dictated that plural nouns should take plural verbs—after his time people said the United States IS, and not, the United States ARE.

Hostile juries found verdicts for him when the law was against him. Stephen Vincent Benet illustrates this power in *The Devil and Daniel Webster* when Webster won over the Devil's own hand-picked jury. With his magnificent voice Dan'l held 50,000 people spellbound at the First Bunker Hill Oration, and at Plymouth he moved a multitude to tears. A deep hush, charged with emotion, lay over the Senate when he spoke. Whence came this tremendous power?

Commentators use the metaphors of natural forces, the power of the sea, the wind, lightning and thunder. Lightning from his eyes, thunder from his mouth—speech that had the violence of a hurricane. James Russell Lowell describes him: "Webster should be a conductor to gather from every part of the cloud of popular indignation the scattered electricity, which would waste itself in heat lightning, and, grasping it in one huge

[299]

Left: *Grace Fletcher Webster, Daniel's first wife, painted in 1827 by Chester Harding (Dartmouth College portrait).* Right: *Caroline LeRoy Webster, his second wife, about 1830.*

thunderbolt, let it fall like the messenger of an angry god among the triflers in the capital." One thinks of Odin, or Thor, or Jupiter, or even Jehovah. These titanic powers were ascribed, most amazingly to this man while he was still alive. He did not need to pass into myth before the legends began to arise.

He became known as the man "who can do anything." He saved a College and a Nation, twice averted war with Great Britain, fixed boundaries and established the Constitution for what it was. His popular fame lay in smaller things: school children for generations read and recited his defense of a woodchuck; he took to court the case of a horse with a broken leg that was dragged through a wall; he took an axe in his hand to break down a door illegally nailed up, and he drew the picture of a murderer trying to slink away from his own conscience in such terms that all who heard or read shuddered as at tragedy. When he walked through State Street in Boston, business was suspended as people rushed out to see him pass. "He stood nearly six feet high," said Senator Samuel W. McCall. "His head was one of the largest ever seen on human shoulders. He had a dark 'gunpowder' complexion, a broad and lofty brow, and large, deepsunken, black eyes that would blaze with intensity in moments of excitement." Truly he was "a great actor lost to the stage," the ideal of a Roman Senator, a giant, a titan.

Around Searles' Hill, New Hampshire, which he called Mt. Pisgah, with just a crossing over of the line into Franklin (did somebody make that line crooked in order to get the old home place into Franklin?), one passes through a wilderness, almost as dense today as it was when Dan'l's father Ebenezer hewed himself a log cabin. The cabin is gone, but a portion of a second house where Dan'l was born is there in its old place. It seems that both Lanman and Harvey in writing of the place declare that only the cellar was there when they saw it. But the Webster Birthplace Association, with the New Hampshire Historical Society, worked on the theory that the old house had been carted away, and indeed the portion

Dartmouth College's famous "Black Dan" portrait, painted by Francis Alexander in 1835.

[301]

in which Webster was born was found tucked into the rear portion of the house next door. It was restored to its old place and is today a shrine.

Franklin has really honor enough in the possession of Elm Farm, now a part of the Dan'l Webster Home for Orphan Children. It's a lovely place in among the trees where "the boy grew older," where the young Dan'l hung his scythe on an oak.

Dan'l went from Elm Farm to Exeter. Although he was but a year there, the importance of Exeter's influence cannot be minimized. For here he first encountered academic life and thought. It was at Exeter that he was slanted toward college, and Dartmouth.

Dartmouth was very dear to his heart, and once at the meeting of the Boston Alumni he stated that his speech before the Supreme Court in behalf of the College was his favorite speech. In Hanover, New Hampshire, one finds Webster Hall, with its tablet—"Dartmouth College, Founded by Eleazar Wheelock; Refounded by Daniel Webster"—and the old Webster House where he lived in his senior year.

Christian Meadows' engraving of Dartmouth College in 1851; Webster elm (cut down in 1951) in foreground.

The citizens of New York presented Daniel Webster with a fine, silver-mounted carriage, harness, and span of horses—"the most elegant piece of workmanship ever turned out in this country." Cost for coach, harness and horses: $2500.

Stories of Black Dan'l abound in the Webster Country, some great, some trifling. Did he but stop to ask for a cup of water from a well, that cup became sacred. Where he spent a night, the fact is usually recorded on a sign outside the building. The legends are legion, but they are all big. In Plymouth where the assertion is sometimes made that he spent his first day in court, the old building is now a library. In Fryeburg, Maine, where he was principal of the Academy and made a famous Fourth of July Oration one may find, in the old Registry of Deeds office, the copying made in his own hand. The building where he taught has burned down, but the students there not too long ago used to shout in public, as we have it from Tom Ward of Fryeburg (whose brother there used to make beautiful ash wood bats for the National League):

> "We do as we should,
> We talk as we ought;
> We come from Fryeburg
> Where Dan'l Webster taught."

Webster fables are of the heroic quality of the Middle-Ages—they point to him as outwitting somebody or other; if he had debts they were greater than anyone else's, if he drank, and he did like his liquor as did most public men of that day, he drank more than was good for him. In popular legend he might have been a Nuremberg alderman who could empty a

[303]

five-gallon tankard at one breath. Or Loki, drinking a large portion of the sea.

Webster rose to fame in Portsmouth, New Hampshire, that "quaint old town." He was there from 1806 to 1816 after a few years at Boscawen, and the training under Christopher Gore in Boston. The building in Market Street where he had his office is now the printing establishment of Blaisdell & Son. Many of the New Hampshire stories about Webster stem from this period when he was still "riding circuit," and it was here that he was first elected to Congress, first made his entrance into politics and publicly demonstrated his position as a defender of the Constitution. The beginnings of the Dartmouth College Case were here—its subsequent settlement in the Supreme Court.

It was in Marshfield, however, more than anywhere else, that Webster felt absolute freedom from national cares. The fields were richer than the rocky soil at Salisbury, the air was fresh and tangy from the ocean, and out beyond lay that other power in which he exulted, the sea. The hills, the fields, and the sea. He loved to walk the hills, to work in the fields, arising at four in the morning when he was home, inspecting his stock, feeding the cattle or admiring his rare imported llamas.

Marshfield, too, had another great solace for him. The people who lived there. Baffled and in sore pain after the reception of that Seventh of March speech, he returned to Marshfield to find his neighbors lined up along the road for miles to welcome him.

There lived on the outskirts of Marshfield in 1922 a retired school teacher by the name of Mary Ann Ford. At that time she was about 85 years old. She was 15 on that night of October in 1852 when Webster lay dying at Marshfield. Like others in the neighborhood she had been constantly listening for the tolling of the church bell which would mark the end of a great career. Everyone knew that the end was near. Everyone knew that Webster lay in his bed so that his eyes would be fixed on the American flag hoisted within his view on the mast of the boat that lay in the little body of water behind his house. At night the carriage lantern was hoisted beside it, so that the dying eyes could see the emblem which stood for all that he had struggled for during his life. "When my eyes shall be turned for the last time on the Meridian sun, I hope I may see him shining bright upon my united, free, and happy country. I hope I may not see the flag of my country with its stars separated or obliterated, torn by commotion, smoking with the blood of civil war." So he had said in what many consider his greatest moment.

Daniel Webster's farm at Marshfield, Massachusetts (top), *where he could find "absolute freedom from national cares"* (bottom).

At 2 o'clock in the morning he died. They dressed him in the blue Revolutionary coat with its gilt buttons, white cravat, vest, pantaloons and gloves, silk hose and patent leather shoes. He was laid on a table in the great library of the Marshfield home. His last words "I still live" still rang in the ears of those about him, words that were to be more true than he thought—or did he, in the dark mystery of that great mind, know that he had joined the immortals?

Mary Ann was listening for the bell. At 7 o'clock in the morning she heard it—the first sad tolling—then the Three Strokes in the old New England fashion denoting that the deceased was a male—then the 70 single strokes, one for each of the eventful years of Dan'l's life. Hardly had the tolling finished before the carriage wheels began to rumble on the little bridge down the road. They were coming, coming from Boston, from New York, from Washington, to attend the funeral of the departed giant. The funeral was on the lawn in the midst of some 10,000 people, and then he was laid away in the cemetery beneath the solid stone with the plain lettering.

In a sense, however, his fame had just begun. The storm which had arisen after the Seventh of March Speech died away. Even Whittier re-

The Webster obsequies in New York—the funeral car.

lented. The Abolitionists may have been swayed by grief or by pure personal affection, but they realized at last that the man had fought for them as well as for all Americans. Perhaps they relented somewhat, perhaps they saw the light, that the North was not yet strong enough to take its position alone. Webster had undoubtedly amalgamated the Union.

There are statues to Webster in many cities, memorials, halls, libraries, and even a whistle-stop on the Boston & Maine railroad. There is the painting of Webster's "Reply to Hayne" in Faneuil Hall, Congressional and Senatorial group pictures, and there are portraits in every New England town and village. Truly no other man was such a target for portrait painters. That however which is imperishable is the reality in the form of legend and tradition which exists in men's minds. He was one of the most impressive men in all history. He was Emerson's Yankee with Wings, he was Jack the Giant Killer, he was Roland and Amadis and Robin Hood all in one. Truly a child of earth with a magnificent brain, and he carried as the chief impact, the idea that the preservation of the Union under the Constitution was the very first concern of all real Americans. That there was a Union to pass on to Lincoln to be saved was perhaps the great work of his life. END

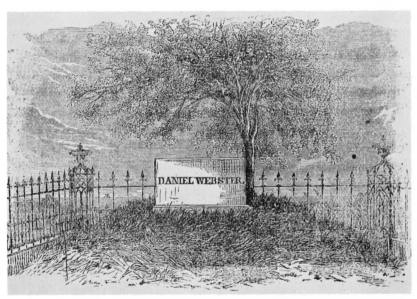

"Old Dan'l's" tombstone in the Marshfield cemetery.

[307]

P. T. Barnum's Gold Mine

by Maudie M. Dabrowski

In the mid 1840s, nearly everyone in the world had heard of General Tom Thumb and today, more than a century later, his name lives on. No other midget has so captured the public's imagination nor achieved the fortune and lasting fame of little Charlie Stratton, born in Bridgeport, Connecticut, in January of 1838. What lies behind his unusual fame? Probably these two factors hold the answer: first, P. T. Barnum's tremendous flair for showmanship with the important element of perfect timing, and secondly but no less important, Tom's wit and piquant personality as a child. Barnum's choice of the name General Tom Thumb was another stroke of Barnum genius and must have heavily contributed to the child's success.

Had Barnum been content with merely exhibiting the Little General in his American Museum in New York, it is doubtful that Tom Thumb's name would have become a household word. What made him a world sensation was the glamor which surrounded him—audiences before every crowned head in Europe, before the Kings, Emperors, or Queens of England, Russia, France, Spain and Belgium, making Tom Thumb the pet of London and Paris society, furnishing him with beautiful costumes and jewels and his own small fine carriages made by the Queen's carriage maker in London. Everyone wanted to see the miniature child who had charmed the Queen of England, but when they saw him they fell in love with him for himself, for Tom Thumb had a roguish, saucy way with him that was endearing.

Except in size, Charles Sherwood Stratton was a perfectly normal, healthy child. There was no deformity of proportion, he was a beautifully formed miniature with golden hair, rosy cheeks, and a quick wit and intelligence. At age four and a half when Barnum took him over, the little

General Tom Thumb (from a daguerreotype)

general was only 25 inches tall and weighed 15 pounds; he had stopped growing at age five months. Years later, at about age 14, he resumed growth and eventually reached a height of 35 inches. There were two normal daughters older than Tom in the Stratton family and many years later, a normal son.

Tom's father, a carpenter by trade, was bitterly ashamed of his tiny son. Mrs. Stratton was a cleaning woman at the Sterling House in Bridgeport and often carried her little boy to work in a market basket. He was a pet of Mrs. Fairchild, wife of the tavern keeper, and it is she who brought Tom to the attention of Barnum's half-brother, who ran the rival Franklin House. When a delay in transportation forced Barnum to spend a night in Bridgeport, Mrs. Fairchild, dressing the child in a blue velveteen suit she had made for him, arranged an interview between Tom Thumb and the showman. (Although Barnum was reasonably successful and very well known at the time, it was actually through Tom Thumb that he founded his later great success and fortune.) Barnum was enchanted with the beautiful tiny boy and induced his mother to go to New York with him on a four week contract at three dollars a week. Barnum says in his

[309]

Phineas Taylor Barnum, mentor, exhibitor and friend of Tom Thumb.

memoirs that he had no idea at the time what a gold mine he was acquiring.

Mrs. Stratton and Tom arrived in New York in November 1842. Barnum hired a tutor and a dancing master for the child, but he himself coached Tom afternoons and evenings in jokes, verses, and skits. The amazing five-year-old prodigy was ready for his debut only two months later. Barnum advertised him as an English import, 11 years of age. The performances, three a day with many private appearances in the evenings, were a game to the child. He strutted about in a pert and impish way, exchanging quips with the audience, and overnight became the darling of New York. Fashionable carriages lined the street outside the museum, the papers were full of him, his picture was in every shop window. At the end of the four week contract, Barnum raised Tom's salary to $25 a week and later to $50, then after two years, following the first European tour, the Strattons shared equally with Barnum in the immense profits. A day's average was $500. On one of his European tours, Tom's share was close to a million dollars.

At the end of the second year, after touring the Eastern seaboard, Barnum decided it was time for a European tour. The day they sailed seven-year-old Tom Thumb performed at the museum until 11 A.M.; the boat sailed at noon. More than 80,000 people had stormed the museum to see him; 10,000 turned out to see him off, and he was escorted aboard by the City Brass Band. Despite his mother's presence, the tutor and the dancing master, it was hardly a healthful, and certainly not a normal environment for a child. It is small wonder that at 20 Tom Thumb was jaded and world-weary; there is always an undertone of the pathetic in his story. Consider this schedule for a child of seven, according to the *New York Evening Post* of January 16, 1844: "A few hours more remain for General Tom Thumb to be seen . . . as the packet in which he has engaged passage to England does not sail today, in consequence of the easterly winds now prevailing. He may be seen throughout the entire day and evening and at three and seven o'clock P.M. there will be grand performances. . . ."

In the Barnum group sailing to Europe were Tom and his tutor, Mrs. Stratton and her husband who would act as ticket-taker, and Barnum. After a stormy 19-day crossing they landed at Liverpool. Barnum had planned to go at once to London to try to present Tom Thumb first to the Queen, knowing that a Command Performance would establish them securely, but upon arrival there learned that the Royal Family was in mourning, and although it was not impossible to gain an audience, the chance was now much less likely. Barnum plotted his *coup d'état* cannily. He rented a furnished house in the most fashionable part of Mayfair and from this social stronghold issued invitations to a series of receptions to members of the nobility and London editors. Horace Greeley, one of Barnum's close friends, had given him a letter of introduction to the impeccable Edward Everett, American Ambassador to the Court of St. James. Barnum says in his memoirs that it was to this letter he owed his ultimate success in getting Tom before the Queen and so launched to fortune. While impatiently awaiting the audience, Barnum finally decided to show Tom to the public. He hired Egyptian Hall, and besides daily appearances the child gave many evening performances at houses of the nobility; his first patroness was the Baroness Rothschild. Everett finally arranged a meeting at his house between Barnum and Mr. Murray, Master of the Royal Household, a Sunday breakfast at which Barnum dropped the hint that the General was about to go to France to see Louis Philippe. Murray rose to the bait and assured Barnum that Her Majesty would probably like to see Tom first. The day of the command performance, Barnum, publicity wise, had a placard placed on the door of the exhibition hall: "Closed this evening, General Tom Thumb being at Buckingham Palace by Command of Her Majesty." From this time on the pounds, shillings, and pence rolled in like a tidal wave.

One of the most beguiling and wistful portraits of Tom Thumb as a child is to be found in Barnum's description of this first of three royal visits. Barnum had been instructed that under no circumstances were they to address the Queen directly and that they must at all times face her, so that when they left her presence, they must back out bowing. The Queen and a large family group awaited them in the royal picture gallery. Tom Thumb, seven years old and big as a minute, trotted smartly down the long gallery, bowed solemnly, and piped directly to Victoria: "Good evening, Ladies and Gentlemen!" The Queen was enchanted by the child's simplicity and took his hand in delight to lead him about. Tom informed Her Majesty that he found her paintings "first rate" and told her he should like to see the Prince of Wales. The Queen regretted that H.R.H. was in bed (where the little General should have been) but invited him to come again to meet the Prince. (Years later on a trip to New York the future King Edward looked up the little General.) After an hour's performance in which Tom Thumb danced the hornpipe, impersonated Napoleon, sang several songs and posed as Grecian statues, backing-out time came. Barnum, six feet two, managed well but poor Tom's little legs were unable to keep up, and when he saw Barnum yards behind him, he turned and ran a few steps, quickly faced the Queen and bowed low in respect, continuing by this method to reach the end of the long gallery. This time Victoria *was* "amused," but not so her pet spaniel who dashed for the General's legs. The terrified little boy raised his tiny malacca cane and thrashed out at the dog while everyone there went into further gales of laughter. Victoria sent Barnum a bag of gold coins and to Tom, her first of many gifts—a pearl bibelot ornamented with emeralds.

After a tremendous success in England Barnum took the General to Paris where he was presented many times to the royal family. Tom Thumb became the rage of Paris as Le General Tom Pouce; a smart new boulevard cafe was named for him. Aside from his regular appearances, this amazing child soon appeared in a play. "Petit Poucet," speaking his part in French!

The General became a familiar sight on the streets of Paris in his carriage five feet long and a foot wide. It was drawn by four matched ponies and on the box sat two small children dressed as coachman and footman in sky-blue livery trimmed with silver lace, cocked hats on their powdered wigs. As the carriage rolled down the Champs Elysées, thousands cheered the little General as he bowed left and right. This carriage and the ponies were taken along as part of the theatrical equipment on all their trips throughout Europe, and caused a sensation wherever they appeared.

The Barnum party next went to Spain, where Tom attended a bull

The Thumbs' tiny brougham and ponies created quite a stir in Exeter, N.H. The General and his wife, Lavinia, are standing, right. (Photo by Frances Lawrence)

fight as guest of Queen Isabella, then on to Belgium and further triumphs. The newspapers of that day report that on their return trip to France the Barnum carriages were held up in the mountains and Tom Thumb kidnapped; the whole world awaited breathlessly until Tom was found by shepherds in a cave. Since Barnum makes no mention of this colorful episode in his memoirs it was undoubtedly more of the famous Barnum "humbug" which paid off heavily at the box office.

Upon their return to America, Barnum says that Tom's ". . . friends found that he had not increased in size during the four and a half years of his absence, but they discovered he had become sharp and witty, abounding in foreign airs and graces; in fact, that he was quite unlike the little, diffident country fellow they had formerly known . . . He was an apt pupil, and I provided for him the best of teachers . . . The General left America a diffident, uncultivated little boy; he came back an educated, accomplished little man . . . he went abroad poor, and he came home rich."

Tom's father spent $30,000 of Tom's earnings on a large and impressive house in Bridgeport, putting into it a suite of rooms filled with exquisite miniature rosewood and mahogany furniture, much of which Mr. Stratton himself made. In a curio cabinet were displayed Tom's jewelled ornaments, gifts of royalty—a Tom-size gold snuffbox set with turquoises, a tiny gold watch from Queen Adelaide, a ruby brooch from Victoria, an emerald and diamond stickpin from Louis Philippe. In the stables stood

[313]

Left: *General Tom and Lavinia Thumb;* right: *Commodore George Washington Morrison Nutt and Minnie, Lavinia's sister.*

horses and ponies and the carriages made for Tom in England. It was the first home the child had known since he had left Bridgeport almost five years before, but he was soon put back to exhibiting, accompanied by a tutor while his family remained at home. The next several years were spent either at the museum in New York or touring here and in Europe.

In 1862 when the General met Lavinia Warren, his future wife, he was living in Bridgeport, making few public appearances, and at last enjoying his yacht and ponies. He was an active member of the Masonic Order, a wealthy man with extensive real estate holdings and well able to retire upon his vast earnings.

Mrs. Tom Thumb was born Mercy Lavinia Bump in Middleboro, Massachusetts in October of 1842, one of eight children; of these only Lavinia and her younger sister, Huldah, were not of normal size. Lavinia's full growth was 32 inches.

Unlike Tom Thumb, who had been taken by P. T. Barnum at the age of five and had never known a normal home life, Lavinia grew up in a good family background and received an unusually good education for that day. Upon graduation from Middleboro Academy, she taught school there. Such was her dignity and force that although every child in her classes was taller than she, she had no difficulty maintaining discipline! Lavinia's dignity was a great part of her charm; although she was a little person in a Brobdingnagian world, and because of her size this world pampered and petted her, she always behaved as though she were of full

[314]

stature. The contrast of adult behavior in a miniature body heightened the touch of faery and goes far to explain the feting she received here and abroad.

When Lavinia was 20, a cousin who had a floating museum on the Mississippi came to visit and by holding forth visions of travel here and in Europe, overcame her strong reluctance to display herself and to capitalize on her diminutive size. She returned to the South with him and spent a year on his showboat. P. T. Barnum heard of Lavinia Warren (the stage name she took) in 1862. Since Tom Thumb was in semi-retirement, Barnum's current attraction was Commodore Nutt, son of Major Rodnia Nutt of Manchester, New Hampshire. The Commodore was not drawing the audiences that Tom Thumb had, and Barnum was eager to sign up Miss Warren, who was both pretty and intelligent. This he did, though Lavinia drove a hard bargain.

Soon afterwards, General Tom Thumb visited New York and dropped into the Museum to see Barnum, where he caught sight of Lavinia Warren. Immediately, without even getting himself introduced to the lady, he rushed into Barnum's office, trembling with excitement and piped: "Mr. Barnum, that is the most charming little lady I ever saw, and I believe she was created on purpose to be my wife!" Barnum refused to comment. Tom Thumb continued, "Now, Mr. Barnum, you have always been a friend of mine, and I want you to say a good word for me to her. I've got plenty of money, and I want to marry and settle down. I really feel as though I must marry that young lady! I hope you will favor my suit to her?"

Barnum then replied: "Well, General, I will not oppose you in your suit but you must do your own courting. But I tell you, Commodore Nutt will be jealous of you, and, more than that, Miss Warren is nobody's fool. You will have to be careful if you want to succeed."

Tom abandoned his yacht and ponies and settled in his sister's house in New York, visiting the Museum every day to call on Miss Lavinia. Commodore Nutt did grow very jealous and resented Tom's daily intrusions. One day when they were alone in the dressing rooms, he could contain his fury no longer. Out shot the Commodore's little fist, knocking Tom Thumb flat to the floor—little Nutt was wiry and alert while Thumb, eight years older, had grown slow and portly, but although the Commodore had all the physical advantages, in their suits of Miss Warren the General held the advantages of wealth and leisure, poise and worldliness. (Miss Warren told Barnum she considered Nutt a mere boy.) Plotting

[315]

his suit carefully, Tom Thumb waited for what he felt was appropriate time and then asked Mr. Barnum to invite Lavinia to Barnum's house in Bridgeport for a weekend. When Nutt heard of the proposed trip he insisted Barnum invite him, but before Nutt could arrive by train after the evening performance in New York, Tom Thumb had laid the ground well for the success of his own suit—he met Miss Warren at the train in his best carriage, his coachman dressed with a broad ribbon on his hat and a new silver buckle. He took Lavinia for a drive, showing her first his own impressive house with its suite of midget-sized rooms filled with exquisite little furniture—carved sofas and chairs made in France, the beautiful mahogany canopy bed given him by Queen Victoria, curio cabinets filled with diamond studded bibelots from every crowned head in Europe, even a library with small books especially printed and bound and a miniature pool table. (Years later, in 1921, all this beautiful little furniture was sold for $300. What a charming museum it would make today in the town of Middleboro.)

In their drive around Bridgeport, Tom Thumb did not fail to point out his many real estate holdings, his yacht, his large stable and carriages. After dinner that evening, to which Tom Thumb brought his mother to meet Lavinia, he and Miss Warren played backgammon. He had already told Barnum he intended to propose that evening before the Commodore arrived. At nine o'clock Barnum yawned and said he would like to retire, but that someone must remain up to welcome the Commodore. Tom volunteered if Miss Warren would remain to keep him company. For an account of the proposal, we are indebted to Barnum's small daughters who eavesdropped from the stair landing. First, the General showed Miss Warren several insurance policies and mortgages he held, proving to her what a smart little business man he was and how extensive his holdings. His point made, he then said, "So you are going to Europe . . ." Lavinia answered, "Yes, I will be invited to appear before the Queen of England, the Emperor and Empress of France, the King of Prussia, the Emperor of Austria, and at the courts of any other countries we may visit. O, I shall like that; it will be so new to me!"

"Yes, it will be interesting indeed. I have visited most of the crowned heads," said the suave little man, "but don't you think you'll be lonesome in a strange country? I wish I were going over, I know all about the different countries, and could explain them all to you." Lavinia admitted that would be very pleasant.

"Would you really like to have me go?" asked the General as his arm

The Duke of Wellington admired the General's impersonation of Napoleon.

boldly encircled Lavinia's tiny waist, "Don't you think it would be nicer if we went as man and wife?"

Lavinia demurred that she did think this was very sudden, but he swept all her doubts away, and by the time the forgotten little Commodore rang the bell, Tom Thumb had won his prize.

The wedding of Charles Stratton (Tom Thumb) and Lavinia Warren took place at Grace Church, New York City, on Tuesday, February 10, 1863, when the General was 25 years of age and his bride 22. A raised platform was built before the altar so that the wedding group could be seen. Governors, Civil War Generals, and New York Society attended.

President and Mrs. Lincoln sent as their gift "a gorgeous set of Chinese fire screens." Mrs. Cornelius Vanderbilt gave them "a coral and gold set brooch, earrings and studs." There were tiny silver tea services and trays, a Sèvres dinner service, and what Lavinia loved most of all, a miniature silver plated sewing machine at which she spent many happy hours when she was settled in her new home. The wedding reception was held at the Metropolitan Hotel where the bride and groom received standing atop a grand piano. Lavinia's sister Minnie (Huldah), and Commodore Nutt served as attendants.

Upon their marriage, Barnum had generously released Mrs. Thumb from her contract, and following a wedding tour which included a visit with the Lincolns at the White House, the bride and groom retired to private life at the Stratton house in Bridgeport with Tom's mother (his father had died several years earlier). Perhaps there was a personality clash, for soon the General and Lavinia built a house in Middleboro, Massachusetts, opposite her mother's house, but they never really settled down. Barnum says in his recollections that "The General and his wife had been accustomed to excitement, and after a few months retirement they again longed for the peculiar pleasures of a public life. . . . They . . . have since travelled several years in Europe and considerably in this country, holding public exhibitions more than half the time, and spending the residue in leisurely viewing such cities . . . as they may happen to be in." In addition to this restlessness there set in a flagrant recklessness with money. Although as a child Tom Thumb, according to Barnum, was miserly, at maturity he became a profligate spender, wasting thousands upon houses, jewels, horses, carriages, and yachts so that when he died suddenly of apoplexy at his summer house at Wareham, Cape Cod, at age forty-five, on July 15, 1883, he left a very small estate to his widow. He was buried with full Masonic honors at Bridgeport, Connecticut.

What of Tom Thumb as a personality? There is no doubt that he was an enchanting child; he charmed Victoria into three visits, the great Duke of Wellington repeatedly called upon him and befriended him, Louis Philippe invited him to the royal birthday celebration as a guest. It is interesting to notice in Barnum's writings how little of the General's personality as an adult comes through, yet we get a distinct picture of Tom Thumb the child—as a blithe, outgoing, unaffected little boy. Although the following is quoted out of context, which is always unfair, it seems to pretty well sum up not only what Barnum felt for Tom Thumb but what Tom Thumb the man felt about himself as others regarded him: "That is my piece of goods. . . ." As one reads in Barnum's memoirs the strains put upon the little General as a small child, it makes an almost unbelievable story as well as a pathetic one: "Besides giving daily entertainments, the General appeared occasionally for an hour, during the intermissions, at some place in the suburbs; and for a long time he appeared every day at the Zoological Gardens . . . and when the General had gone through his performances on the little stage . . . he was put into a balloon which . . . was then passed around the ground just above the people's heads . . . one

Under two feet high and 16 pounds at the outset of his career, Tom Thumb grew to a height of almost three feet.

day, a sudden gust of wind took the balloon out of the hands of half the men . . . and had not an alarm been instantly given . . . the little General would have been lost. In addition to other engagements, the General frequently performed in the play, Hop O' My Thumb." But compared to the children of that unenlightened day before child labor reforms, when children worked in mills or did piece work in dank cellars, little Tom Thumb was fortunate.   END